Crossing the Schism

CATHOLICS AND PROTESTANTS
SHARE THE SAME CORE BELIEFS

John D Smatlak

John D. Smatlak

Copyright © 2019 John D. Smatlak.

All rights reserved. No part of this book may be used or reproduced by any means, graphic, electronic, or mechanical, including photocopying, recording, taping or by any information storage retrieval system without the written permission of the author except in the case of brief quotations embodied in critical articles and reviews.

This book is a work of non-fiction. Unless otherwise noted, the author and the publisher make no explicit guarantees as to the accuracy of the information contained in this book and in some cases, names of people and places have been altered to protect their privacy.

WestBow Press books may be ordered through booksellers or by contacting:

WestBow Press
A Division of Thomas Nelson & Zondervan
1663 Liberty Drive
Bloomington, IN 47403
www.westbowpress.com
1 (866) 928-1240

Because of the dynamic nature of the Internet, any web addresses or links contained in this book may have changed since publication and may no longer be valid. The views expressed in this work are solely those of the author and do not necessarily reflect the views of the publisher, and the publisher hereby disclaims any responsibility for them.

Any people depicted in stock imagery provided by Getty Images are models, and such images are being used for illustrative purposes only.
Certain stock imagery © Getty Images.

Scripture taken from the NEW AMERICAN STANDARD BIBLE®, Copyright © 1960,1962,1963,1968,1971,1972,1973,1975,1977,1 995 by The Lockman Foundation. Used by permission.

THE HOLY BIBLE, NEW INTERNATIONAL VERSION®, NIV® Copyright © 1973, 1978, 1984, 2011 by Biblica, Inc.® Used by permission. All rights reserved worldwide.

ISBN: 978-1-9736-5665-4 (sc)
ISBN: 978-1-9736-5666-1 (hc)
ISBN: 978-1-9736-5664-7 (e)

Library of Congress Control Number: 2019902917

Print information available on the last page.

WestBow Press rev. date: 3/13/2019

This book is dedicated to my wife, Liz, who joined me through each step of my crossing.

I deeply appreciate the advice and encouragement given by friends, family members and clergy.

John Smatlak

Contents

Preface ix

Introduction xi

Chapter 1   Do You Believe in Miracles? 1

Chapter 2   Placing Limits on Miracles 9

Chapter 3   How Far the Divide 23

Chapter 4   A Window into Fundamentalism 27

Chapter 5   Christianity in Review 39

Chapter 6   Indoctrination and the False Narrative 51

Chapter 7   Myth 1: We Interpret the Bible Literally 65

Chapter 8   Myth 2: The Bible Is the Sole Authority 69

Chapter 9   Myth 3: We Are More Holy 83

Chapter 10 The Treadmill 97

Chapter 11 Myth 4: There Is One Correct Doctrine 103

Chapter 12 Myth 5: Catholic Beliefs Are Wrong 111

Chapter 13 Relics 125

Chapter 14 Different Catholic Worship Practices 131

Chapter 15 Indulgences 145

Chapter 16 Early Protestantism 153

Chapter 17	Post-Reformation Report Card	165
Chapter 18	Unum versus Requiem	173
Chapter 19	The Worldwide Church	187
Chapter 20	A Long Crossing	195
Chapter 21	A Short Crossing	203
Chapter 22	My Antenna Went Up	209
Chapter 23	From Tiny Seeds	215

Epilogue 219

Catholic Terms and Phrases 225

Common Catholic Prayers 237

Suggested Reading 245

Notes 247

Index 289

Preface

After many years of marriage to a practicing Catholic, the light bulb finally came on. I figured it out. I now understand the major differences between Catholics and Protestants, and how those differences started.

As a Protestant Fundamentalist, I was raised to believe Catholics behave in strange ways. They pray to dead people, worship Mary, and believe in mystical powers of old clothing and bone parts. Catholics also never share communion with anyone except themselves.

Shortly after being married, I learned that Catholics think Protestant Fundamentalists behave oddly. They meet for worship in plain buildings, stay to themselves most of the time, and fail to enjoy many of life's celebrations. Fundamentalists also think everyone outside of their group is going to hell when they die.

I knew the Catholic views of Fundamentalists were not true. I wondered why Catholics believe those false ideas. I asked questions and read about Christian history. It seemed many Catholics didn't know Fundamentalists personally, and believed things they heard without verifying their accuracy.

After I befriended more Catholics, I learned many of the things I believed about Catholics weren't true, either. Once I understood the truth, I realized Catholics and Protestants share the same core Christian beliefs. They just have different worship practices. Protestants misinterpret Catholic worship practices. Catholics underestimate the faith of Protestants.

I don't think any Christian should necessarily change their style of worship. However, while learning the truth about Catholicism, I gained new insights into my own faith. I want to share what I learned. I hope it increases your faith in Christ and shortens your crossing over the divide between Catholics and Protestants.

Introduction

Growing up in a Fundamentalist Christian church gave me a strong foundation for the development of a personal relationship with Christ. During my adult life, I had the rare opportunity to learn more about Christian doctrine from the perspectives of mainstream Protestant denominations and from the Catholic church. The knowledge gained from such a wide variety of worship practices across many parts of Christianity increased the clarity with which I viewed my religion. It also helped me realize all Christians share the same core beliefs.

I learned Christians grow stronger in their faith once they see their religion from new and different perspectives. Although Christianity is based on love, some groups within the Christian religion misunderstand other Christian groups and treat them with a lack of trust. Different Christian groups hold interpretations of the Bible that conflict with each other. However, some consider only their own interpretations to be sacred. In addition, many Christians were taught "myths" in their youth which continue to keep them from living in harmony with other Christians today.

As Christians, we often focus too much on our differences, and not enough on our similarities. There is no need to have as many versions of Christianity as we have today. With so many different denominations of this one religion, modern Christianity is splintered and fragmented.

The divide between Catholics and Protestants is Christianity's greatest weakness. Seeing the Christian religion through the lens of a single denomination constrains its growth. It is better to view Christianity as the sum of its parts. It is one religion, which competes with other religions worldwide. Christians make up nearly a third of the world's population. The commission Christ gave to his disciples was to expand Christianity worldwide. Success will not be achieved until large Christian groups work together, with mutual love and trust.

This book is based on my personal reflections of a Fundamentalist Christian upbringing and Christian experiences with mainstream Protestantism and Catholicism. It includes observations of Catholicism through the eyes of Protestants, and observations of Protestantism through the eyes of Catholics. The book is written from a layman's perspective, after decades of attendance in a wide variety of Christian churches, travel experiences to holy Christian sites throughout the world, and research.

CHAPTER 1

Do You Believe in Miracles?

Some walk so a loved one will be healed. Some walk so they, personally, will be healed. Some walk to show their Christian faith. Others walk for spirituality. Some pilgrims walk the final six miles. Others walk from a small town located twenty miles away. Many pilgrims walk the ninety miles north from Albuquerque, New Mexico; it takes them one week to complete the pilgrimage. Young or old and healthy or lame, they walk. Those who make the pilgrimage say they feel closer to God.

On Good Friday each year, an estimated thirty thousand people gather at a small church, called El Santuario de Chimayo, in the rural town of Chimayo, New Mexico. El Santuario de Chimayo was built in 1816. It was donated to the Archdiocese of Santa Fe in 1929 and is still an active Catholic church today.

The Crucifix in Chimayo

In 1810, Bernardo Abeyta, a farmer, was praying when he saw a light emanating from the ground. He followed the light and uncovered a wooden crucifix buried there. A crucifix is a cross with a representation of Jesus hanging on it. His body is upright along the longer part of the cross with arms outstretched and hands nailed to the side pieces of the cross. His feet are nailed to the bottom part of the main length of the cross. The Chimayo crucifix is approximately six feet tall and mostly light green.

Three times, the Chimayo crucifix was moved to a church in another village. Three times, the crucifix disappeared and was found upright, back in the same hole in Chimayo. After realizing the crucifix was meant to stay in Chimayo, Bernardo Abeyta built a small private chapel to house it. Six years later, the private chapel was replaced with a small adobe church. The church has twin front towers with belfries, wooden doors, a wall-enclosed garden, and an arched gate with a cross on top.

As you enter the front door of the church, you immediately step into the back of the sanctuary. It is primitive in nature with white walls, rustic wooden beams in the ceiling, and small wooden pews. The Chimayo crucifix is in the front of the sanctuary, centered on the altar. The church is dimly lit and smells of earth and wood. Stations of the cross, a series of fourteen illustrations representing the successive incidents during Jesus's progress from his condemnation by Pontius Pilate to his Crucifixion and burial, hang on the side walls. Lighted candles are in the rear of the church, along with a small font.

El Santuario de Chimayo, the small adobe church built by Bernardo Abeyta, is the destination for many who pilgrimage by foot to arrive by Good Friday of Holy Week each year. Their intent is to celebrate the risen Christ on Easter morning and to pray for healing. The sacristy, a room adjacent to the sanctuary, contains racks of crutches and braces left by those who were healed. The sheer number of crutches and braces demonstrates the power of this holy place and provides evidence of the miracles performed during the past two hundred years. Following extensive investigations, the Catholic Church officially recognized some of the healing miracles attributed to El Santuario de Chimayo. However, most of the healings are not reported to church officials.

On the ground in a small side room just off the front of the sacristy is an eight-inch hole where the Chimayo crucifix was originally discovered. Many people who make the pilgrimage to El Santuario de Chimayo believe the dirt is holy and want a small amount to take home. They place some into a small cannister for their personal use. Later, they mix it with water to make mud that can be applied to the skin during prayer for healing. As the dirt is removed, it is necessary to replenish the supply. A priest blesses dirt from elsewhere on the property and places it into the hole. My wife, Liz, and I placed some of the blessed dirt into a small cannister and brought it home to have a remembrance of our holy and sacred pilgrimage to El Santuario de Chimayo.

Outside the church are many shrines with notes of praise for answered prayers. There are other notes that request healing. Boards displaying photographs of those who experienced healing and those requesting healing have been placed around the property outside the sanctuary. Candles and rosary beads are left by pilgrims on shelves near the display boards, so their prayers may continue after they depart Chimayo. Because the church is so small, a large area with outdoor seating near a tributary feeding Santa Cruz Lake is available for those who want to rest and pray.

After we spoke to the priest about recent changes to the site to better handle crowds of people, we completed our tour of El Santuario de Chimayo. Liz and I returned to our rental car to continue our visit through the region. As we traveled north on narrow, two-lane roads through a rural countryside, we noticed a group of men walking toward us along the opposite side of the road. Most were in single file. A few were walking side by side. As we approached, we counted thirty men on a pilgrimage to El Santuario de Chimayo. The lead man was holding a crucifix chest high; the top of the crucifix remained above his head out of respect for Jesus. Many of the men wore jerseys with religious words imprinted on them, such as "Jesus" and "Prayer."

Our visit was in early June, and we did not know why these men were making a pilgrimage to the church well after Good Friday of Holy Week. But for whatever reason, it was clear that these men believed in miracles and were unashamedly living out their personal Christian faith with humility and selflessness.

An exact replica of the Chimayo crucifix.

Crutches and braces left in the Chimayo sacristy.

The Black Madonna in Jasna Gora Monastery

Four million Catholic and Orthodox Christians from across the world make a pilgrimage to the Jasna Gora Monastery in Czestochowa, Poland, every year. They come to southern Poland to see a four-foot-tall portrait of Mary and her young son, Jesus, painted by the Gospel writer, Luke. It is believed that Luke painted it on the tabletop of a table built by Jesus during his time as a carpenter.

It was while Luke was painting Mary that she recounted to him the events in the life of Jesus that would eventually be used in his Gospel. The portrait is called the Black Madonna because the colors darkened after centuries of soot residue from lighted candles. The painting is considered sacred and has been associated with many miracles of healing.

When Liz and I traveled through Poland, from Warsaw to Krakow, we stopped in the small town of Czestochowa to visit the Jasna Gora

Monastery. Crowds of people visit this site daily and wait in a long line to see the Black Madonna, some in hopes of being healed. The painting hangs on a dark altar with silver angels and candles around it. For those who do not have the hours required to wait in line, there is an exact replica of the painting in a side chapel.

In 1430, Hussite raiders stormed the Jasna Gora Monastery and stole the Black Madonna. The Hussites placed the painting in a wagon, but their horses refused to move. An angry robber pulled his sword and gashed the painting twice along Mary's cheek. When raising his sword for a third blow, the robber fell to the ground in anguish and died. The Black Madonna remained with the Jasna Gora Monastery. Many Christians believe the horses' refusal to move and the death of the robber were miracles.

Jasna Gora is considered Poland's most sacred destination and one of the world's most popular pilgrimages for Catholics. A 140-mile pilgrimage walk from Warsaw to the Jasna Gora Monastery occurs every August. Many of the pilgrims come to pray for miracles of healing.

Jasna Gora Monastery.

An exact replica of the Black Madonna.

Now I Believe

After personally seeing the crutches and braces in El Santuario de Chimayo, I believe many miracles of healing occurred there. After personally seeing faithful visitors seated in the pews in silent prayer, I believe there will be more miracles of healing there. After personally seeing the thirty men walking along the road, I believe most Chimayo pilgrims hold a strong faith in Christ.

After seeing so many people of faith at the Jasna Gora Monastery, I believe there will be more miracles there. After learning of annual walking pilgrimages from long distances to see the Black Madonna, I believe those Catholics have a strong faith in Christ. Because I previously became aware of many miracles of healing associated with the greater Roman Catholic Church throughout the world, I tend to believe in many miracles associated with Catholicism.

However, my tendency to believe in Catholic miracles is relatively recent. Several decades ago, I did not believe in Catholic miracles. I was raised in a conservative Protestant church that taught that many Catholic beliefs were false beliefs. This teaching developed a bias in my mind against Catholicism. I was skeptical of the Catholic Church. Whenever I heard of any Catholic miracles, I discounted and ignored them. I had a psychological barrier that did not allow me to view Catholic miracles as real miracles. But as I learned more about Catholic worship practices and the history of Christianity, my perspective changed.

Miracles are what Jesus used to spread his ministry, to spread Christianity. Jesus taught the disciples to perform miracles with the power of the Holy Spirit. After Jesus ascended to heaven, he left behind the Holy Spirit for Christians to continue performing miracles. The disciples taught other early church leaders to perform miracles as Christianity spread further into the world.

Christians believe God's power is unlimited. Choosing not to believe in miracles because they occurred within a different Christian group is not consistent with the views of Jesus and Christianity. A refusal by Christians to learn about miracles in other Christian groups is not in accordance with Christ's ministry. All Christians should take the time to learn more about God's many miracles across the world from the past and the present.

A psychological barrier between Protestants and Catholics originated five hundred years ago with the Protestant schism in its break from Catholicism. Ever since that time, a bias against the Catholic Church was passed down from Protestant parents to their children over many generations. The same bias still exists in many Protestant Christians today. While I am a recipient of that bias, I somehow learned to cross the schism between Protestants and Catholics. I gained a respect for the holiness of the Catholic Church. I remain Protestant but respect both Catholic and Protestant beliefs. There are many examples of Christian miracles in both Protestantism and Catholicism. All of God's miracles can be appreciated if people learn to cross the schism of bias that divides the different forms of Christianity.

CHAPTER 2

Placing Limits on Miracles

The city of Santa Fe, New Mexico, founded by Spanish colonists in 1610, is steeped in Christian and Catholic history. Even the city's full name as founded remains "La Villa Real de la Santa Fe de San Francisco de Asis," which means "The Royal Town of the Holy Faith of Saint Francis of Assisi". For this reason, Liz and I wanted to visit the city to see the holy sites where miracles occur and to experience the rich beauty and inspiration of their Catholic chapels.

One of fourteen outdoor stations of the cross in Santa Fe.

JOHN D. SMATLAK

The Loretto Chapel Staircase

In the downtown plaza area of Santa Fe, there is a former Roman Catholic chapel named the Loretto Chapel. More than 140 years ago, the Catholic archbishop rendered the services of a French architect to design and construct the chapel. It was fashioned after the St. Francis Cathedral project in Paris. The chapel is a Gothic-style design, complete with spires, buttresses, and stained glass windows imported from France. It was built from locally quarried sandstone and took five years to complete. It was officially consecrated in 1878.

The Sisters of Loretto is a Catholic religious institute that strives to bring the healing spirit of God into our world. The Sisters were early collaborators with the Jesuits in their missionary endeavors among Native Americans. In the 1870s, their work spread to the American Southwest, where the Sisters established a school for girls, which was unheard of during that time in history. The school was named the Academy of Our Lady of Loretto.

Over the years, the Sisters of Loretto gained a reputation for educational innovation, as well as racial and religious tolerance. By the 1890s, they had opened girls' schools across the American Midwest, ran parochial and mission schools, and founded two colleges. Their work continues today and has transformed itself into a larger Loretto Community. It includes Loretto Sisters with vows and members without religious vows, as well as volunteers.

The Loretto Chapel, completed in 1878, is ornate both inside and out. The interior walls are white with colorful, recessed, stained glass windows. Interior columns are white with gold trim on top. The altar in the front of the chapel is white marble. Three-dimensional stations of the cross hang on the side walls, and a choir loft is in the rear. Although the chapel is no longer used for regular worship in the Catholic diocese, many weddings are still held there because of its beauty.

When construction of the chapel was completed, one design flaw remained: the architect never included a way to access the rear choir loft, which is twenty-two feet above the chapel floor, and the nuns did not want to use a ladder. Local carpenters were unable to design a staircase that retained all the seating space in the chapel's small footprint.

The Sisters of Loretto prayed for nine straight days to St. Joseph, patron saint of carpenters, for help from God in solving this dilemma. Catholics refer to this type of nine-day prayer as a Novena. During a Novena, devotees make petitions through worship of Jesus and request intercession from a saint. They may express love and honor by kneeling, burning candles, or placing flowers in the church.

Shortly after the Novena, a gray-haired stranger appeared on a burro. He brought three old carpentry tools with him and said he would build the staircase, but he required complete privacy. After six months, the staircase was complete, and the stranger disappeared, without being paid. There is no record for the purchase of wood. He left behind a tightly wound, spiral staircase using thirty-three steps while making two complete revolutions. Only square wooden pegs were used to fasten the pieces together. There was no column or bracket attachment to a wall or pillar for support.

Modern architects, engineers, and physicists marvel at the design of this staircase, which uses no exterior support. The full weight of the entire staircase rests on the bottom step. Some believe the small diameter of the inner spiral acts like a center pole. The double-helix shape and wooden pegs add stability to the stairs. They conclude that the very design of the staircase is what provides its stability. There is no known staircase with the same design.

In 1996, a sample of wood from the staircase was sent to a laboratory for analysis. It was determined to be made of spruce. Spruce is known to be a soft wood and would not be a good choice for a staircase. However, the lab analysis concluded the density of this wood matched the density of hard wood. The staircase wood is inconsistent with any kind of known spruce.

Unfortunately, the Academy of Our Lady of Loretto closed in 1968, and the property was sold in 1971. It was then deconsecrated as a Catholic chapel. The chapel remains now as a private museum operated and maintained, in part, for the preservation of the Miraculous Staircase and the chapel itself. Access to the choir loft via the staircase is now closed due to safety regulations and the preservation of the historic miracle staircase. As Liz and I toured the chapel, we noticed the addition of handrails and an iron brace attached to the choir loft column in order to provide support for the aging wooden staircase. Although we did not see the staircase exactly the way it was originally built, we saw a picture of the staircase without the handrails and brace.

There are several different stories that explain the staircase in nonmiraculous terms. Skeptics studied the history of the Loretto Chapel and developed rational and repeatable explanations for the staircase that were not miraculous. Most of these explanations were developed more than a hundred years after the staircase was built. At the time the staircase was built, the Sisters of Loretto believed Saint Joseph built it. They believed their Novena prayers were answered directly by the patron saint they used for intercession with Jesus. Then and now, the Sisters of Loretto believe in miracles.

The Loretto Staircase.

Our Lady of Lourdes

In 1858, Bernadette Soubirous, a peasant girl of fourteen, saw an apparition of Mary, the Mother of Jesus, near Lourdes, France. Bernadette was collecting firewood with two companions near the Gave River when she noticed a bright light coming from a cave, or grotto, near the riverbank. She watched as a lady of great beauty emerged from the grotto wearing a pure white robe with a blue sash. She had a rosary in her hands and yellow roses at her feet. She appeared more brilliant than the sun. The lady smiled peacefully and asked Bernadette to say her rosary. When Bernadette finished her prayers, the lady had vanished.

Bernadette felt compelled to return to the grotto two more times. During her third visit, the lady spoke to her. She asked Bernadette to return to the grotto every day for fifteen days. She also asked Bernadette to tell the priests to build a chapel there. She told Bernadette to pray for the conversion of sinners. The lady revealed herself as "Mary, the Mother of Jesus." She also referred to herself as the "Immaculate Conception." Mary told Bernadette that although she could not promise her happiness in this world, she did promise happiness would be waiting in heaven. Mary shared three secrets with Bernadette, but Bernadette never revealed them.

Bernadette's visits to the grotto began to attract crowds of people. Only she had the ability to see and hear Mary. The crowd watched as Bernadette followed each of Mary's instructions. In compliance with one of Mary's requests, Bernadette scraped away the soil until an underground spring appeared. Currently, that spring provides twenty-seven thousand gallons of water every day. The grotto at Lourdes quickly became a sacred site for worship. Believers use the Lourdes holy water from the spring to perform miracles of healing.

In 1864, the Catholic Church built a statue of Mary in the grotto, using the shape and colors as described by Bernadette. In 1870, church officials built a small parish at Lourdes. A three-story basilica, which holds four thousand people, was added in 1889. An additional underground basilica, which holds twenty thousand people, was constructed in 1958.

Every year, more than five million people from around the world visit the Lourdes shrine, in the foothills of the Pyrenees Mountains. The town of Lourdes has a population of fifteen thousand. In all of France, Paris is the only city with more hotels than Lourdes.

At age twenty-two, Bernadette became a nun in the order of the Sisters of Charity and devoted her life to praying for the conversion of sinners. She remained sickly throughout her life but never returned to Lourdes to bathe in the healing waters. Bernadette died at age thirty-six. She was buried on the convent grounds in Nevers, France.

Her body was exhumed thirty years later, in the presence of two doctors and church leaders. One of the doctors selected by the Catholic Church to examine her body was an atheist pathologist. Church leaders purposely selected a known atheist so the examination results would be believed.

The examination showed no decomposition of the body. There was no odor from her body other than the smell of roses. Her clothing was rotted. The metal in the rosary she was holding failed. However, her body was completely untouched by the laws of nature. The Catholic Church refers to this phenomenon as an incorruptible body. Shortly after this exhumation, the atheist pathologist converted to Catholicism.

There are dozens of Catholic saints determined by the Vatican to have incorruptible bodies. Some are in Rome. Others are found throughout the world. Some are on display in glass coffins. Others are interred under church altars, buried underground, or placed in church basement crypts.

Of the five million people who visit Lourdes in southwest France every year, at least half a million are sick and hope to be cured miraculously. There are two hospitals on the complex to care for (but not treat) the sick. The number of miraculous healings at Lourdes is substantial but unknown. There were seven thousand cases of healing reported to the Vatican to request official confirmation as miraculous. So far, the Catholic Church officially recognized seventy cases as miraculous, after completing a thorough investigation of each case.

Our Lady of Fatima

Fatima is a small village in Portugal, located about eighty miles north of Lisbon. It is a famous Catholic pilgrimage site that is, ironically, named after the daughter of Mohammed, the prophet of Islam. On the thirteenth of each month, from May through October every year, nearly one hundred thousand pilgrims come to Fatima. Many pilgrims walk from Lisbon. Some walk the last miles on their knees.

On May 13, 1917, three shepherd children from Fatima were tending sheep. They saw a bright light and an apparition of Mary, the Mother of Jesus, standing near an oak tree. The children were Lucia dos Santos, age nine, and her cousins, Francisco Marto, age eight, and Jacinta Marto, age six.

Mary asked the children to pray the rosary for world peace, for the end of World War I, for sinners, and for the conversion of Russia. Mary referred to herself as the "Angel of Peace" and the "Lady of the Rosary."

Mary promised the children she would return on the thirteenth of each month for the next five months. In response to a question from Lucia, Mary said she came from heaven. According to Lucia, Mary wore a white mantle edged in gold and held a rosary in her hand. She appeared more brilliant than the sun.

As the three children reported each successive apparition, the crowds grew larger. Only the children could see and hear Mary. Because of growing doubts and skepticism among local adults, Mary told the children she would let the town's people know the children saw a real apparition from God.

During the children's sixth and final apparition, sixty thousand people arrived to watch; they saw the sun dance in unusual motions. Although the people could not see or hear Mary, they could see the sun moving in strange directions. Many finally believed what the children reported. October 13, 1917, became known as the "Day the Sun Danced."

Throughout the six apparitions, Mary shared three secrets with the children. Lucia began to reveal the secrets in 1927. The first secret was a prediction that peace was coming and World War I was ending (this came true a year after the Day the Sun Danced).

The second secret was a prediction of the immense damage Russia would do to humanity by abandoning the Christian faith and embracing Communist totalitarianism. Mary also spoke of trials that would afflict the world through war, starvation, and persecution of the church in the twentieth century unless the world made reparations for sins. This prediction presaged World War II. Mary also shared a vision of hell and encouraged the church to pray that peace comes upon the world and trials be averted.

The third secret was revealed by the Vatican in the year 2000. It referred to a "bishop in white" who was shot by a group of soldiers. Many people believe the third secret was about the assassination attempt on Pope John Paul II on May 13, 1981, in St. Peter's Square, shortly after the fall of Soviet communism. John Paul also believed he was part of the third secret and credits a "Mother," Mary, with helping to guide the bullet in order to save his life. May 13, 1981, happens to be the sixty-fourth anniversary of the first apparition in Fatima. It is also the ongoing Feast of Our Lady of Fatima Day, a religious holiday in the Catholic Church since 1930.

During the second apparition, Mary revealed that the two younger children would be taken to heaven soon, but Lucia would live longer. Due to a flu epidemic, Francisco died in 1919, followed by Jacinta in 1920. Lucia grew up and became a Carmelite nun. She died in 2005 at the age of ninety-seven.

Approximately four million people visit Fatima each year. Many go there to pray for world peace and for sinners, as Mary requested. There are also reports of physical healings. Many unbelievers are healed when Christian loved ones pray and use dirt or water from Fatima on their ailing body part. The miracle healings are both physical and spiritual.

Our Lady of Guadalupe

On December 9, 1531, a humble peasant named Juan Diego was walking to church in the morning hours. Juan Diego was born in Mexico under Aztec rule. He converted to Catholicism and was now fifty-seven years old.

While walking, Juan Diego heard strange music. He later described the music as the beautiful sounds of birds. Juan Diego changed direction to investigate when he suddenly saw an apparition of the Virgin Mary. She was surrounded by a ball of light as bright as the sun. Mary calmed Juan Diego and identified herself as the "Mother of the True God."

Mary and Juan Diego were standing on Tepeyac Hill, the site of a former Aztec temple, just northwest of Mexico City, Mexico. Mary brought a message of love and compassion for the world. Mary told Juan Diego to ask the bishop to build a church on the site of the apparition.

Juan Diego did as he was instructed. The bishop refused. Juan Diego reported back to Mary. She told him to ask the bishop again the next morning. Juan Diego met with the bishop again. This time, the bishop requested a sign from Mary before he would agree to build a church. Juan Diego again reported the bishop's response back to Mary.

Mary instructed Juan Diego to take some roses and keep them hidden inside the front of his tilma, an outer garment worn by men, until he meets with the bishop for the third time. Juan Diego complied with her instructions. Upon meeting the bishop, Juan Diego opened his cloak and let the roses cascade to the floor. Both men were astonished to see a beautiful painting of Mary on the front of Juan Diego's tilma. The bishop realized it was a sign from Mary and knelt before it. He agreed to construct a church on Tepeyac Hill, as Mary requested.

In the painting, Mary stands just as she first appeared to Juan Diego, a native princess with a mestizo face and high cheekbones. Her head is bowed, and her hands are folded in prayer to God. Under her feet is a crescent moon, a symbol of the Aztec religion. One message from the painting is that she is more powerful than Aztec gods, yet she herself is not God.

Symbolism throughout the painting communicated many messages to the Aztec people. During that time, Aztecs worshipped the sun. Out of fear the world would soon end, they practiced daily human sacrifice of Aztec children to symbolically feed the sun with blood. In the painting, Our Lady of Guadalupe is shining as bright as the sun. Her long hair is a sign of virginity. She is pregnant with a son who was also sacrificed, giving up his body and blood to pay the price for all humankind. Mary shows a deep love for all people; there is no need for any further human sacrifice. Within six years of the apparition, six million Aztecs converted to Catholicism.

Today, the Basilica of Our Lady of Guadalupe houses the original cloak and image of Our Lady of Guadalupe. The garment and painting would normally deteriorate within twenty years. But now, 470 years later, scientists verified both the cloak and the image show no sign of decay.

In 1921, new government leaders in Mexico plotted to destroy the Catholic Church. Their first target was Our Lady of Guadalupe. A bomb with dynamite was hidden in a basket of flowers and placed at the base of the garment with the painting of Our Lady of Guadalupe inside the church. The explosion cracked some of the marble in the church. Windows in houses outside of the church were blown out. The painting and garment were undamaged. Even its glass cover remained unbroken.

The site is visited by ten million people each year. People with olive-colored skin from across the world are especially comforted by Our Lady of Guadalupe. The church is known for many miracles, cures, interventions, and conversions to Christianity.

Padre Pio's Stigmata

Francesco Forgione was born on May 25, 1887, in Pietrelcina, a small village in southern Italy. His parents were peasant farmers who worked long hours. The family was very religious and prayed together often.

As Francesco grew up, he decided he wanted to become a priest in the Capuchin order to devote his life to help the poor. His father traveled to America for work to save enough money to pay for Francesco's education. It was a large sacrifice for this loving family.

Francesco was deeply devoted and worked very hard. On August 10, 1910, after completing seven years of study, Francesco was accepted into the Capuchin order of priests and ordained. As a new priest, he took the name Padre Pio. Because of his deep faith and devotion, a large group of parishioners grew to love and support Padre Pio.

On September 7, 1910, while praying in Piana Romana, near his family's farmhouse, Padre Pio received the invisible stigmata. He felt himself pierced with a lance, and a wound in his side remained. On September 20, 1918, while praying alone after Mass in the Friary Chapel in San Giovanni Rotondo, Padre Pio received the visible stigmata. There were five wounds of Christ on his hands, feet, and side.

Genuine stigmata wounds are distinct from any wounds arising from pathology. Genuine stigmata wounds are located where Christ's wounds were located. Pathological wounds are more randomly located. Genuine stigmata wounds bleed more heavily on Good Fridays. Pathological wounds do not. Blood flow from genuine stigmata wounds do not harm the individual and cannot be treated with medication.

Padre Pio was greatly inconvenienced and personally embarrassed by the stigmata. He kept the wounds on his side and bleeding feet wrapped with clean cloth. He tried to keep the bleeding wounds on his hands hidden from view by wearing gloves. Padre Pio lost about one cup of blood each day. His wounds never closed or worsened. A sweet odor emanated from his wounds instead of the smell of blood. He lived with this condition for fifty years, until his death in 1968.

Padre Pio lived his entire life in the spirit of poverty and charity. He reconciled thousands of people to the Christian faith. Among Padre Pio's most important works is a hospital, La Casa Sollievo della Sofferenza (the Home for the Relief of Suffering). It is located on a mountain in San Giovanni Rotondo, next to Our Lady of Grace Church and Friary. The hospital was dedicated in 1956.

Padre Pio was canonized a saint by Pope John Paul II on June 16, 2002. Every year, eight million pilgrims visit the rural town of San Giovanni

Rotondo, in southern Italy, where Padre Pio lived as a priest. Christian believers make this pilgrimage for increased spirituality and for new miracle healings. There are many documented miracle healings associated with Padre Pio. There are many more miracles that are not reported.

Our Lady of La Vang

Persecution of Catholics in Vietnam began in 1640 and escalated in 1798, when the ruling party attacked Catholics and destroyed churches. Over one hundred thousand Catholics were killed. Many remaining Catholics fled to the remote La Vang Forest. They struggled with hunger and cold weather. The Vietnamese Catholics prayed the rosary together each night.

One evening, a beautiful lady appeared with an infant in her arms. She smiled at them tenderly and said, "My dear children, don't be afraid. I am the Mother of God and your Mother too. We know your suffering and heard your prayers. All your aspirations will be satisfied. Have full confidence in God and stay strongly faithful to Him. You may gather some leaves and make a drink for healing your illness." Mary disappeared and reappeared many times.

Because of these apparitions, La Vang became a holy site where many miracles of healing occur. In 1901, a church was built on the site. In 1928, a larger church replaced the old one. The Vatican cannot officially recognize the apparitions because Vietnam does not recognize the Vatican and still opposes any appointment of cardinals. In 2013, there was a report that a statue of Mary at the site had wept tears for years.

Which Miracles Don't You Believe?

There are other stories of widely known miracles around the world. I am also personally aware of lesser known miracles of healing in both Protestant and Catholic churches. According to Jesus and his disciples, miracles of healing are one of the signs that a church is a true Christian church.

Most Christians believe in miracles. They more easily believe in miracles where someone is healed of a physical affliction. They believe a lame person could miraculously walk again. They believe someone with cancer can be miraculously healed through prayer. They believe blind people could regain their sight through the miracle of prayer. They believe someone with deafness can hear again.

Some Christians are less comfortable about believing in miracles where a person from the Bible comes back from heaven in a way that you can see them and speak with them, commonly called an apparition. They may not believe it was truly Joseph who built the Loretto staircase. Many Protestants are uncomfortable about believing in miracles where Mary, the Mother of Jesus, appears and speaks.

Some Christians are uncomfortable with using holy water or holy dirt from sacred sites when praying for a miracle. In Lourdes, they may not drink or wash with the water from the underground spring used for healing. In Chimayo, they may not take a small cannister of blessed dirt back home with them. They may feel that prayer, by itself, is enough to request a miracle from God.

Other Christians are uncomfortable with the idea that God can move objects around. In Chimayo, they may not believe it was God who moved the crucifix back three times to where it was found. In Fatima, they may not believe the sun really danced. They may believe there are other earthly explanations for both situations.

What the Old Testament Tells Us about Miracles

There are many childhood stories from the Old Testament that display the miraculous power of God. God told Noah to build an Ark to save his family and the animal kingdom from a great, impending Flood. God protected Daniel when he was in the lion's den. God helped direct David's sling when he killed Goliath. God protected Jonah in the belly of a whale. God separated the Red Sea to help the Jewish people leave Egypt. There are many more stories of God's miracles in the Old Testament.

What the New Testament Tells Us about Miracles

In the Gospels of the Bible's New Testament, we learn that Jesus performed many miracles of healing. Jesus restored sight, healed the sick, healed a paralyzed servant, healed a man's withered hand, healed a deaf man, healed a cripple, cast out demons, replaced an ear that was cut off, and raised people from the dead. People who exhibited their faith in him were healed of physical afflictions. Their faith in Jesus's power to heal was all they needed.

However, Jesus sometimes used dirt or water to assist in the miracle of healing. When healing a man who was blind from birth, Jesus mixed spit with dirt and placed the mud on the man's eyes. Jesus then told the man to go and wash in the pool of Siloam. When healing a man who was deaf and mute, Jesus first touched the man's ears, then spit on His own hand. Jesus then proceeded to use His fingers to touch some of the spit and place it on the man's tongue.

Jesus also performed many miracles that did not involve healing. He was born to a virgin, turned water into wine, walked on water, fed five thousand people, filled a fishing net bursting full of fish, helped Peter catch a fish with a coin in its mouth, calmed a storm, met with people after being resurrected from the dead, and ascended into heaven. Jesus even arranged for three apostles to meet with apparitions of Moses and Elijah, more commonly called the Transfiguration. God the Father spoke directly to those three apostles as they met with the apparitions.

An angel met with Mary to announce the virgin birth of Jesus. An angel spoke to Joseph in a dream. The Spirit of God descended like a dove after Jesus was baptized, and then God the Father spoke directly to man. An angel rolled the stone away from the tomb of Jesus and spoke to Mary Magdalene.

So everything about the miracles at Chimayo, Loretto, Jasna Gora, Lourdes, Fatima, Guadalupe, San Giovanni Rotondo, and La Vang is consistent with what we know about miracles from the New Testament and Christianity. Instead of asking Christians if they believe in miracles, it is much more informative to better understand why some Christians feel uncomfortable with certain types of miracles.

Limitations on Our Experience with Miracles

Christians today are divided into numerous different groups and denominations. Like me, many Christians were raised in an environment that not only taught a narrow set of beliefs consistent with one specific Christian church, but also encouraged bias against other Christian churches. While being raised in a very conservative Protestant church, I learned to have a bias against the Catholic practice of honoring Mary. I learned to have a bias against the Catholic practice of praying to saints for intercession. I also learned to have a bias against the Catholic practice of using holy water blessed by a priest.

Some types of miracles are more aligned with the views of specific Christian churches and not with others. The use of holy water in performing miracles is more aligned with Catholic practices. Apparitions of Mary are also more aligned with the Catholic practice of honoring Mary. In my case, my personal bias hindered me from understanding or even learning about any of the widely known miracles summarized in these first two chapters.

Miracle healings occur daily at some of these holy Christian sites. Each year, millions of Christians visit the holy sites where miracles occur. Many Christian believers make an annual pilgrimage walk to a place where miracles occur just to be closer to God. Throughout most of my adult life, I was largely unaware of these miracles and these sites. Because of learned biases, my eyes were closed, my ears could not hear, and my heart was not open to the possibility of Catholic miracles.

My Christian experience with miracles and with God was unfairly limited during much of my life. Many other Christians, due to no fault of their own, are also unfairly limited from knowing the full power of God's miracles. For a variety of reasons, many Protestants and some Catholics still miss the full experience of God's grace.

Skeptics can always rationalize a miracle. They can always develop a way to explain a miraculous event as nonmiraculous, rational, and repeatable. It is a question of what limits they place on God's power.

Any ability to believe in both Catholic and Protestant miracles is affected by many life experiences, including the church in which you were raised; any religious bias you were taught by your parents; your understanding of the history of Christianity and Protestantism; and your exposure to different worship practices within the Christian religion. This book examines each of these areas, which can impede your crossing of the schism between Protestants and Catholics. With a better understanding of the cause of biases and other impediments, barriers are reduced, and our hearts and minds are opened to the great things God does for us and his great love for us.

CHAPTER 3

How Far the Divide

The Catholic Church has been in existence for over two thousand years, since the time of Christ. It is the original Christian church. About five hundred years ago, there were three schisms or breakaways from the Catholic Church. First, the Orthodox church split from Catholicism, in what is known as the Great Schism. Next, Protestants broke away from Catholicism, in what is known as the Protestant Reformation. Finally, the Anglican church separated from Catholicism, in the third major schism.

Both Orthodox and Anglican religions have similar worship practices to the Catholic Church. Generally, their church buildings are ornate. Sanctuaries set the tone for a spiritual experience with stained glass windows, burning candles, statues of Jesus and other Christian leaders, and elaborate altars. Their services are full of Christian symbolism, rituals, and tradition that hark back to the time of Christ.

Protestantism, however, made the most significant changes in Christian worship practices following their schism from Catholicism. Generally, Protestant church buildings are very simple. Sanctuaries appear more like plain auditoriums than a place of worship. Protestant services also reflect simplicity, with little or no Christian symbolism, rituals, or tradition. As the generations and centuries passed, the divide between Protestants and Catholics became more distant and more entrenched.

Level of Bias Determines the Distance of the Divide

Many Protestants believe in the miracles that occur within the Protestant religion. Many Catholics believe in the miracles that occur within the

Catholic religion. Fewer Protestants believe in Catholic miracles. Fewer Catholics believe in Protestant miracles. This situation should prove troubling to most Christians.

There is only one God in all of Christianity. Any and all miracles, whether Protestant or Catholic, are performed by that one God. There is no separate Protestant God. There is no separate Catholic God. We all share the same God.

There are many skeptics, both external to Christianity and within the Christian religion. Skeptics rationalize miraculous events into human-made events that are rational and repeatable, not divine. When people have a bias against any belief in God, they rationalize all miracles as human-made events that can be explained scientifically.

When Protestants have a bias against Catholics, they tend to rationalize Catholic miracles as human-made events. When Catholics have a bias against Protestants, they tend to rationalize Protestant miracles as human-made events. Higher levels of bias result in more miracles rationalized as human-made events. Lower levels of bias result in fewer miracles rationalized that way.

Based on my personal experience in Christian circles, higher levels of bias appear to exist in more conservative Christian organizations. Mainstream Christian organizations appear to exhibit less bias. This seems to be true for both Protestants and Catholics. Levels of bias within Christianity are typically passed down through families from one generation to the next. Christians are partly a reflection of how they were raised.

Many Protestants feel unwelcome in a Catholic church. Protestants are not permitted to participate in Holy Communion because they are not Catholic. This sets the tone for feeling unwelcome. In addition to not feeling welcomed, Protestants are unfamiliar with the Christian symbolism and rituals used in a Catholic service. They have difficulty following and understanding the service, which makes them feel even more unwelcome.

Many Catholics feel unwelcome in a Protestant church. Conservative Protestant churches believe most Catholics need to be saved because they are not real Christians. In addition, the simplicity of the Protestant church building, sanctuary, and service make most Catholics feel like they are in an auditorium, not a place of worship.

Knowledge Can Decrease the Distance of the Divide

You understand your own Christian beliefs more when you learn from sources external to your own denomination or your own type of Christianity. The experience and viewpoints of others is key to a richer and fuller knowledge of your own Christian views. It's only when you learn about the perspectives of other Christians that you more fully understand your own Christian beliefs and grow stronger in your faith. Many Christians confine their source of knowledge to one church, one denomination, or views passed down in their family for generations. Gaining knowledge about the entire Christian religion can open doors of understanding. It can also decrease the distance of the schism divide between Protestants and Catholics.

Liz and I were invited to a Seder meal in the home of some Jewish friends. We viewed it as an opportunity to learn more about the Jewish religion in an authentic and intimate setting. We were not disappointed. There were readings from a Jewish handbook in both English and Hebrew throughout the different courses of the meal.

Each page of the booklet reads from left to right. However, the pages are organized to begin in the back of the booklet and read from back to front. The first page is on the right. The second page is on the left. We each took turns reading aloud. The main topic of the booklet was the Old Testament exodus of Jews from Egypt.

An empty chair was left at the dining room table for the Prophet Elijah. A small plate of food was placed in a special plate on the table for Elijah. At some point during the meal, one of the children was asked to open the front door to allow Elijah to enter.

Judaism does not accept Jesus as the Messiah who was prophesied in the Old Testament. People of Jewish faith still await their Messiah to come. Judaism interprets the book of Malachi in the Old Testament to mean Elijah will return to announce the new Messiah. Jews do not accept Jesus as the Messiah because John the Baptist, instead of Elijah, came to announce him.

I was already aware of the basic views of Elijah and Jesus within Judaism. However, it was not until I experienced a Seder meal in the home of Jewish friends that I gained a full appreciation of their interpretation. Seeing the actionable expressions of waiting for Elijah to come to announce a Messiah added dimension to my previous textbook knowledge.

Practicing Jews pass on the history, culture, and stories of their religion to their children through rituals like the Seder. Over thousands of years, Judaism successfully used rituals to pass on their religious beliefs in a consistent manner from one generation to the next. My experience of attending and participating in a Seder meal added a richness and fullness to my understanding of both Judaism and Christianity.

Our Jewish friends had no intention of converting us to Judaism. Our Christian beliefs were not under any threat by learning more about Judaism. On the contrary, by learning more about Jewish tradition and beliefs, we increased the quality of our own Christian beliefs, since Christianity has its roots in Judaism.

Learning about the history of Christianity, how it began, the three schisms, and the growth of Protestantism provides a framework for Christian understanding. Learning when and how your version of Christianity began, developed, and changed over the generations locates your belief system within the wider framework. Learning about the Christian beliefs of your ancestors, how they developed, and how they changed over time adds new texture to your own Christian beliefs.

Gaining knowledge about the history of the Bible, when different parts of the Bible were written and by whom, and which parts are more influential than others enlightens your perspective. Learning about religious writings that were once included in the Bible but later removed is critical to your overall Christian knowledge. Learning about different doctrinal views among the various Christian religions and denominations, different worship practices among Christians, and different symbolism and rituals used among various groups adds structure and clarity to understanding your own beliefs.

Many times, when we fail to educate ourselves about the views of other Christians, we jump to conclusions about those other Christians that are false. It's when we take the time to really understand the views of other Christians that our own views become clear. As our own Christian views become clear, the distance of the divide between Protestants and Catholics diminishes.

CHAPTER 4

A Window into Fundamentalism

I just arrived at my high school gym class. Normally, the high school boys held gym class separately from the girls. The boys had a male gym teacher. The girls had a female gym teacher. There were separate locker rooms. The two groups usually participated in different programs, with the boys' activities a little more physical in nature. But for two weeks, the boys and girls would take gym class together, in order to learn how to square dance. I was directed to sit on one of the bleachers on the side of the gymnasium and watch while the other students learned to square dance.

I did not participate because I brought a note from my parents to explain my religious beliefs against dancing. Even though my gym teacher honored my note without question, I could tell he thought my religion was silly. Most of the boys and girls in the gym class also thought my religion was silly. Right then, I agreed with that sentiment and began to question many of the things I was taught in my Bible-based church.

Understanding the Fundamentalist Mind-Set

Protestant Fundamentalists have a very different view of the world than mainstream Protestants or Catholics. The best way to understand the mind-set and belief system of Fundamentalists is through examples and stories of real-life situations. To provide a window into the world of Fundamentalism, I will share many of my personal experiences of growing up in the fundamentalist Christian and Missionary Alliance church. Not every Fundamentalist shared the same experiences. However, most

Fundamentalists shared similar experiences and developed views of the world that resulted in the same Christian Fundamentalist mind-set.

Slovakian Heritage

All four of my grandparents were born in Slovakia; they worshipped in the Lutheran church and then came to America to have a better life. After their arrival in the United States, they all attended a Fundamentalist Christian church that was part of a Protestant denomination called the Church of God, based in Anderson, Indiana. My grandfather on my father's side was particularly independent and adventuresome. At age sixteen, with the blessing of his family, he left his home in Slovakia with one suitcase and the clothes on his back, took a train and then a ship to the United States, and never saw any members of his family again. However, he did keep in contact through letters.

He worked in a steel mill, then met and married a Slovakian woman who also emigrated to the United States. They started a Slovakian Church of God in their home in Pennsylvania. When the church grew large enough, they moved it to a separate building nearby and hired a preacher who could speak in the Slovak language, like the parishioners.

When he first arrived in America, my grandfather initially attended a Lutheran church. However, he did not understand the service because it was spoken in English. My grandfather spoke very little English upon his arrival in the United States. He changed to a Church of God, where everyone spoke his native language. In order to become settled in this new country, where a new and unfamiliar language was spoken, he looked for assistance from other Slovakian immigrants who arrived in America before he did. They helped him obtain housing and food, and then showed him how to get a job. They also invited him to attend an informal church where he could understand the worship service in his own language, even though it was not the Lutheran denomination in which he was raised.

Because he appreciated the assistance he received from fellow immigrants, my grandfather wanted to help other Slovakian immigrants upon their arrival in America. Once my grandfather married, he and his wife opened part of their home to take in temporary boarders who recently arrived from Slovakia. Those new immigrants had a place to live and food to eat, until they gained employment and moved to a place of their own. The boarders were also invited to attend a church where their native Slovakian language was spoken.

Once the first boarders became settled and moved out on their own, new Slovakian boarders moved in. A rotation of new immigrant boarders in their home continued. One of the families who boarded at my grandfather's home was the family of my grandfather on my mother's side, before she was born. That is how my mother's parents were introduced to the Slovakian-speaking Church of God, which they also chose to attend instead of the Lutheran denomination in which they were raised.

My grandparents on my mother's side eventually moved to Connecticut for a permanent job in a brass mill and attended a Slovakian-speaking Church of God there. My maternal grandfather lived most of his adult life in Connecticut, surrounded by an ethnic community of Slovakian immigrants. He continued to speak in his native Slovakian language and never really assimilated to an English-speaking American life.

The Church of God denomination owned a campground in eastern Ohio, where families from congregations in the northeastern part of the United States met together for one week each summer. The campground had a large tabernacle for church services, a dining hall, and dormitories. A tabernacle is a large building with open-air windows and doors, lots of simple wooden pews, and unfinished-wood ceilings and walls. Church services were held there each morning, afternoon, and evening. Some of the services were in Slovak. Some were in English. My parents met at that church camp.

Three of my uncles were Fundamentalist Christian preachers. My mother's oldest sister married a Church of God preacher, who pastored a Slovakian church in western Pennsylvania. They had sixteen children together. My father's oldest sister married a preacher and moved to a remote area in the mountains of Idaho, where he pastored camp visitors and rural parishioners. That uncle hunted deer and moose for food and traveled by snowmobile during the severe winter seasons. My father's youngest brother became a Church of God preacher in the Seattle area. He and his wife later moved to different churches in southwest Canada, where they obtained dual citizenship with the United States and Canada.

I grew up during the 1960s and 1970s in a small town in western

Pennsylvania. We were poor, but as children, we did not realize it at the time. My father worked as a scheduling clerk at a steel mill, where they manufactured railroad cars. My mother stayed at home to raise five children. We owned our house, but we shared bedrooms. I attended a Fundamentalist Christian church that was part of a Protestant denomination called Christian & Missionary Alliance. The church was a very simple building, without stained glass windows, statues, paintings, or any other ornate decor. I attended Sunday School class and worship service every Sunday morning, church service each Sunday evening, and prayer meeting each Wednesday evening.

My life revolved around the church. I joined the Youth Fellowship group and served as president for a year. I attended a weekly youth Bible study group. I played for the church basketball team and later for the church softball team. Because our youth group regularly socialized together, most of my friends attended the same church.

Our family always ate meals together and prayed out loud before each meal. Each summer, I stayed at two church campgrounds for one week each and attended church services several times each day. One family campground was the Church of God campground in Hubbard, Ohio. The other was a Christian & Missionary Alliance campground, called Mahaffey Camp, in western Pennsylvania.

Explanation of Fundamentalist and Evangelical

The term "Fundamentalist Christian" means different things to different people. The same is true with the term "Evangelical Christian." The most common characteristic used to differentiate them from other Christians is the degree of legalism in which they believe. Legalism is the belief in laws, or rules, you must follow to be considered Christian.

There are different degrees of legalism within the Evangelical and Fundamentalist communities. Evangelical is a vaguer, umbrella term that can also include the Fundamentalist community. Generally, Fundamentalists are considered more legalistic (have more laws) than Evangelicals. There is a range of denominations that identify with those terms, some more legalistic than others.

At some point, many Fundamentalists stopped use of the term

Fundamentalist and adopted the term *Evangelical* instead. There are Fundamentalist Protestants, as well as Fundamentalist Catholics. Evangelicals can also be either Protestant or Catholic. For brevity, I will use the term *Fundamentalist Christian* to generally convey someone who is very legalistic and Protestant.

Many of my examples draw from my experiences growing up in the Christian & Missionary Alliance church in western Pennsylvania. When I share my experiences with a legalistic upbringing, I do not intend for it to reflect negatively on the Christian & Missionary Alliance denomination, nor on the Church of God denomination. The level of legalism is not necessarily consistent across all the churches in a denomination. One church can be much more legalistic than other churches in the same denomination. Also, individual churches and denominations change over time and may be very different today than they were during my youth.

Church Camp for Families

I have fond memories of Mahaffey Camp, which I attended for a week each summer. This church camp was owned by the Christian & Missionary Alliance denomination and was located about one hour's drive from home. Mahaffey was a regional camp that drew families from many Christian & Missionary Alliance churches in western Pennsylvania. Approximately three thousand adults and youth attended. Many of my church friends were there with their parents. The camp had a variety of housing arrangements available for church families to vacation together economically.

My father initially brought a small travel trailer that some members of my family would use. Other family members would stay in tents. With little plumbing available, we used large outhouses that were built to handle crowds of people. My father later purchased a used, permanent trailer that could house more people. The larger trailer had a water hook-up for use with cooking and bathing.

Mahaffey Camp also had about two hundred small cottages on the grounds, with indoor plumbing. They were owned by church members who were more financially fortunate. Dormitories were available to preachers and their families, in return for work in volunteer jobs during camp. They performed many duties like dining hall service, youth group leadership, music director, bookstore sales, and toilet paper roll replacement in the outhouses.

During some years, I camped in a tent on an open field, with one or two of my friends. We purchased inexpensive meals in the dining hall. We hiked one mile through the woods to a cold stream to bathe. There was one place along the shallow stream with a small pool of water ten feet deep. Except for the sheer coldness of the water, it was the perfect spot to bathe. After my father bought the large trailer, I chose to shower there instead of the freezing stream.

While at camp, we attended many church services in both the main tabernacle and the youth tabernacle. The sermons almost always challenged us to be better Christians than we were, through more sacrifice and increasingly higher expectations. However, we also found time to play with other teenagers in the river across the street from camp.

Without many planned activities for youth, we walked along the dirt roads through camp to visit different church families at their tent or trailer locations. After the evening service each night, we bought milkshakes from the back of the snack store on the campground and socialized with teenagers from other churches. Each year, near the end of camp, an outdoor baptismal service was held for Christian believers who wanted to be baptized by total immersion in water.

One family from our home church always invited the entire church to their trailer site on the last Saturday night of camp to eat mountain pies. Mountain pies were two pieces of bread with pie filling in between. We usually had a choice of apple, blueberry, or cherry pie filling. My favorite was blueberry. Each piece of bread was buttered on the outside. Each mountain pie was toasted individually over an open fire in special iron tongs. The butter kept the bread from sticking to the iron tongs. The tongs had long metal rods leading to wooden handles on the end so the cook would not get too close to the fire. The mountain pie was served on a paper plate because it was too hot to hold in your hands.

The Church of God campground in Hubbard, Ohio, also a family camp, was smaller than Mahaffey Camp and more lightly attended. Most of the people stayed in dormitories. The public restrooms had indoor plumbing and showers. Our family usually squeezed into a one-room dorm with two double beds. Youth activities were limited to organized softball games and a few other group events. I always looked forward to visiting with relatives and friends at this camp. Because many of them were from distant places, we did not see each other very often. Church services usually included choir music in both English and Slovak. At some point, the camp closed due to limited attendance and insufficient financial support. The property was then sold.

Fond Memories of Home Life

I also have pleasant memories of many visits in my childhood home with extended family members. When aunts, uncles, and cousins from my dad's side of the family visited, we usually all sat in the living room to sing old-time Gospel hymns together, while someone played the piano. It made me feel good just to be part of a large family group. When it was time to leave, someone always prayed out loud to ask God to protect them while they traveled back home.

There was also one aunt and uncle on my mom's side of the family, Aunt Sue and Uncle Jim, along with their children, who would occasionally visit us from Ohio. They seemed to be extra religious. Shortly after they arrived, Uncle Jim prayed out loud and thanked God for their safe travel. He also prayed again just prior to their departure back home. My siblings and I knew we could not watch television while they were visiting. Prior to their arrival, my mother would drape a cloth across the top and front of the television as a reminder to keep it turned off. Aunt Sue and Uncle Jim did not own a television. It was against their religious beliefs. So my parents respected their beliefs by keeping our television turned off when they visited. They were very friendly people and always brought fruit for everyone to enjoy. While I enjoyed their visits, I also missed watching television and never understood why they believed it was sinful to watch it.

As a child, I was taught to follow a long list of laws, or rules, in order to be Christian. I learned that dancing, drinking alcohol, going to a movie theater, not treating Sunday as a day of rest, smoking tobacco, swearing, and growing long hair were all sins that could cause me to go to hell when I died. I was taught that members of the Methodist church, next door to where I lived, engaged in sinful practices because they did not interpret the Bible literally, like Fundamentalist Christians do. In addition to that, some of their members smoked cigarettes in the parking lot right after church, which was a clear indication of sinfulness. I was taught that Catholic practices were sinful because they worshipped Mary and statues, directly breaking two of the Ten Commandments. Many Catholics also smoked cigarettes and drank alcohol, which provided additional evidence of their sinful ways. Because our family was Fundamentalist Christian, I was taught that I needed to live differently than the worldly people at school and in our neighborhood.

My parents did not have wedding rings or any engagement ring. Rings and other jewelry were too ornate to wear. It was considered sinful to wear jewelry that would draw attention to oneself and away from God.

My dad taught Sunday School for middle school boys, served as the Sunday School treasurer, and was head usher. I often helped him by serving as an usher during the Sunday morning, Sunday evening, and Wednesday evening services. In addition to financially supporting the church, my parents also sent money to several television evangelists.

Even though my parents were very active in the Christian & Missionary Alliance church for decades, they never actually joined that church as members. They were more comfortable with the Church of God denominational policy of having no formal church membership, to avoid development of an earthly organizational hierarchy. Just being a Christian and, therefore, a member of Christ's universal church was sufficient to be welcomed into the local church. The Church of God denomination believed there was no need to also join a separate, human-made religious organization. At times, church membership can make church seem more like a business than a religion.

Memories of Church Life

I remember when one of our local Christian & Missionary Alliance church members moved to a different state for a new job with a much higher salary. Like Aunt Sue and Uncle Jim, he also seemed to be extra religious. He began to tithe 90 percent of his income back to his new church and only kept 10 percent for himself and his family. They continued to live in a modest home.

Another one of our local church members went into the seminary, earned his doctorate degree, and became president of the Christian & Missionary Alliance seminary. Later, he became president of the entire U.S. Christian & Missionary Alliance denomination. Our local church members were very proud of his accomplishments in service to God.

Through all these experiences, it became evident to me that people with the highest number of religious rules and the highest amount of sacrifice were considered the most religious in the Fundamentalist community. By not dancing, not drinking alcohol, not swearing, not going to a movie theater, not watching television, being active in the church, praying out loud in public, tithing more than 10 percent, and becoming a preacher or missionary, you would be considered more religious, would be more respected in the church, and would gain favor over others in God's eyes. Those who could not comply with an increasing number of rules and higher levels of sacrifice were considered less religious and would not gain favor in God's eyes.

Church sermons were educational in nature but usually focused on how to become a better Christian. Biblical text was cited and interpreted in a manner that set higher expectations, required more sacrifice, and added new rules to follow. It was similar to being on a treadmill that goes faster and faster. Those who continued to become better Christians through more sacrifice and additional rules were rewarded with more respect. Those who could not meet the ever-increasing expectations were left with feelings of guilt.

I was fine with being a Fundamentalist Christian, until I reached high school. It was there that my exposure to people from other Christian denominations increased. It was in high school that I began to question and research many of the things I was taught. Some of the people I knew from different denominations seemed very religious. Even though they sometimes did things that I was taught were sinful, I no longer believed they would go to hell. I always heard everything we believed was based in the Bible. However, I never saw anything in the Bible about dancing, movie theaters, tobacco, or long hair being sinful. I also never saw any mention in the Bible about Methodists and Catholics engaging in sinful practices. Because most people in the world were not Fundamentalist Christians, I did not believe so many people would be condemned to hell, and only Fundamentalist Christians would go to heaven. The teachings I learned from my Fundamentalist Christian church just didn't seem right.

While in high school, I asked a Catholic girl I met at school out on my first date. She seemed to be conservative and very religious. We went to a movie at a movie theater. Not only was it my first date, it was also the first time I went to a movie theater. Even though we never dated again, I really enjoyed the movie. Word spread back to my preacher that I saw a movie. He invited me to a private meeting in his study at the church. I was asked questions about my religious beliefs concerning going to movies and other rules. Without any fear or shame, I replied that our church interprets the Bible literally; I read the Bible and never saw anywhere in it where movies and dancing were sinful. He was kind in his response but shared his concern that the youth leaders in our church were becoming less religious.

I was the middle child of five. We all inherited some of my grandfather's independent and adventuresome nature (I may have received a larger dose than others). All four of my siblings married someone with a Christian & Missionary Alliance background. My two younger sisters married preachers. Shortly after college, I met a religious girl, and we eventually decided to get married. There was one problem: she was Catholic. I was not sure how my family would react. She was also concerned about how her parents would react to me being a Fundamentalist Protestant. However, it all worked out fine. Any misgivings anyone held were kept private, and both of us felt welcomed into each other's family. I am sure my parents prayed that Liz would become a Fundamentalist Christian, and I am sure Liz's parents preferred I become Catholic.

Catholic and Mainstream Protestant Exposure

We were married in a Catholic church. At the wedding reception, wine was available to guests. The champagne toast used either real champagne or apple juice at assigned seats, depending on each person's religious beliefs. Years later, we had two children and had them baptized as infants in the Catholic church. They were also dedicated as infants in a Disciples of Christ church. At age twelve, they were confirmed in a Presbyterian church. We raised them while attending both Protestant and Catholic churches. Liz typically went alone to a Catholic Mass early Sunday morning, and then our entire family attended a Protestant church together. Liz even taught Sunday School in a Protestant church. On Christian holidays, our entire family attended a Catholic Mass together.

Because of numerous home relocations associated with career opportunities, I had the good fortune to regularly attend a large variety of Christian churches from different denominations throughout my adult life. During college, I occasionally attended a United Methodist church with beautiful stained glass windows in downtown State College, Pennsylvania. After college, while living and working in northern Virginia, I attended a variety of churches but never settled on any particular one as a home church. Shortly after I married, we moved to Suffolk, Virginia, and attended a United Church of Christ church and a Catholic church for two years. We moved to Hampton, Virginia, and attended Disciples of Christ and Catholic churches for four years. Liz and I then moved to South Boston, Virginia, and separately joined Southern Baptist and Catholic churches there for four years. We moved to Roanoke Rapids, North Carolina, and attended United Methodist and Catholic churches for one year. Finally, we moved to Richmond, Virginia, and attended Presbyterian and Catholic churches for over twenty years.

These widely different experiences greatly enriched my understanding of Christianity. When possible, I found a large church with a pastor who held a doctorate degree in religion, and where there were many children the same age as our children. During my adult life, I had significant exposure to the following Christian churches: Christian & Missionary Alliance, Church of God, United Church of Christ, Disciples of Christ, Baptist, independent, Methodist, Presbyterian, and Catholic. I have seen many devout Christians in each of these churches. I also had a more limited exposure to many other Christian churches. From this lifelong experience, I better understand the core Christian principles that hold true throughout the Christian community.

Core Beliefs of Christians

All Christians believe Christ died so we can have eternal life. It is through faith that Christians believe in Christ. They also love others as Christ loves them. These are the core beliefs of all Christians, whether Catholic or Protestant.

CHAPTER 5

Christianity in Review

I stared at the *Pieta*, a beautiful marble sculpture by Michelangelo, which portrays Mary holding the lifeless body of her son, Jesus, across her lap. I never experienced such emotion from a piece of stone before. Although Mary was much older when Jesus died, Michelangelo portrayed Mary as a young woman, around the age of nineteen. That is how he pictured her in his mind. He portrayed Jesus more accurately, in his early thirties. That unique depiction of a younger Mother and older Son was part of the artistic genius of Michelangelo.

Further past the *Pieta* and above my head was the tallest dome in the world. Artwork completed by some of the world's master artists could be seen in every direction. St. Peter's Basilica, in the Vatican, is the beautiful and ornate headquarters of the Catholic Church in Rome.

On a wall in a side room, there is a simple plaque listing the names of popes who led the Catholic Church. Peter's name is listed first. While reading that plaque, I fully comprehended for the first time that the Catholic Church was the original Christian church. The mythical impression I had since a child that the Fundamentalist Christian church was the original and one true Christian church was dashed forever. The Vatican has some of the best artwork in the world, but the most impactful piece for me was the simple list of Catholic popes on a wall plaque, starting with Peter.

Many Fundamentalist Christians, other Protestants, and even a few Catholics are unaware of the historical facts around the origins of Christianity and Protestantism. It's not because the history was misrepresented. It's because the history of Christianity was rarely discussed in most Christian churches.

While growing up in a Fundamentalist Christian church, I was ingrained with the concept that our Fundamentalist Christian views were from the one true church. During that time, I proudly referred to myself as a *Fundamentalist*. Much later, when the term *Fundamentalist* gained a negative connotation, my church began using the word *Evangelical* instead of *Fundamentalist*. In church, I studied the scripture and was often reminded that Fundamentalist Christian views were the correct views, but I heard very little about the history of the Christian church. This approach of learning Christian doctrine from the one true church without knowledge of church history gave me the false impression that our Fundamentalist Christian church was also the original Christian church.

When I studied church history in high school, I learned Protestantism was relatively new and broke away from the Catholic Church. I learned that Martin Luther, who started the Protestant break, initially only wanted to make changes to the Catholic Church, not break away from it. I think it is important to review some of the history of Christianity and Protestantism. This knowledge helps to provide an accurate framework from which to gain a proper perspective of Christian beliefs and interpretations.

Jewish Roots of Christianity

The roots of Christianity are based in Judaism. The Jewish Bible, or Hebrew Bible, is commonly referred to as the Old Testament by most Christians. The Old Testament begins with the story of creation and tells the history of the Jewish people up to the time of Christ. It covers a period of Hebrew history that spans more than two thousand years. In addition to the historical books of the Hebrew nation in the Old Testament, there are also books that contain the poetry and prophecy of Israel.

In contrast, the New Testament tells the story of Jesus and the early Christian church. It spans a time period lasting less than one hundred years. Many prophecies in the Old Testament about the coming Messiah are confirmed by eyewitness accounts in the New Testament.

The death of the future Messiah was prophesied in the Old Testament chapters of Isaiah 53 and Psalm 22. Both books were written hundreds of years before the birth of Christ. The book of Isaiah was written seven hundred years before Jesus was born. They foretell details of Christ's death, including a prophecy that Christ would be killed with no broken bones. Roman soldiers typically broke both legs of those crucified to ensure death. John chapter 19, written after Christ's death, confirms the Old Testament prophesies, including Roman soldiers lancing Christ's side instead of breaking his legs.

People of Jewish faith also believe in the prophesies of the coming Messiah contained in their Hebrew Bible, or Old Testament. However, they do not believe Jesus is the true Messiah. They interpret chapters 3 and 4 of the Old Testament book of Malachi to mean the prophet Elijah will announce the arrival of the Messiah. Christians believe John the Baptist served as the messenger for Elijah. Judaism still waits for Elijah to come and announce their Messiah.

Jesus was raised as a Jew in the Middle East in the area now known as Israel. Jesus attended the Jewish temple in Jerusalem and studied the laws of Judaism. The sect of Judaism known as Pharisees interpreted the Ten Commandments into thousands of laws with practical definitions. The Pharisees then proceeded to teach the laws, judge those who broke the laws, and enforce punishment on lawbreakers. For example, a walk to the synagogue on the Sabbath of more than a specific number of steps breaks the law of not working on the Sabbath.

Preparing meals on the Sabbath is considered work, which also breaks that law. Simply eating a meal on the Sabbath is not considered to be work. More famously, as Jesus pointed out to accusing Jewish leaders, helping a distressed animal out of its distress on the Sabbath is not considered to be work, but healing sick humans on the Sabbath is considered work and breaks the law.

Today's Reformed Jews are considered more progressive and maintain fewer and less strict laws than Orthodox Jews. Even in Reformed Jewish synagogues, playing musical instruments on the Sabbath is considered work and breaks the law. So they typically employ non-Jewish musicians to play musical instruments on the Sabbath.

The Ten Commandments are considered the foundation of all law and the principles of reverence for God and respect for other people. Additional laws, now more than several thousand years old, are listed in the first five books of the Old Testament, primarily in the books of Deuteronomy and Leviticus. Many more laws were added by the scribes and Pharisees. The entirety of Jewish law is normally referred to as the Scribal Law. The Scribal Law was passed on orally until the third century, when it was recorded in writing for the first time. The English version of the Scribal Law is approximately eight hundred pages in length.

Under this oppressive system of laws, called legalism, the common religious people were forced to make sacrifices and constantly live with feelings of guilt because they could not possibly follow all these laws. Jesus came to free people from the burden of this extensive legalism and to refocus Christianity on love, instead. He also came to expand Christianity beyond Jewish men, to all people across the world, including Gentiles, women, and slaves. With oppressive legalism gone and a new focus on love, Jesus also said Christians should not judge others. Only God can see what is in a person's heart and be the judge of right and wrong, not Pharisees and not Christians.

The Original Christian Church

So the original Christian church began with Jesus in the Middle East in approximately AD 30 and grew out of Judaism. That original Christian church, which began under the leadership of the apostles, is known today as the Catholic Church. The apostle Peter is considered by many to be the first leader of the Catholic Church, followed by a long line of apostolic popes. Because Jesus is quoted in the Bible to say, "upon this rock I will build my church," many Christians believe he named Peter, which means "rock," to be the head of the early Christian church. Peter is buried under the stone altar on the main floor, directly below the dome of St. Peter's Basilica, in the Vatican in Rome, Italy.

The apostle Peter was also singled out by Jesus to lead the Christian church one other time. After the resurrection and before his ascension to heaven, Jesus met with his disciples a third time. After eating bread and fish for breakfast, Jesus told Peter to "tend my lambs," "shepherd my sheep," and "tend my sheep." Jesus previously called himself the Good Shepherd but knew he would soon ascend to heaven. Jesus gave the assignment of shepherding the Christian church to Peter (who would also die on a cross and requested Roman officials to crucify him head down, to indicate a lesser stature than Jesus).

The original apostles were instructed by Jesus to expand Christianity to the entire world. The apostle Paul was tasked with traveling the farthest to start Christian churches in Greece, Turkey, Italy, and other places around the Mediterranean Sea and beyond. Paul is buried beneath the Papal Basilica St. Paul Outside-the-Walls, in Rome. Mark, author of one of the four Gospels, learned much about Jesus and Christian expansion from both Peter and Paul. Mark is buried in St. Mark's Basilica in Venice, Italy.

St. Mark's Basilica in Venice.

The apostles began Christian churches in countries both inside and outside of the Middle East for all converts to join. Some of the early Christian churches struggled with the change from legalism to love. Out of habits learned under Judaism, many of the early Christian church leaders fell right back into the practice of laws and enforcement of those laws within the church.

The *Didache*

In order to ensure more consistency in the early churches as they expanded worldwide, the original apostles wrote a book in the first century called the *Didache* (did'-a-kee), to document early church teachings and church organization. This book was not included in the Bible. One of the directives in the *Didache* called for only accepted Christians to be permitted to take Communion. At that time, there were new Christians in leadership positions in the church who ran those churches with many laws like the Pharisees ran Judaism. By not allowing them to participate in Communion, they could better control the early churches to focus on love, instead of laws. Catholics still follow this directive today by limiting Communion to only members of the church. The early Protestant churches also followed this directive but then changed in more recent times to a Communion policy open to all believers.

The Bible

The official Bible was canonized in 382, about 350 years after Christ died, when a group of religious scholars agreed on which books should and should not be included. The Old Testament was already accepted long before by the Jewish people. The New Testament had twenty-one books that were generally accepted as apostolic by the end of the second century, with more books pending further review. The books of Hebrews, James, 2 Peter, 2 John, 3 John, and Revelation were the most controversial but were finally accepted into the Bible two hundred years later, by the end of the fourth century. Upon final approval, the New Testament contained twenty-seven books, with Revelation as the last, and most controversial, book to gain approval for inclusion in the Bible.

The Crusades

From 1096 to 1291, the Catholic Church waged eight Crusades, or holy wars, against Muslims for control of the Holy Land. These were violent wars in a medieval period fought in the name of religion. There were sites near Jerusalem that were considered sacred to both religions, and each wanted control.

Christian Schisms

The Catholic Church was the home of a unified Christian religion for nearly fifteen hundred years. Then the Christian religion suffered three major schisms. The three Christian schisms occurred in succession and were Orthodox, Protestant, and Anglican.

The first schism involved the separation of the Orthodox Church and is often called the East-West Schism or the Great Schism. It occurred over many years through a gradual estrangement among church leaders. The Byzantine emperor wanted to consolidate more power in Constantinople, capital of the East, and reduce power in Rome, capital of the West. In 1054, the Orthodox Church, which was under the influence of the Byzantine emperor, began separation from Rome over minor doctrinal disagreements. By 1450, the Orthodox Church had completed the amicable separation from the Catholic Church. Church doctrine and worship practices in Roman Catholicism and the Orthodox Church remain very similar.

The Protestant schism, or Protestant Reformation, occurred in 1517, after Pope Leo X was elected head of the Catholic Church. In addition to being pope, Leo was also the government leader of two city-states in Italy. Upon election as pope, Leo abused church parishioners by charging money for forgiveness of sins. Believers revolted and left the church to become Protestants. Extensive changes were made to Protestant doctrine and worship practices immediately following the Protestant schism. Wars broke out between Catholics and Protestants. There was significant loss of life. Following the Protestant Reformation, Lutheranism dominated northern Europe, and Presbyterianism dominated Scotland. Calvinism spread in smaller parts of various countries in Europe.

The Anglican schism occurred in 1534 after the Roman Catholic pope refused to grant a marriage annulment to King Henry VIII, who was king of England and head of the Anglican Church (the Anglican Church is also known as the Church of England). This schism occurred when England's Parliament passed a series of statutes denying the pope authority over Anglican churches. The separation was amicable. Few doctrinal or worship practices changed as a result of this schism.

It is important to note that each of these three schisms involved a government leader who exercised control over the church. If there had been adequate separation between church and state, all three of these schisms would have been avoided. All Christians today would be Catholic.

JOHN D. SMATLAK

The Rise of Unholy Popes

During the fifteenth century, the pope was not only the religious leader of Catholicism, but also the government leader of the Papal States, a city-state that is now known as central Italy. As government leader, the pope would sometimes go to war with countries that invaded one or more of the neighboring city-states. The leaders of each remaining city-state in Italy worked hard to have their family members placed into high-level positions in the church. Their goal was to someday have a family member elected as pope to gain political control of a larger territory and to expand their influence through control of religion across the entire Roman Empire.

In the early 1400's, immoral leaders from many of Italy's city-states successfully pressed their children, grandchildren, and other family members into the priesthood. Over time, some of them rose to the levels of bishop, archbishop, and cardinal. Some were better than others at hiding their immoral lifestyles. In 1455, the first immoral government leader from a city-state family, Alfons de Borgia, was elected pope. Pope Alexander VI (Borgia) wasted no time in appointing many additional city-state family members and others who were friendly to his regime as new cardinals. Because cardinals elect all new popes, holy leaders no longer controlled the Christian religion. The Catholic Church failed to have adequate safeguards in place to keep their religion from being hijacked by immoral government leaders.

Corrupt city-state families controlled the church for one hundred years. The new, unholy popes focused on government control, not on Christianity. Pope Alexander VI kept a mistress. Other popes had numerous illegitimate children. Nepotism also allowed city-state popes to appoint family members as dukes over specific territories in order to enrich and extend their family dynasties. City-state popes encouraged war to maintain and increase the size of their empire. Access to Holy Communion was used as a weapon. Communion was withheld from entire countries during times of war. They also abused church members to increase the treasury to pay for war and for their lives of privilege and decadence.

Because of long-term papal abuse, many people throughout Europe wanted reforms in the church. Church leaders met at the Lateran Council from 1513 to 1517 to determine whether to reform the church. Reformers were decisively defeated. Church leaders chose money, corruption, and family enrichment over religion. In 1517, after the failure to reform the church following sixty years of abuse by unholy popes, Martin Luther challenged the Catholic Church so intensely that his challenge led to the Protestant Reformation.

Close to the time of the Protestant Reformation, the printing press was invented. That development could have allowed the Bible to become available to parishioners in their own language. However, unholy popes blocked availability of the Bible in any language except Latin, in order to better control church members. Their primary goal was to increase the church treasury, at the expense of spreading the Gospel of Christ.

Sola Scriptura

In 1517, Protestants broke from the Catholic Church because of unholy practices by Catholic leadership. To protect from further unholy interpretations by unholy church leaders, Protestants created a new belief at that time, called *sola scriptura* (by scripture alone), which basically means the Bible is the sole authority of church doctrine, not church leaders. Catholics believe in a dual source of revelation: the Bible and tradition. Tradition was removed from being a source of church doctrine under Protestantism. Fundamentalist Christians later narrowed their *sola scriptura* belief to also mean the Bible can be read and fully understood by the average person.

Within fifty years of the Protestant Reformation, holy leaders in the Catholic Church once again replaced city-state family members and began to regain control of the church. New holy leaders of the Catholic Church began work on reforms to the church. However, it was too late to restore the rift between Protestants and Catholics.

At some point after the Protestant break from the Catholic Church, Martin Luther placed seven books from the Bible's Old Testament in an appendix and referred to them as the lesser books. Many Protestant denominations later removed them altogether. These seven books remain in the Catholic Bible and in a few Protestant Bibles today. The books that were removed were Tobit, Judith, Wisdom, Sirach, Baruch, and the two books of Maccabees; sections of Esther and Daniel were also removed. In my Fundamentalist Christian church, I was told the Catholic Bible had seven extra books. Now that I understand the historical timeline, it is more accurate to say Fundamentalist Christians have seven fewer books in their Bible.

Because tradition, history, and historical church documents remained with the Catholic Church following the Protestant Reformation, Protestants were left with only the Bible. That is another major reason they place such an emphasis on the Bible today with a *sola scriptura* perspective. That is also why most Fundamentalist Christians never heard of the *Didache* and do not know Peter is buried at the headquarters of the Catholic Church in Rome, Paul is buried in Rome, and Mark is buried at St. Mark's Basilica in Venice.

The Impact of Immigration on Christian Unity

During the twentieth century, tens of millions of people relocated to the United States and Canada from Europe, Africa, and other places to have a better life and for religious freedom. Like my grandparents, many Protestants who did not speak English very well sometimes changed denominations after their arrival in America, in order to worship together with people from their home country who spoke the same language. They often started new churches using poorly trained pastors.

In Catholic churches, Mass was spoken in Latin worldwide until 1964. Catholics who emigrated to America were familiar with hearing Mass in Latin, so there was less of a need for them to change to a different church. Yet Catholic immigrants still attended Catholic churches in groups of people with the same ethnicity. Both Protestant and Catholic ethnic churches grew in number. As a result of large waves of immigration, language differences and cultural differences often fostered an increase in the fragmentation and splintering of the Christian religion.

The Expansive Christian Church Today

Today, the Catholic Church owns many religious buildings in Israel, where Jesus lived most of his life. Liz and I met a Franciscan monk in Washington DC at the Franciscan Monastery of the Holy Land in America. He explained to us that the Catholic Church constructed church buildings in Israel to protect holy sites that were important during the life and death of

Jesus. Some of the sites are shared with Jews and Muslims, because they also consider them to be holy in their religions. The Franciscan order of monks has the responsibility to maintain those sites for visitors to the Holy Land. The Franciscan monk we met spent most of his career in the Holy Land. Now that he was eighty years old, he was semi-retired and gave tours in America at a monastery that houses a replica of the tomb of Jesus and other Holy Land sites.

In addition to control of important Holy Land sites, the Catholic Church built a vast network of excellent universities. In the United States, some of the well-known Catholic universities include Notre Dame, Georgetown, Villanova, Catholic University, DePaul, Gonzaga, St. John's, Duquesne, Loyola, Marquette, Holy Cross, Fordham, Thomas Aquinas, Seton Hall, and Boston College. Worldwide, the Catholic Church also has excellent universities in Belgium, Bavaria, Switzerland, India, Japan, Italy, England, and many other countries. Protestant Christians have a network of small colleges and universities that include Wheaton College, Texas Christian University, Liberty University, Baylor University, Grove City College, Dallas Baptist University, Pepperdine University, and Regent University.

After two thousand years, Christianity has grown to be the largest religion in the world, with 2.2 billion people, almost one-third of the world's population. Of those, 1.1 billion, half of all Christians, are Roman Catholic. By comparison, here are approximate numbers of people in other Christian groups: Orthodox at 262 million; Anglican at 85 million; Lutheran at 78 million; Baptist at 73 million; Presbyterian at 56 million; and Methodist at 27 million. The Christian & Missionary Alliance has 6 million people. The Church of God denomination based in Anderson, Indiana, has fewer than 1 million people.

CHAPTER 6

Indoctrination and the False Narrative

Years ago, my brother and I took our father and our father's friend on a vacation to Slovakia to visit family and to see the towns where their parents grew up. We stayed with my mother's relatives in Gerlachov, a small town near the Tatras Mountains. This was the third trip there for my father's friend. Even though he knew the address of his relatives, he had trouble finding them.

In the town where we stayed, I noticed that houses were numbered sequentially throughout the town, regardless of what street they were on. The houses on the first street were numbered one through eight. The houses on the next street over were numbered nine through sixteen, and so on. When I reviewed the address on mail in the house where we stayed, I discovered that the postal address used in Slovakia was different from the postal address used in the United States. We place the street name immediately after the house number, but Slovakia places the name of the town right after the house number. Where we have the town, they name the nearest major city. I asked my father's friend to let me see the address of his relatives, and then located their town on a map. It was a three-hour drive away. We went there the next day, and I watched as they had a joyous family reunion.

My father's friend had a filter on his brain about postal addresses. He was only familiar with how one country arranges a postal address. His mind assumed, through that filter, that all countries arrange their postal addresses the same way. That caused him to continue to look in the wrong city for a street that did not exist. He could have made a dozen trips to Slovakia in search of his relatives, but his filter would have kept him from success every time. All of us have filters that keep us from seeing the whole truth. It's only when we learn about the perspectives of others, that we begin to more fully understand.

False Narratives

False narratives, or misguided beliefs, are also very prevalent. False narratives are similar to filters, but instead of being developed on your own, they are planted in your mind by others. Many politicians tell false narratives in politically correct terms so we believe them. Members of the media often repeat false narratives, which make them more believable. At times, public schools are more focused on an education according to political agendas than educational principles. Some of our greatest universities routinely shut down speech that disagrees with their false narratives, to not risk any challenge to their false narrative. Scientific research studies are occasionally completed only to support a false narrative, regardless of facts or science. Labels and names are sometimes used to deceive the public in support of a false narrative. It requires more work than ever to discern truth from fiction. Once you accept and believe a false narrative, it is very difficult to unlearn it.

Partisan politics produces people with extreme views on both liberal and conservative sides, who are intolerant of any opposing view. Political extremists occasionally turn violent, damage property, and fight police to stop the opposing political view. Some political extremists parade the Confederate flag in a very public way, in a purposeful attempt to hurt certain segments of society. Other political extremists form Nazi groups that stockpile weapons and ammunition, in preparation for mass killing of those they hate. Extreme views are easily developed by an immersion in one-sided information without verification of its accuracy. Engagement with a group of like-minded people reinforces the false narrative.

I once met an environmental extremist in northern Virginia who lived very frugally in order to minimize his personal impact on the environment. In our one-on-one discussion, he shared with me that he can justify the murder of industrial executives he believed to cause pollution. The reason he can personally justify the murder of these executives is because of his belief that the pollution they create causes equal loss of life. He was a soft-spoken individual, in his early thirties, who lived his life according to his environmental ideals. He was a true believer and very dangerous.

Several years after meeting the environmental extremist, I attended a five-week, executive business training program at the University of Michigan in Ann Arbor with other businessmen from around the world. One training session was taught by an environmental professor. The professor taught us how to statistically calculate the impact of pollution on people, by using several examples. With his simplified analysis, each contributing factor is found to be a singular cause of death. In one example, car exhaust is a contributing factor to death from emphysema. Using statistics, the professor showed that if twenty thousand people per year die from emphysema, then two thousand deaths per year are caused by car exhaust. He then used a similar analysis to show two thousand deaths per year are caused by industrial smokestacks. The problem with his analysis is that it is wrong. Car exhaust may be a contributing factor in people dying from emphysema, but based on proper analysis, you cannot conclude that car exhaust ever directly killed numerous people on its own.

Based on my previous training in statistical analysis, it was clear he was using correlations and extreme assumptions not normally accepted in technical academia. He never even excluded other causes of death in people with emphysema, like cancer, auto accidents, or heart conditions. With the use of his type of environmental math, instead of real mathematics, the same people are killed multiple times, but by different causes. In addition to me, all my peers in this class were upset with this professor's lesson, based on faulty analysis and false narratives. We demanded that our time no longer be wasted on faulty instruction. But from this experience, I better understood how the environmental extremist I met in northern Virginia came to believe his extremist views. He and his peers were trained for years on a false narrative using improper statistical analysis by college professors in upstanding universities. He believed the false narrative he was taught.

Techniques Used by Cults

Based on my personal experience, it appears many Fundamentalist Christians believe some false narratives that survived over multiple generations. As a young Fundamentalist Christian, I believed many false narratives and repeated them openly to others. Over the years, I was occasionally challenged on some of those statements. I slowly realized many of my facts were inaccurate. That made me begin to doubt many of the other facts I learned in my Fundamentalist Christian church. I searched the Bible for either corroborating evidence or conflicting evidence. Conflicting evidence was easy to find. I viewed myself as logical and did not understand how I could be fooled into a belief in false narratives that were obviously inaccurate.

Later in my life, I learned why I was so susceptible to a belief in false narratives. Once while traveling, I happened to meet an expert on cults. He helped many people extract themselves from cults and is occasionally interviewed about cult topics on television programs. He shared with me how most cults begin with false narratives. I do not mean to imply the church in which I grew up was a cult. It was not. False narratives are common in many parts of society, including politics, education, and religion, as well as cults.

My happenstance meeting with the cult expert was an eye-opening opportunity to learn about false narratives. He explained there were destructive cults like ISIS, the country of North Korea, and the Church of Scientology, where people are at risk of loss of life. ISIS cult members believe they go to heaven after committing mass murder and suicide. The entire country of North Korea lives in abject poverty and near starvation but still believes their government leader to be a god. Scientology members occasionally place the lives of their children at risk by avoiding certain medical procedures.

The cult expert also gave examples of mild cults like the Moonies and the Mormon church, where the primary risk is families becoming separated because of cult beliefs. The leader of the Moonies declared himself to be God, held mass weddings after he acted as matchmaker, and focused on fundraising to become personally wealthy. Mormonism is polytheistic and believes that Jesus and Satan are spirit brothers. Non-Mormon family members are not permitted in the temple for any reason, including family weddings and funerals. There are many cults across the world, and many more people who believe false narratives.

You may think there was initially something very wrong with people who joined destructive cults. But most of them were normal people who fell victim to leaders who were able to manipulate their minds into believing a false narrative. In the murder-suicide of nine hundred Americans from a cult in Jonestown, Guyana, an upstanding American medical doctor was the person who prepared the punch laced with cyanide for everyone to drink, including himself. There are many more examples of normal, everyday people involved in terrible acts after becoming entrapped in a cult.

A common thread through all cults is the ability to convince someone that a false narrative is true. The techniques used to accomplish this type of indoctrination are simple. They include the following: provide evidence of leader credibility; repetition and reinforcement of the false narrative from different cult leaders; take up large amounts of time to limit any ability to think clearly; and limit interactions with people and literature from outside of the cult. Conflicting views are considered wrong and are not tolerated.

These techniques can indoctrinate and control someone's thoughts on a single subject within one week. Parents have a special ability to pass on false narratives to their children. The parent-child bond provides a pre-established leader credibility, which allows false narratives to be passed on easily from generation to generation, lasting hundreds of years.

False Narrative Examples

For example, there is a long-standing feud between Palestinians and Jews that continues across multiple generations. A Muslim friend of mine shared with me his view of relations between Muslims and Jews in the Middle East. He grew up in Kuwait, moved to the United States as an adult, and explained how his grandfather lost his home and all the land he owned in Palestine, when Israel became a country after World War II. My friend told me Palestinian children are taught in school, and reinforced by their parents at home, that Jews are bad people who should be pushed into the sea. When their parents attended school before them, they were also taught this same false narrative. Their grandparents before them were taught the same thing.

The belief in this false narrative results in a refusal by Palestinians and some Muslim countries to even acknowledge Israel's right to exist. That is one of the main reasons positive change between Israel and the Palestinians is so elusive. My Muslim friend personally accepts the right of Israel to exist, but even he misunderstood the timeline around ownership of Palestine.

He believed Muslims were in Palestine as early as 1915, long before Israel became a nation in 1948, and had the stronger case to control that land. He was surprised when I pointed out Jewish people owned that land for centuries before Christ lived, and well before the word *Palestine* was created.

A change in his perspective was easy, because he was well educated, logical, and open to new ideas. But a change in the beliefs of the entire Palestinian population and many other Muslims is not as easily accomplished. This is one of many examples where indoctrination techniques are used on a large population to create widespread belief in a false narrative, which is then passed on from generation to generation.

Even three of the original apostles, Peter, James, and John, were victims of being trained under a false narrative. I heard a Presbyterian sermon on the Transfiguration, where Jesus went up to a mountaintop and saw Moses and Elijah. Peter, James, and John, were also there. God spoke and said, "This is my Son, whom I love; with Him I am well pleased. Listen to Him." The pastor explained that the reason God told the apostles to listen to Jesus is because they still did not understand what Jesus said. Peter, James, and John, like all Jewish men at that time, were trained since they were children to believe the Messiah would arrive with great power. He would once again take the throne of David and be king. Contrary to that belief, Jesus said he would be crucified on a cross in Jerusalem and then be resurrected. The Messiah would come in servanthood with suffering and death, not with the earthly power Jewish men expected.

Peter, James, and John did not understand. They could only process information that reinforced what they already believed in the false narrative they learned in their youth. Some call it belief in a false narrative. The pastor called it cognitive dissonance. In either case, the apostles filtered out all information that was inconsistent with their original belief. They never really understood what Jesus meant until after the resurrection.

Leader Credibility

One of the cult techniques used for indoctrination is to establish leader credibility. As a child, I certainly had the highest regard for my parents. They raised five children in a respectful environment. They attended church regularly, and they worked hard. They passed on to me the same values and beliefs their parents passed on to them. At church, the pastor, elders, and Sunday school teachers were all respected leaders. They reinforced religious beliefs similar to those I learned at home. The leaders who taught me had a lot of credibility. I very willingly believed the things I learned from them. My siblings also adopted similar values and religious beliefs. It is very easy to adopt the beliefs of a leader once they establish credibility with you. It is especially easy to adopt the core beliefs of loving parents.

The Fundamentalist False Narrative about Drinking Wine

The largest painting in the Louvre Museum in Paris is *The Marriage at Cana*, by Paolo Veronese. It is approximately thirty-two feet wide and twenty-two feet high. It hangs on the opposite wall facing Leonardo da Vinci's *Mona Lisa*. This large painting was taken from Venice and brought to the Louvre by Napoleon Bonaparte as part of the spoils of war. The painting depicts the Gospel story of the miracle performed by Jesus of turning water into wine. The wedding hosts ran out of wine during a wedding celebration in Galilee attended by Jesus, his disciples, and his mother, Mary. Mary asked Jesus for help. Jesus directed the servants to fill six clay pots with water, each holding up to thirty gallons, then miraculously turned the water into fine wine. This was the first miracle ever performed by Jesus.

As a young boy, I was taught by my Fundamentalist Christian church that drinking alcohol was a sin. This view was repeated many times at church and was reinforced at home by my parents. It did not matter that the Bible clearly told a story of Jesus turning water into a fine wine for wedding guests to enjoy after the first pots of wine ran out. It did not matter that Jesus drank wine at the Last Supper. It did not matter that during one of his many explanations about the differences between Judaism and Christianity, Jesus said, "Nothing that enters a man from outside can make him unclean.... What comes out of a man is what makes him unclean ... from within, out of men's hearts." Every church member could read in the Bible that Jesus drank wine, and he declared what you eat or drink is not sinful.

But through repetition and reinforcement from church leaders and parents, I was completely convinced drinking alcohol was a sin. I was also convinced Catholics and other Protestant denominations were made up of sinners because they drank alcohol. This is an example of the second cult technique used to establish mind control: repetition and reinforcement. When I read the Bible sections about Jesus drinking wine, I never thought about it being a contradiction to what I believed. Because I was already indoctrinated to a false narrative, I was unable to process information that disproved the false narrative. The cult technique of using repetition and reinforcement was very successful.

When directly confronted with evidence from the Bible about drinking wine, many Fundamentalist Christians propose an alternate view, which is, they choose not to drink alcohol to avoid causing new Christians to stumble. This view originates in Paul's first letter to the church in Corinth, Greece. Prior to conversion to Christianity, many of the pagan people in the Corinth area worshipped idols. After they converted to the Christian religion, they still could not bring themselves to eat the meat that was offered to idols by others. Paul recommended stronger Christians in the Corinth church also avoid eating this meat, so new and weaker Christians would not be offended and leave the early Christian church. Paul offers this advice to the church in Corinth in response to a very specific problem at that church.

Not causing new Christians to stumble is also tied to the Jewish dietary laws concerning the eating of meat. Paul again addresses this issue in his letter to the church in Rome. In the Roman letter, Paul explains the issue in a more formal and general manner, compared to his letter to the Corinthians. Under Jewish law, meat had to be handled in a specific manner in order to be considered clean to Jews. Because Gentiles did not handle meat in this way, Gentiles were considered unclean, and Jews were not permitted to associate with them. After Jews initially converted to Christianity, many of them continued their practice of only eating meat according to Jewish dietary laws.

Because the early Christian church consisted of both converted Jews and converted Gentiles, there was a real risk to Christianity when Jewish members of the Christian church would not associate with Gentile members of the same Christian church. A temporary solution was put in place for Gentiles in the handling of meat, to make Gentiles clean enough for Jews to associate with them. For Gentiles to prepare meat in a similar manner as Jews was only a temporary solution until the culture changed and Jewish members of the Christian church learned how they handled meat was unimportant under Christianity. The rationale used by the apostles for this temporary solution was to avoid causing new Christians to stumble.

I heard a sermon by an Anglican preacher in Arlington, Virginia, who pointed out that weak Christians were the ones who held onto old laws. Because they were new to Christianity and still weak in their faith, they held onto old laws until their faith grew stronger. During this transitional period, experienced Christians with a stronger level of faith might comply with old laws when in the presence of the weaker Christians to avoid causing the weaker Christians to stumble. The preacher went on to say, experienced Christians should not hide the fact that they do not comply with old laws, but they should also be careful not to flaunt it in front of weaker Christians until they are able to develop a mutually respectful personal relationship with those new Christians.

During early Christianity, both converted Jews and converted Gentiles drank wine. There was no need to worry about causing new Christians to stumble over drinking wine. The wine used back then was more diluted than the wine of today, but people could still become drunk with wine.

After reaching high school, because Jesus drank wine, I questioned whether that was really a sin. I was then told drinking alcohol was a sin because it caused new Christians to stumble. It never occurred to me to ask who those new Christians were. I simply believed the newest false narrative I was taught. Later, when I reflected upon that false narrative, I realized there were no new Christians at risk of stumbling. This idea was being used as another way to justify living under laws. If experienced Christians temporarily follow a law to avoid causing a new Christian, who they can name specifically, from leaving the Christian religion, they show Christian love. Experienced Christians who follow a law to gain favor from God are weak in their faith. Weak Christians do not rely on faith in God but try to earn their place in heaven through compliance with laws governing behavior. However, choosing not to drink alcohol for health or other nonreligious reasons is perfectly acceptable.

Legalism in Christianity

The cult expert I met was not of the Christian faith, but he understood more about the New Testament than any Christian I knew. He mentioned that

Christians do not have any rules they must follow. As evidence, he cited Paul's letter to the Galatians. I read Galatians before but never noticed Paul said there were no rules. This piqued my interest, so when I returned home, I read the book of Galatians again. To my surprise, he was right.

The leaders of the early Christian church in Galatia set up some rules for all church members to follow and tried to enforce them. A complaint came to Paul from church members, and he responded with a statement about no rules in Christianity, saying we are not justified by works. Galatian church leaders then accused Paul of just trying to be liked by everyone in the church by having no rules. I cannot imagine Paul, an educated Pharisee who at first imprisoned Christians and then began missionary journeys to start new Christian churches in distant lands, wanting to be liked by everyone. That's not how I pictured Paul's personality. Yet he did say no rules. Once again, because I was indoctrinated as a child to believe there is a long list of rules that, if violated, are sins, I was not able to correctly read and understand the plain text in the book of Galatians. I could not see the whole truth because credible leaders, using repetition and reinforcement, were successful in controlling my thought process.

Paul did not believe any laws were needed in the Christian church. He even argued that if there were laws, then Christ died needlessly. But other apostles, like James, believed compliance with many laws was necessary to be Christian and we are justified by works. Because of this difference of opinion between apostles, you can find supporting evidence of both views in the Bible. In addition to those two views, some Christians believe you are saved by faith alone, but then, being a Christian requires you to show good works through obedience to some laws. Catholics and most Evangelical Christians hold this belief. This third view, which incorporates some of Paul's beliefs and some of James's beliefs, is also supported by evidence in the Bible.

Control of Time and Information

Another cult technique used to establish mind control is to limit exposure to information from outside of the cult. Fundamentalist Christian leaders are very successful in the control of literature and movies seen by church members. I noticed when a new best-selling book or new blockbuster movie concerning Christianity is released, there is always some well-known Fundamentalist Christian leader who makes a public comment about it. The comment is a message to all Fundamentalist Christians about whether they should read the book or see the movie.

Bill O'Reilly and Martin Dugard wrote a book titled *Killing Jesus*. It is a wonderful look at the history of Christ's Crucifixion. As part of their preparation to write the book, much research was done on the culture and customs of those times. Shortly after the book was released, a message was delivered to Fundamentalist Christians that the book did not include the resurrection. That was code for Fundamentalist Christians to not read this book. *Killing Jesus* was written by a Catholic, not a Fundamentalist Christian. O'Reilly clearly communicated that he personally believed in the resurrection. However, he wanted to expand book sales beyond Christians by not including the resurrection as historical fact in this book.

I read the book two times because I was so moved by what I learned about the culture of that time and by what Jesus went through. I sent copies of the book to some of my Fundamentalist Christian friends. But, sadly, they never read it. They were indoctrinated to only read literature written by and approved by other Fundamentalist Christians.

Another cult technique used for mind control is to take up large amounts of time. While growing up, much of my free time was monopolized around the church. I attended church services three times each week. I joined the youth group and Bible study. Most of my friends attended the same Fundamentalist Christian church. Two weeks each summer would be spent away at Fundamentalist Christian church camps. All of this limited my exposure to any views outside of the Fundamentalist Christian church. Through repetition, reinforcement, and control, I was very susceptible to a belief of the Fundamentalist Christian false narratives, or myths. Any level of intellect or logical thought had no impact on the susceptibility to believing in myths.

The last similarity to cults is the belief that the organization's view is the correct view, and everyone else is wrong. From my experience with several other different Protestant denominations, Fundamentalist Christians are the only Protestant group who believes their interpretation of the Bible is correct and other denominations are incorrect. Fundamentalists do not easily tolerate other perspectives. All other Protestant denominations

I experienced have a set of main beliefs. Yet they understand they may not necessarily be correct. They respect the views of other denominations because they understand no one can know for sure which view is correct.

Aside from similarities, there are also important differences between cults and Fundamentalist Christians. One major difference between a cult and a Fundamentalist Christian church is when someone leaves a cult, they will come under intense pressure to return to the cult. When someone leaves a Protestant Fundamentalist church, there is typically no pressure placed on that person to return.

Catholic Example of False Narratives

The use of cultlike techniques is not confined only to Protestant Fundamentalists. Catholics also believe their doctrine is the only correct doctrine. Because they were the original Christian church and retained much of the tradition from the time of Christ, they believe any church doctrine in conflict with their doctrine is wrong.

In addition, the Catholic religion has a Catholic Fundamentalist institution known as Opus Dei, meaning "Work of God" in Latin, which uses cultlike techniques. Only about a hundred thousand Catholics, out of 1.1 billion worldwide, belong to this organization. Opus Dei members are Catholics who desire to increase their holiness through a higher level of personal sacrifice with more time spent in prayer, living more simply, and giving more money toward works of charity. Some members also choose to live celibate lives. They all have a desire to live their lives in a more saint-like manner.

A friend of our family is a member of Opus Dei. Although approved by the Catholic papacy as a Catholic institution, this little-known group sometimes uses the same techniques cults use to recruit and retain new members. While membership comes from all walks of life, recruitment appears to target some of the best and brightest Catholics, who are very religious and have a heart for service to others. In order to establish indoctrination, they first establish leader credibility, then repeat and reinforce false narratives about holiness, take up large amounts of time, and limit interactions with people outside of Opus Dei. The organization is shrouded in secrecy and has gained a reputation for elitism and an intolerance of other religious beliefs. Unlike cults, Opus Dei members are free to leave the group at any time, without pressure to return. Although leaving Opus Dei does require permission from the organization, permission is not unduly withheld.

I am not suggesting that either Opus Dei or Protestant Fundamentalist Christian churches are cults. However, I am suggesting they sometimes employ similar techniques used by cults to indoctrinate false narratives. This results in a belief in myths and the inability to see the whole truth.

I once believed many false narratives about the Christian faith. Through an increased exposure to a variety of mainstream Protestant denominations and Catholicism, by reading religious books from outside of Christian Fundamentalism, and from a personal interest in the history of Christianity, I finally realized the errors in my past beliefs and moved beyond the false narratives. Some of these false narratives may also be found in Protestant denominations other than Fundamentalist ones, but my personal experience with false narratives is within Fundamentalism.

After I recognized many of my views were false, I was finally open to understand that Catholics and other Christians share the same core Christian beliefs that make us all Christian. I also grew to understand that Christians could have very different worship practices and still treat each other as brothers and sisters in Christ. Unfortunately, during the time I still believed in the false narratives, I was unable to see the whole truth.

Based on the understanding gained from a lifetime of ecumenical Christian experiences, I will expose five common Protestant Fundamentalist myths, uncovered from my own past beliefs. Each exposed myth provides further insight to the whole truth. Each new insight serves as a bridge to Christian unity.

CHAPTER 7

Myth 1: We Interpret the Bible Literally

I believed it. I really did. There was no doubt in my mind. I wasn't the only one who believed it. My parents believed it. My brother and sisters believed it. My preacher and Sunday school teacher believed it. The church deacons believed it. We all believed it. However, it was obviously untrue.

The first myth I learned as a Fundamentalist Christian youth was that Fundamentalist Christians interpret the Bible literally. Fundamentalist Christians even use this myth of a literal interpretation of the Bible as sort of a badge of honor that elevates their view on Christianity to a superior position over other Protestant denominations and superior to Catholics. The problem is that it just isn't true.

While growing up in a Fundamentalist Christian church, I heard this claim of literal Bible interpretation over and over. I not only believed it but also repeated it many times. I still hear it from others who remain in Fundamentalist and Evangelical Christian churches. Fundamentalist Christians hear it and say it so much that many believe it without question. Yet they fail to take an objective review of the facts.

There are many examples of where Fundamentalist Christians do not use a literal interpretation of the Bible. I will share two of them. But these two examples are very important and well-known ones.

Christian Communion with Consecrated Bread and Wine

In the story of the Last Supper in the Gospels, Jesus says, "This is my body," and "This is my blood." These words are repeated by Christians every time they take Communion. Catholics do very much interpret these particular words of Jesus literally, and they really do believe the bread and wine used during Communion become the body and blood of Jesus when consecrated by a priest. The highlight of every Mass is Communion, and it is served at every Catholic service. You must be a member of the Catholic Church to partake of the bread and wine during Communion. Church membership is the method used to ensure that anyone who participates in Communion agrees that Jesus intended for his words to be taken literally in this case.

Orthodox Christians have a similar belief about Communion. The Orthodox religion believes the Communion elements of bread and wine spiritually turn into the body and blood of Jesus when consecrated. Catholic and Orthodox Christians usually refer to Communion as the Eucharist. The Lord's Supper is another term that is also synonymous with Communion and the Eucharist.

Lutheran Christians believe the consecrated elements of bread and wine are the true body and blood of Christ. Episcopal Christians and Anglican Christians also believe in the real presence of Christ in the Eucharist. There are minor, technical differences among these religious groups, like whether you can dip the bread into the common cup of wine, whether the bread should be leavened or unleavened, and how long the presence of Christ remains in the consecrated Communion elements. Yet they all generally believe the consecrated bread and wine used during Communion spiritually turn into the body and blood of Christ. They interpret the words of Jesus literally, on this issue.

On the other hand, Fundamentalist Christians believe the bread and grape juice served at their Communion are only symbols of Christ's body and blood. Fundamentalist Christians certainly do not take these words of Jesus in a literal sense. Fundamentalist Christians mentally add an extra word to these quotes from the Bible in their nonliteral interpretation: "This is a *symbol* of my body."

As in most Protestant churches, the highlight of a Fundamentalist Christian service is the preacher's sermon. Communion is typically served on a monthly basis and is open to nonmembers who believe in Christ. Some Protestant churches serve Communion eight times per year. There are a few Fundamentalist denominations that serve Communion only once per year.

Approximately 70 percent of Christians in the world today believe the elements of bread and wine used during Communion are the true body and blood of Christ. That belief has been held by Christians for two thousand years, since the time of Jesus. Only 30 percent of Christians in the world today treat the Communion elements as symbols, and that view has been held for less than five hundred years. I am not suggesting the minority view is wrong. However, I do think it is important to understand the facts and history of Communion, to place this important Christian belief in proper perspective.

In the Bible's book of John, Jesus says something similar to "This is my body," but in a much more direct and explicit manner. When teaching in the Israeli town of Capernaum on the Sea of Galilee, Jesus said, "My flesh is real food and my blood is real drink. Whoever eats my flesh and drinks my blood remains in me and I in him." Catholics interpret these words literally. All my Lutheran grandparents interpreted this quote literally. They believed the Communion bread and wine become the body and blood of Christ when consecrated. Fundamentalist Christians do not interpret these words of Jesus literally.

Many of the Protestants who change to Catholicism often do so because of the Catholic belief in Christ's presence within the Eucharist. I met a Catholic priest who was a former Protestant minister. One of his primary reasons to change to Catholicism was to truly receive the body and blood of Christ during each Communion. We also have a family friend who was raised as a Methodist but became an Episcopal priest because of the Episcopal belief that the consecrated bread and wine used during Communion become the body and blood of Christ. A literal interpretation of these words of Jesus can serve as a powerful way to attract and retain Christian believers.

Whoever Believes Will Go to Heaven

The second example of using a literal interpretation is one of the most important verses in the Bible. John 3:16 says, "For God so loved the world, that He gave His only begotten Son, that whoever believes in Him should not perish, but have eternal life." Presbyterians and some other mainstream Protestants interpret this verse literally. If you believe in Jesus, you will go to heaven. That is all that is needed. However, Fundamentalist Christians believe, to have eternal life, you must believe in Jesus and are required to perform works through compliance with rules. Some of those rules may include not remarrying after divorce, not smoking cigarettes, and not being drunk with wine. Because there is no second requirement included in this verse, the Fundamentalist Christian interpretation is not a literal interpretation.

Like Fundamentalist Christians, Catholics also do not interpret this verse literally. Catholics believe you are saved by faith, but then, good works are also required after accepting Christ. The required good works of Catholics are different from those of Fundamentalist Christians. Catholics do not interpret this verse literally, but they never claimed to interpret the Bible literally.

Parables and Metaphors

These are just two examples of biblical quotes that are not interpreted literally by Fundamentalist Christians. There are many others. In addition to the many direct examples, Jesus often spoke using parables and metaphors as an effective method to communicate moral lessons that were new concepts within the Christian religion. Parables and metaphors are almost never intended to be taken literally. Jesus also spoke cautiously with the Pharisees because he had to be careful to not reveal his true beliefs until the timing was right to go to the cross.

Utilizing simple mind control techniques and methods, like repetition, reinforcement, and control, many Fundamentalist Christians came to believe they interpret the Bible literally. This myth was passed on from one generation to the next for hundreds of years. A review of some obvious facts shows the myth to be untrue.

CHAPTER 8

Myth 2: The Bible Is the Sole Authority

During the Protestant Reformation, Martin Luther is credited with the origination and name of the concept of *sola scriptura*. Luther was upset with the leadership of the Catholic Church due to abuse of power and believed that the decisions made by church leadership must align and comply with the scriptures. The Catholic Church historically believed decisions on church doctrine are based on a combination of scripture and tradition.

At that time, the pope raised money under his authority using tradition, but in violation of both scripture and Catholic teaching. *Sola scriptura* means "by scripture alone," but Luther never actually rejected the use of tradition. He personally respected the writings of the early church fathers. He considered the Nicene Creed binding on the church. He continued his personal participation in Confession. He continued to honor the Blessed Virgin Mary. Luther's intention with *sola scriptura* was only that tradition not take priority over the Bible. Tradition was still to be used and appreciated. However, unlike Martin Luther, Fundamentalist Christians interpreted the name *sola scriptura* literally, whereby they removed and ignored tradition altogether.

The second myth I learned as a Fundamentalist Christian youth is the Bible is the sole authority for Christian doctrine, and the Bible can be read and correctly interpreted by the average person. Remember that Protestants were part of the original Catholic Church for the first fifteen hundred years. They initially believed church doctrine resulted from a combination of scripture and tradition.

The original apostles, who learned about Christianity directly from Jesus and started the early Christian churches, were part of their tradition. Early church writings, including early Greek and Hebrew Bible manuscripts, the *Didache*, the Apostolic Canons, and the Apostolic Constitutions, were part of their tradition. Early church worship practices, practiced by and written in the *Didache* by the apostles, were part of their tradition. Early church leaders, who learned about Christianity directly from the apostles, were part of their tradition. At the Protestant Reformation, when Protestants justifiably broke away from the Catholic Church, they necessarily left much of their tradition and historical writings behind. The only document they brought with them was the Bible.

Protestants could no longer trust Catholic leadership to interpret church doctrine and wanted to eliminate the risk of any human leadership from subjective interpretations of church doctrine in the future. So in the year 1517, Protestants created the new idea of *sola scriptura*, which generally means the Bible is the sole authority on church doctrine. Tradition, along with its corresponding human interpretation, was no longer a source for the development of doctrine. Fundamentalist Christians went even further in narrowing their *sola scriptura* views with a declaration that the Bible can be read and fully understood by the average person. This narrowing view is also part of the second myth believed by today's Fundamentalist Christians.

Language Translation Obstacles

There are obvious problems to overcome in order to believe in *sola scriptura*. Accurate language translation is the first obstacle to be overcome by average people interpreting the Bible. The books of the Bible were originally written in the Greek, Hebrew, and Aramaic languages. Translating the Bible to the English language often results in misunderstanding. The English language has a limited number of words compared to the other languages, so the use of general words replaces the very specific words that were originally used in the Greek, Hebrew, or Aramaic version.

The most commonly used example to illustrate this point is the single English word *love*, which is used in the translation of each of the five Greek words: *agape*, *eros*, *philia*, *storge*, and *xenia*, representing five different types of love. Expertise in the original languages used in writing the scripture would allow for a clearer understanding of its true meaning. Obviously, the average person is not well versed in Greek, Hebrew, and Aramaic.

An example of an unresolved language translation error is the English translation of the Lord's Prayer. In one line of the Lord's Prayer, we ask God to "lead us not into temptation." This English translation implies that God would actively tempt us, which is not correct. A more accurate English translation has been under study since 1988 by a group of Catholic biblical scholars. Their current (yet unapproved) proposal to revise the English translation of this line in the Lord's Prayer is "abandon us not when in temptation." This wording more accurately implies that God only passively allows us to be tempted, because of our sinfulness. Average people who read the Bible on their own would not likely even notice this error.

Another language translation error is the name *Jehovah*. The original Hebrew word for God is *YHWH*, which does not have any vowels. We know from Greek records how it was probably pronounced, because the early Greek translation included vowels. The correct translation is most likely *Yahweh*. Near the end of the first century, Jews began substituting the name *Adonai* for YHWH when reading or speaking aloud because they were fearful of breaking the Second Commandment, which is taking the name of the Lord, your God, in vain. Adonai means "Lord" and was viewed as a safer word to use when speaking in public.

Over time, Jews added the vowels of the word Adonai over the top of the word YHWH in publications, so they would remember to substitute the word Adonai for YHWH when they read aloud. In the thirteenth century, Christians incorrectly translated the word YHWH with Adonai vowels, into the word *Jehovah*. The name *Jehovah* was created in a translation error by combining two different words, in an inaccurate belief that it was one name. Most Catholics are unfamiliar with the name Jehovah because it is not used in the Catholic Church. My niece, who has a PhD in religious studies with an emphasis in Hebrew, is aware that the name Jehovah was incorrectly translated. The average person does not have that understanding.

Knowledge of Ancient Culture

Expert knowledge of the culture and customs of different time periods is also critical to the correct interpretation of scripture. Bible scholars analyze ancient writings in order to better understand the culture, customs, and regulations during the time of Jesus. This type of knowledge allows for more accurate interpretations of the Bible.

The discovery of the Dead Sea Scrolls from 1946 to 1956 provided new information about Judaism and early Christianity. The Dead Sea Scrolls included both biblical and non-biblical manuscripts. The non-biblical manuscripts contained previously unknown information on culture and regulations, as well as new biblical commentary. To read and interpret the Bible on your own, without knowledge of historical culture, causes much distortion of the real meaning. The following two examples, which I learned from two different sermons in a Presbyterian church, illustrate this point.

Jesus said if someone wants your coat, give them your cloak, also. Many Fundamentalist Christians today interpret this to simply mean they should give their possessions away to help others. But under Judaism at that time, church leaders (Pharisees and Sadducees) would often loan money to poor farmers, then go to collect payment on that debt before the crops were in. They could then take part of the farmer's land as repayment of debt and enhance their wealth. It was Jewish custom to give your debtor your coat as a sign that you will repay your debt by the end of the day and get your coat back. A cloak is an undergarment, that if removed after removal of your coat, would leave you naked. Back then, nakedness did not embarrass the naked individual, but it did embarrass others who would see the naked individual. Jesus intended to communicate that someone who was asked to repay their debt unfairly should comply but also publicly embarrass the church official who was collecting the debt.

Jesus also said if you were asked to carry someone's things for one mile, you should offer to carry them for two miles. Many Fundamentalist Christians today interpret this to simply mean they should work hard to help other people. But in the days of Jesus, Palestine was under Roman occupation. Roman laws were forced on the occupied people. Under Roman law, a Roman soldier was to be respected. Every Roman soldier had the legal authority at any time to order an individual in an occupied territory to carry his things for him for up to one mile. This authority was used to force a man named Simon to carry the cross of Jesus to Golgotha after Jesus became too weak to carry it any further. It was believed by the Roman government that a requirement for someone to carry their belongings for more than one mile would risk an uprising that could result in fewer taxes being paid, so the law limited it to one mile. Jesus intended to communicate that you should comply with the law of your occupiers, but also try to undermine the occupiers with a temptation to their soldiers to disobey their own laws.

With these last two examples, it is easy to see that under *sola scriptura's* clear-to-the-average-reader belief, the correct interpretation of the scripture is nearly impossible to ascertain. These examples also make it clear that clergy with doctoral degrees in the study of the New Testament; Greek, Hebrew, and Aramaic languages; and historical cultures can be invaluable for accurate interpretations of the Bible. The Catholic Church and large, organized denominations of Protestants all have biblical scholars in their organizational hierarchy to help develop church doctrine based on accurate interpretations of the Bible. Independent churches and small, Fundamentalist Christian denominations are at the highest risk of teaching improper and inaccurate church doctrine, in addition to false narratives.

Gifts of the Holy Spirit

Some Fundamentalist Christians think they know when the Second Coming will occur. Jesus considered this blasphemy. Jesus told the disciples that even he, the Son of God, did not know when the Second Coming would occur. He went on to say, only God the Father knows. Even being filled with the Holy Spirit does not mean you know what God the Son knows or what God the Father knows. We are still human, with general human knowledge.

Fundamentalist Christians believe the average person can accurately interpret the Bible with the help of the Holy Spirit. This is untrue. In jumping to this conclusion, they conveniently ignore two parts of the New Testament. The first is the story in Acts where the original apostles, who were filled with the Holy Spirit, still disagreed with each other on Christian doctrine, most notably whether Gentiles must follow Jewish law to be Christian. Being filled with the Holy Spirit does not mean you have a higher power of knowledge to better interpret the scriptures. If Jesus did not know when the Second Coming would occur and the apostles could not agree on church doctrine after being filled with the Holy Spirit, then average Fundamentalist Christians cannot accurately interpret scripture on their own, even when filled with the Holy Spirit.

The second part of the Bible that is ignored is in Paul's first letter to the Corinthians. Paul explains there are different kinds of special gifts given to us by the Holy Spirit. Each of us is given our own manifestation of the Spirit. One person may receive wisdom; another may receive the word of knowledge. Others may receive the gift of faith, the gift of healing, the ability to produce deeds of power, the gift of prophecy, the ability to distinguish between different kinds of spirits, different kinds of tongues, or the power to interpret tongues. It is clear in Paul's letter that the ability to accurately interpret the Bible is not the single gift the Holy Spirit gives to every average Fundamentalist Christian. Even if that single gift was given to every average person, we would not end up with so many different interpretations and such a fragmentation of our religion. The one Holy Spirit would share the same interpretation with everyone.

After repetition and reinforcement of a myth about Bible interpretation, Fundamentalist Christians are unable to objectively see the conflicting evidence that is plainly written in the Bible. The myth is believed. The truth is unseen.

The Bible's Books and Written Letters

Many Fundamentalist Christians believe the religious scholars who determined which books to include in the Bible when it was canonized in 382 were filled with the Holy Spirit, and therefore, the books were selected according to God's will. They believe every word in the Bible is true and accurate. Because of their focus on every word being true, Fundamentalist Christians sometimes tend to read and interpret the scripture in a more detailed manner. They read the Bible verse by verse, which causes them to understand it literally rather than reading an entire passage, chapter, or book to gain a more general view of the bigger picture.

History shows there was much discussion and disagreement among the religious scholars about which books should be included in the Bible. The debate over the four most controversial books of James, Jude, Hebrews, and Revelation went on for two hundred years. In the end, scholars agreed to include all four controversial books because they would add a historical perspective, even though some of what was written in those books was viewed as questionable. The general view at the time was, the inclusion of more books was better than the inclusion of fewer books. The parts of the controversial books that were accurate would provide good information when the Bible was read from a big-picture perspective. The parts of the controversial books that were either inaccurate or unclear would be left for future historians to debate. Other books, that were mostly incorrect, were left out of the Bible altogether.

Much later, when Martin Luther published a German New Testament, he separated the four controversial books in the table of contents to indicate they were the lesser books. Luther, a biblical scholar, was particularly upset with the book of James because of its focus on laws and justification by works. Luther believed the book of James was in direct opposition to the views of Peter, Paul, and the rest of the New Testament.

Fundamentalist Christians believe every word in the Bible, canonized in 382, is true because the religious scholars at that time were filled with the Holy Spirit. But shortly after the Protestant Reformation in 1517, more than a thousand years after the Bible was canonized, seven books were removed from the Old Testament by many Protestant denominations. Only the remaining portion of that Bible is used by Fundamentalist Christians today.

In Martin Luther's Bible, with a German translation, those seven books were initially moved to an appendix at the end of the Old Testament. Luther did not believe them to be part of the scriptures but still considered them to be useful to read. The time period covered by those books was the most recent of all the books in the Old Testament but still prior to the birth of Christ.

Much later, after Luther's German publication, Lutheran Christians dropped those books altogether. As mentioned previously, it remains unclear why those seven books, originally selected by scholars who were supposedly filled with the Holy Spirit, are no longer included in the Fundamentalist Christian Bible. Not only were those books removed, they are not typically even referenced for background information. The logic appears to be flawed when you take a divinely inspired Bible, make revisions, and still consider it to be divinely inspired.

In the New Testament, the four Gospels were not recorded until decades after the death of Jesus. Prior to having them available in written form, the information was passed on orally. Matthew wrote the Gospel of Matthew from a Jewish perspective, beginning with a long genealogy that is historically important to Jews. Matthew was a Jewish tax collector. The Gospel of Mark is the closest recorded account on the life of Jesus and is probably based on eyewitness information from Peter. It is the earliest and most straightforward Gospel of all.

Luke was the only Gospel writer who was a Gentile. His Gospel is considered more of a universal Gospel, written for Gentiles, women, and slaves. Unlike the other three Gospels, Luke almost never mentions anything from the Old Testament. Luke also gives a special place to women in his writing. Luke was likely a doctor from Macedonia, where women were held in higher esteem than anywhere else. Luke may also have been an artist.

Bible scholars show supporting evidence that the Gospel of John was written much later than the other Gospels, about the year 100, in Ephesus. By that time, Christianity spread significantly throughout the Gentile world, and the Christian church was no longer dominated by Jewish Christians. The Gospel of John was written primarily for this broader audience. The apostle John did not repeat all the stories of Jesus included in the other three Gospels, but he did provide more details about the life of Jesus, especially his early ministry.

Many of the remaining books in the New Testament are just personal letters, not formal epistles, that were written to other individuals or specifically to early Christian churches. Paul wrote many of the letters to churches he personally started. Paul likely became aware of problems or questions from church leaders through letters written to him or from other Christian leaders who passed through those cities. Apart from the book of Romans, Paul wrote these letters to help church leaders better handle immediate and specific issues at their church.

Fundamentalist Christians often misinterpret Paul's writings as laws for all Christians to follow, instead of his intended purpose to offer counseling advice for pressing situations. Because the initial letters written to Paul were not kept, we should understand that Paul's letters are each only one-half of a conversation. It is difficult to properly interpret and fully understand a conversation if you only have access to one-half of it.

The Letter to the Romans is written very differently than Paul's other letters to early Christian churches because Paul had not yet been to Rome and did not personally know those church leaders. In his letter to the

Christian church in Rome, Paul explains his own theological views and the basis of his faith using more formal and thorough explanations. He did not address any immediate problem or issue currently in the church in Rome. It is very likely that the authors of the New Testament letters would have written those letters much differently if they ever imagined they might one day be published in a book for all Christians to read and interpret for thousands of years.

Paul's letter to Philemon addresses the issue of slavery. Philemon was a Christian in the church in Laodicaea, which was in present-day Turkey. There were sixty million slaves in the expansive Roman Empire during the time of Christ. One of Philemon's runaway slaves went to Rome, became a Christian, and worked with Paul. Paul eventually sent him back to Philemon with a personal letter, asking Philemon to free the slave and treat him as a Christian brother in the church.

This was the clearest indication yet that Christianity intended to change people's relationships by abolishing external differences and treating each other with the love of Christ. Under Christianity, there would no longer be a distinction between Greek or Jew, slave or free man, male or female. Over time, the Roman Empire would transition away from slavery to avoid an uprising and significant bloodshed.

Guidance versus Laws

Paul was educated, trained as a Jewish Pharisee, and very knowledgeable of Jewish laws. His primary mission was to spread Christianity beyond the Middle East. Although the early churches Paul started were mostly Gentile and pagan, there were still some converted Jews in them. Paul used his extensive knowledge and training in Judaism to explain to converted Jews how Christianity developed from Judaism. Paul also used his training in Jewish law to help guide early church leaders in how to handle specific problems that arose among church members of different backgrounds. Early pagan Christians had difficulty learning to treat women and others with proper respect. In some of Paul's letters, he offers extensive guidance as a counselor.

Some Fundamentalist Christians tend to focus on Paul's guidance, and to mistakenly develop a long list of rules, or laws, that must be followed and judged on compliance, under their version of Christianity. These laws reinforce the feelings of sacrifice and guilt that Jesus came to change. Some Fundamentalist Christians also tend to dwell on Old Testament directives because of their comfort with legalism. Catholics and mainstream Protestants are prone to focus more on the New Testament Gospel stories of Jesus, who changed the church away from laws and moved to love, without judgment on compliance to laws.

After my son moved to a different city for his first permanent job, he visited a variety of churches seeking to find a home church. He liked one specific church and pastor but noticed the pastor preached from the Old Testament on his first visit. After his second visit, my son called me and indicated he really liked this church except for some lingering discomfort with a focus on the Old Testament. He asked what I thought. I recommended he look for a mainstream organization where he felt comfortable, with a highly trained pastor and congregants his age.

I also suggested, if a preacher gave a sermon from different Old Testament books too often, it is a strong sign the church focuses too much on legalism, and he should consider other churches. On my son's third visit, the pastor continued to preach from a different book in the Old Testament. My son left and never went back. Since then, he found a home church with many people his age, where the pastor has a doctorate degree in religion, and the primary focus is on the New Testament. My son feels very comfortable there.

Growth in New Denominations

I researched the origins of the Christian & Missionary Alliance denomination, the denomination in which I was raised. Even though a Presbyterian minister started the Christian & Missionary Alliance, the denomination grew out of the Holiness movement. The Holiness Church began in the United States in the late 1800s, after the Civil War, and focused on living a holy life without willful sin. Compliance with many rules that govern personal behavior was considered key to achieving a holy life on earth.

The Holiness movement became popular at that time because of a desire to live a perfect Christian life. The founder of the Christian & Missionary Alliance started his own separate, but related, Holiness movement because of his vision to expand the movement worldwide. In addition to the Christian & Missionary Alliance, the Church of God from Anderson, Indiana, the Church of the Nazarene, and many Pentecostal denominations also grew out of the Holiness movement.

Both the US Christian & Missionary Alliance and Canadian Christian & Missionary Alliance organizations have websites. Each website explains the history of their denomination. They refer to their beginnings as part of a movement, but each website fails to identify the movement as the Holiness movement. Further research was required to uncover their true historical beginnings.

Each new denomination that grew out of the Holiness movement created a set of laws to govern personal behavior. Effectively, it was a list of dos and don'ts. Examples include do go to church every Sunday; do read your Bible daily; don't drink alcohol; and don't dance. The list of dos and don'ts varied by denomination.

Over time, the focus on laws to live a perfect Christian life became misinterpreted as laws required to just be considered a Christian. These laws were instilled in children out of fear they may not go to heaven otherwise. Without the use of rituals to pass on their religious beliefs in a consistent manner from one generation to the next, the core message of the Holiness movement became muddled in the first two generations of their existence.

I have a friend who was raised in a Holiness church in rural Tennessee. She explained how offerings were collected in each service. An open Bible was laid on the altar in the front of the church. Everyone filed past the altar by row and laid their offering on the open Bible.

My friend told me each Holiness church owned a campground adjacent to their church building. The local church held special services in a covered, rustic building at the campground for one week each year. The focus of preaching in the camp was on a commitment or recommitment to living a more holy life by adherence to rules that govern personal behaviors. Because there was no overnight lodging available, they would return to their homes each night.

After the close of camp at her church, she described traveling to other Holiness churches nearby to also attend their camps. She would sleep in the home of a relative or friend from each local church while she attended their camp as a visitor. The regional campgrounds of the Christian & Missionary

Alliance and the Church of God I attended in my youth was an idea that likely grew out of the local Holiness campgrounds.

The Holiness church broke away from Methodism after the Methodist Church relaxed their emphasis on sanctification, which is living a holy life helping those less fortunate. As a result, the Holiness church overemphasized sanctification, with a new expectation to live a perfect Christian life based on compliance with laws governing behavior. Prior to the Holiness church separation, Methodism had already split into many different denominations.

Methodism began in England in 1729, when it broke away from the Anglican Church. Methodism started because the Anglican Church was considered too formal and there was not enough emphasis on sanctification and living a perfect Christian life. Methodism can trace its beginning to college students and the Wesley brothers at Oxford University. Poor people gravitated to Methodism, and away from the Anglican Church, because Methodism was less formal. In addition to the Methodist separation, many other denominations also split from the Anglican Church, including many Episcopal denominations.

I also researched the origins of the Disciples of Christ Church, where I attended for four years. The Disciples of Christ started in the United States after two leaders separately left Presbyterianism in the early 1800s and started their own churches. The two leaders later combined their two organizations into one. The Disciples of Christ hold individual freedom of belief and scriptural interpretation paramount, with no official interpretation of the Bible from any organizational hierarchy. They hold Communion weekly and believe in baptism by immersion. There is no formal creed. The name, Disciples of Christ, was initially shared with three other groups. They include the Churches of Christ, the Independent Christian Church and Churches of Christ, and the Christian Congregation. During the late 1800s and 1900s, disagreements among the four groups resulted in the formation of separate denominations.

Presbyterianism began with the Protestant Reformation. They were strongly influenced by Calvinism and have a confessional tradition, where Christians are encouraged to confess their sins corporately and privately. Teaching and ruling elders are ordained in a council, known as a session, and are responsible for the missions of the local congregation.

Failure of the *Sola Scriptura* Experiment

It seems that under *sola scriptura*, many individual Christians find something in their denomination with which to disagree or some new area they felt did not receive enough emphasis, and then start their own independent church or movement. Once their movement grows large enough, it becomes a new denomination. After the original leader steps aside, disagreement within the denomination often results in additional separations. As the total number of denominations increase, the rate at which new denominations grow also increases. There are over thirty thousand separate Christian denominations and organizations in the world today. The total number of denominations continues to grow by more than two per day, on average.

History tells us that Judaism practiced their religion through compliance with many laws controlling individual behavior. Unless Jews worked full-time in Judaism, like a Pharisee or high priest, they found it impossible to comply with all the laws. For two thousand years, animal sacrifices were made to atone for their failure to follow religious law. Then, Jesus came and changed the religion to one based on faith and love, not laws. About eighteen hundred years after Christ died, the Holiness movement in the United States brought back the idea of living a perfect Christian life through compliance with many laws controlling individual behavior. It seems they traveled back to Judaic law during the time before Jesus. Remember, the apostle Paul said compliance with laws means Christ died needlessly.

The Fundamentalist Christian experiment with *sola scriptura*, which was intended to remove subjectivity from Bible interpretations so they would be more accurate and less likely to be abused by church leaders, appears to have failed. Without also using tradition through the guidance of organized church scholars, *sola scriptura* ended up with the opposite effect of its intentions. The Catholic Church has been in existence for over two thousand years. The Fundamentalist Christian churches have been in existence for fewer than five hundred years. During the first fifteen hundred years, there was only one Christian religion, Catholicism, with one set of church leaders. During the last five hundred years, the *sola scriptura* experiment resulted in an explosion in the number of Protestant denominations and independent churches.

The fragmentation of Christianity is so extensive, it is almost unrecognizable from its original form. It is now common practice for someone to start their own denomination without a large central organization of knowledgeable leaders to help interpret the Bible accurately. With widespread acceptance of so many independent Christian organizations, our youth are more susceptible to membership in a growing population of radical Christian cults. With such loss of control, the Christian religion moves along a path of high risk.

Through uncomplicated mind control techniques (including repetition, reinforcement, and control), the myth that the Bible is the sole authority for Christian doctrine, and average people can accurately interpret the Bible, was passed down from generation to generation by Fundamentalist Christians for five hundred years. That myth is not true. It keeps Protestant Christians separate from Catholic Christians. It causes loss of control and irreparable damage to the Christian religion.

CHAPTER 9

Myth 3: We Are More Holy

Without any prior notice, my mother asked me to pray out loud to ask God's blessing on the meal we were about to eat with our family members. When we eat meals together in the privacy of our house, I am happy to comply with her request to pray out loud. But this time, we were in a crowded restaurant. If you knew my mother, you would understand she does not feel superior to anyone. Her motives are pure. She probably felt challenged in a sermon to not be ashamed of her faith and felt guilty unless someone prayed aloud when at a restaurant. She also believes this develops good habits in me. I, on the other hand, do not feel guilted into public prayer and am overly sensitive about exhibitions of my religious views in front of people who may be offended. Out of respect for my mother, I complied with her request. However, I was so uncomfortable in this situation that my thoughts during prayer were not focused on God. Instead, I felt like I communicated to others in the restaurant the insult that "I am holier than thou." Because of this feeling, I also offered a silent apology to those who may have been offended.

The third myth I learned as a Fundamentalist Christian youth is that most other non-Fundamentalist Christian groups are less holy because they follow fewer rules and sacrifice less. Many Fundamentalist Christians believe this inwardly but are careful not to say it out loud. They realize public statements are self-serving and portray themselves as better than others. But when you are around Fundamentalist Christians, you can sometimes sense a few really do believe other non-Fundamentalist Christian groups are less holy.

When I describe the Fundamentalist view that other Christians are less holy, I do not mean Fundamentalists hold that belief from an individual point of view. From a personal perspective, many Fundamentalists do not focus on feeling they are more holy than other Christians. Most Fundamentalists focus more on feeling they have fallen short of the religious expectations placed on them and need to do more. They often feel unworthy because they are not living a perfect Christian life.

However, from a more corporate perspective, they do think their Fundamentalist interpretation of the Bible and the time and effort required to comply with that interpretation make their parishioners, as a group, more holy than Catholic groups and mainstream Protestant groups. They interpret the Bible in a way that requires living a holy life according to rules that control behavior, like not drinking alcohol. They seek perfection or near-perfection in living a holy Christian life by adherence to an ideal set of behaviors. They believe that Catholics and mainstream Protestants interpret the Bible in a manner that has fewer laws that govern behavior, requires less work, and limits the amount of personal sacrifice. Because Catholics and mainstream Protestants have seemingly lower expectations and worse behavior, Fundamentalists conclude they are less holy, as a group.

Just as I did in my youth, Fundamentalist Christians view living a Christian life through a Fundamentalist filter on their brain. They believe that holiness means everyone should strive to live like Jesus, but they judge one's holiness based on compliance with certain laws that govern behavior. Different Fundamentalist denominations focus on different types of behavior they believe is most important. Fundamentalist Christians believe only the most holy will go to heaven, as defined by compliance with behavioral rules. They fear not going to heaven if they do not live sufficiently perfect Christian lives.

The Pharisees had a similar filter under Judaism that was also dependent on complying with many laws that control behavior. They strived for perfection in living a godly life too. Jesus changed the religion away from human-made laws that control behavior. He introduced the idea that holiness can also be achieved through faith and through love. Catholics and mainstream Protestants tend to focus more on faith and love than behaviors.

The Myth that Only the Very Holy Go to Heaven

It's human nature to seek assurance that you will someday go to heaven. Some people work very hard to believe they will be among the chosen few who enter the kingdom of heaven. In doing so, it is common to compare your own holiness with the holiness of others. It's comforting to believe that you are part of a small group who is very holy and that many other Christians are less holy.

Fundamentalist Christians comply with many laws throughout their daily lives in order to be very holy. They also make more personal sacrifices, like giving much of their time and money to the church and those in need, to help secure their place in heaven. They study the Bible. They learn to pray publicly in an extemporaneous manner. They also learn the private phrases used for bonding within their Fundamentalist group. These self-imposed obligations add comfort to the belief that they are very holy and will someday go to heaven. This perspective is not intentional. It is the result of myths learned in their youth.

A belief that you are in a small group of very holy people who are more likely to go to heaven may provide comfort, but it may not be correct. There may very well be enough room in heaven for all Christians, even those who appear to be less holy. When holiness is defined solely by false narratives learned in your youth, it may be time to question those false narratives. It may also be time to listen to different perspectives of other Christians. God may even love non-Christians so much, he plans to give everyone a final opportunity to accept him after death, when they see him face-to-face. We should not limit God only to actions in the earthly ways we understand. With a new perspective on Christianity and a new understanding of holiness that is not based on compliance to rules governing behavior, membership in that small group is no longer required for assurance of everlasting life in heaven.

Compliance with Laws Requires Personal Sacrifice

Fundamentalist Christians typically have a long list of human-made laws that must be followed in order not to sin. Historically, some of these sins include dancing, going to movies, drinking alcohol, smoking cigarettes, having religious statues in church, praying to saints, and remarrying after divorce. They sacrifice to comply with these laws. They teach these laws to others. They watch for those who fail to follow the laws.

The apostle Paul believed Christians accept Jesus through faith alone. Works are not required. There are no laws to follow. Fundamentalist Christians retain a list of laws, even though Paul clearly states in the Bible that "no one will be declared righteous in His sight by observing the law.... Righteousness from God comes through faith in Jesus Christ to all who believe. If righteousness comes through the Law, then Christ died needlessly."

Conversely, the apostle James believed Christians accept Jesus through faith *and* works. They must also follow laws and complete good works for others. Fundamentalist Christians base their legalistic views more on what the apostle James believed and also have scripture to support their perspective. The book of James states, "A person is justified by what he does and not by faith alone."

Jesus never told Christians to live their lives like him. He never set an expectation for humans to be perfect, like God. However, Jesus did tell Christians he loves them. He also told Christians to love others as he loves them.

Judging Others

A legalistic view also makes it very easy to judge others, even if it is unintended. With a list of rules considered to be sins, Fundamentalist Christians will necessarily judge other Fundamentalist Christians and members of other denominations. If you believe a particular action is a sin, and you see someone acting in that manner, you obviously conclude they are sinning. For example, because smoking cigarettes violates the rule about keeping the temple of your body clean, a Fundamentalist Christian who smokes cigarettes is easily judged to be a sinner. Similarly, a Catholic who prays to Mary is easily judged to be a sinner for worship of someone other than God.

Judging others naturally occurs with laws, even if it is not spoken out loud. The majority of Christians, who have no list of laws, are able to more easily *not* judge others. Many mainstream Protestants do not judge others because they don't interpret violations of Fundamentalist laws as sin. They may see individuals who occasionally fail to behave as Christians should; however, they believe everyone has shortcomings in different areas, and God is the judge of those shortcomings.

With their belief in laws and the judging that naturally occurs with required compliance to laws, Fundamentalist Christians seem to ignore repeated Bible verses against judging others, including the admonishment by Jesus in the Sermon on the Mount, "Do not judge." Only God knows what is in a man's heart. In his letter to the Romans, Paul says, "If you judge another, you condemn yourself." In his letter to the Corinthians, Paul also says, "Do not go on passing judgment." Even James, who supports legalism, says, "Who are you to judge your neighbor?" But when other Christians violate human-made laws, there is additional incentive for Fundamentalist Christians to sometimes feel they are less holy. Consistent with myths learned in their youth, it provides Fundamentalist Christians the comfort of believing they are in a small group of more holy people likely to go to heaven.

Most Fundamentalists do not focus on judging others. Nor do they focus on their group as more holy than other Christian groups. These ideas are just accepted in the background. Fundamentalists place most of their attention and effort on continuous self-improvement to live a more perfect Christian life. They place their harshest judgments on themselves after failing to be perfect.

We All Have Different Strengths and Weaknesses

Individuals are all made in their own unique manner, with a unique set of genes and a unique upbringing. Many people are born with some imbalance that is chemically, mentally, physically, biologically, hormonally, or physiologically driven. Any of these imbalances can result in a heavier burden to carry. People often deal with their burdens privately.

Some people have difficulty controlling their temper. They may work hard to control their anger but still show fits of rage. Others may be prone to alcoholism through a genetic makeup that is no fault of their own. They may work hard to remain free of alcohol but still fail often. Some people are born with an addictive personality that can manifest itself in a gambling addiction, a need to control others, or a drug addiction. They may work hard to fight their obsession but still fail over and over. Some people are born with different hormone levels that can result in a range from strong sexual desires to no sexual desire. Those with strong desires may stray outside their marriage even when they have every intention to remain faithful to their spouse.

Simply looking at the results of whether someone complies with human-made laws does not tell the whole story. According to Jesus, it is what is in their heart that matters. Only God knows what is in someone's heart. A person who fights hard and fails to control an imbalance that gives them a higher burden to meet may be judged by God as more welcome in heaven than someone who has no imbalance. Jesus did not focus on laws but on how much faith in God and love for others people have in their heart. Because people have no real ability to see what is in a person's heart, they should not judge others on the results they do see.

When I was in the workforce, my company often provided training for employees. Management employees were trained on many subjects, including financial issues, legal and regulatory issues, motivation, understanding people, and technology. I remember one consultant from San Francisco, who taught how to better understand people. He talked about how he used to become very angry when another motorist passed him at a high rate of speed and then cut him off. The consultant said he believed the speeding motorist was self-centered and took advantage of other drivers for the convenience of an early arrival. Those of us in the training class agreed, because we all had similar experiences.

The consultant then suggested we did not really know why the speeding driver passed other cars. The driver may have just received a call about a child's medical emergency at home and needed to arrive there as quickly as possible to help save the child's life. When you think about it, we just made up the first story about the speeding driver's actions for convenience. We did not know the true intentions. The consultant suggested that if we are going to make up a story anyway, then we should make up a good story, instead of a bad story. By assuming the best about someone, we will lower our own blood pressure, train ourselves to remain more relaxed overall, and may even help to save a life. We can apply this same concept to judgments about people who may have imbalances in their life that cause them to behave differently. We don't know their circumstances or what is in their hearts.

Sanctification

I heard a sermon by a scholarly Presbyterian minister who declared that we receive justification by faith and sanctification through works. Once we become a Christian by accepting Jesus as our Savior, we are saved and will go to heaven. That is justification by faith. However, we should then strive to live better lives by loving others as Christ loves us. That is sanctification through works. Not everyone will necessarily move very far down the sanctification path of works because of varying human frailties. Yet they will still go to heaven.

Under this scenario, with heaven assured, any works that are done to help others are done out of love. By comparison, under the Fundamentalist scenario, where works are required for entry to heaven, Christians are motivated to do them either out of guilt or to earn a place in heaven. This minister cited Saint Francis of Assisi as one of the best examples of someone who moved far down the sanctification path because he chose a life of poverty and caring for lepers and outcasts. His work attracted five thousand followers and later grew into the Franciscan order of the Catholic Church.

The Truth about Tithing

Another law expressed by some Fundamentalist Christian churches concerns tithing. Support of a church financially is an expectation contained in the New Testament and one I routinely follow. Many Fundamentalist Christians have the impression that not tithing 10 percent of your wages to the church is a sin, and this expectation is clearly stated in the Bible. However, the Bible only mentions tithing at a 10 percent level one time. That single reference is in Leviticus, the third book of the Old Testament, along with many other Jewish laws from approximately four thousand years ago. It says, a tenth of your herd or flock shall be holy to the Lord. In those times, animals were periodically killed as a sacrifice to God. The Jewish law meant one-tenth of the herd or flock of animals would be used for sacrifice.

The early Christian church was started about two thousand years after the Jewish law on tithing one-tenth of your herd or flock came into effect. Jesus, the Lamb of God, became the ultimate sacrifice and was killed on a cross. After his death and resurrection, there was no longer any need to sacrifice animals. There was no longer any need to keep a tenth of your herd or flock holy to the Lord.

While the early Christian church was in its initial expansion, Jesus set an example in his ministry by helping widows, orphans, and the poor. He healed them. He fed them bread and fish. He encouraged others to feed the poor. At that time, the only organized assistance available to widows and orphans was through church offerings. Governments did not provide any support to help this impoverished group. In modern times, two thousand years after the start of the Christian religion, it is common practice for most governments to assist widows, orphans, and other disadvantaged classes through the collection and redistribution of taxes. The need for some of the church offerings has lessened over time.

Based on my experience, tithing at a 10 percent level to the church seems to be mostly an American Protestant perspective. During the many times I attended Catholic services in various cities on the American East Coast, I never heard anyone mention anything about tithing at a 10 percent level. Actually, I never heard any recommended tithing amount at all, in any Catholic church. Because of their abundant tradition, lengthy history, and institutional knowledge, the Catholic Church understands how tithing has changed over the centuries. They do not misrepresent any tithing requirement.

While visiting many countries in Central Europe, I learned that each country's government there collects a voluntary religion tax in lieu of church tithes and offerings. People can volunteer to pay the religion tax at a rate of 1 percent of their income and designate which church they attend. The government then sends this money to each taxpayer's church.

Under Judaism, much of their teaching is done using the first five books of the Old Testament, which they refer to as the Torah. That is also where the single biblical reference to tithing at a 10 percent level is located. When it comes to accurate interpretation of Jewish laws contained in the first five books of the Old Testament, Jewish rabbis may have the most knowledge because of their extensive study and understanding of Jewish history. According to some Jewish friends of mine, who practice Reformed Judaism, synagogue dues are currently assessed at a rate close to 1 percent of income. This level of tithing represents the Jewish rabbi view of an accurate interpretation of the tithing law under Judaism in modern times. Most Orthodox Jews still practice tithing 10 percent of their income to charity, not necessarily to the synagogue.

The word *tithe* is an Old English word meaning "one-tenth." The New Testament only uses the word "tithe" in reference to Jews under Jewish law. It refers to "giving" by Christians but never mentions "tithing" by Christians. In the book of Matthew, Jesus called Jewish scribes and Pharisees hypocrites for tithing lesser crops like dill and mint, then told them that tithing should be done with a deep concern for justice, mercy, and faithfulness. In Paul's Second Letter to the Corinthians, Paul talks about giving cheerfully and encourages giving what you can afford. In the First Letter to Timothy, Christians are encouraged to support the financial needs of Christian workers, including preachers and teachers. Chapter 11 of the book of Acts promotes feeding the hungry according to individual means. The book of James says pure religion is to visit and help widows and orphans.

I am not recommending that anyone change their current tithing practices. Small Protestant churches have a need to tithe at higher levels in order to adequately support a pastor and the pastor's family. Catholic churches have less of a financial need to support a priest because a Catholic priest does not have a wife or children. Larger churches do not need higher levels of tithing because many more people help to meet the financial needs of the church. For example, there are over two thousand families who joined the Catholic church where my wife is a member. All churches have varied programs like support for missions or help for the disadvantaged, which require different levels of funding. There are also varying expenses required to support regional and headquarters offices of the larger organization.

However, I do encourage more transparency from churches on what the Bible says about tithing levels and expectations. Tithing 10 percent of your income to a church is fine if you give it out of Christian love. Tithing 10 percent of your income to a church because you were made to feel obligated, or to buy your way into heaven, is un-Christian. Many Fundamentalist Christians still believe tithing 10 percent of income is a Christian expectation worldwide. This belief often requires personal sacrifice for continued compliance. This personal sacrifice further encourages the feeling that other Christian groups who tithe less are not as holy.

More False Narratives about Feeling Holy

Shortly after I married, my Catholic wife was asked by a Fundamentalist Christian friend of mine if she was saved. She didn't know how to answer. She didn't realize that Fundamentalist Christians like to speak to each other using their own private phrasing. If someone who is not a Fundamentalist Christian doesn't understand what it means when asked if they are saved, they are assumed to be a sinner. Fundamentalist Christians use the word *saved* so often in their discussions with each other, they do not realize the majority of Christians in the world do not use that term.

I always appreciated Billy Graham, who, after inviting non-Christians to ask forgiveness for their sins and to believe in Jesus, would also add, "some Christians call that being saved." My wife quickly learned how to properly answer the question on being saved using acceptable private phrasing. Fundamentalist Christians sometimes believe other Christians are less holy because they do not understand the private phrases used for bonding within their group.

Catholics and mainstream Protestant churches, like Methodists and Presbyterians, typically read written prayers during their church services. Fundamentalist Christians usually pray publicly in an extemporaneous manner. Fundamentalist Christians seem to take pride in the use of long, flowing phrases during their extemporaneous prayers. They are also more likely to be seen praying in restaurants, giving thanks for their food. The practice of extemporaneous prayer in public places enhances their feelings of other Christian groups who do not pray in public extemporaneously as being less holy.

Fundamentalist Christians seem to ignore the statement in the Bible by Jesus to not pray purposely to be "seen by people" but to "go into your inner room and shut the door … to pray … in secret." Public prayer and extemporaneous prayer can be very Christian. It's the intent when doing so that matters. Reading prewritten prayers aloud is also very Christian. Praying out loud before each meal is fine, if it is not your intent to do it just to be seen by others. Giving God thanks for your food and not being embarrassed by your faith are good reasons to pray aloud in public. Not praying before each meal is also perfectly fine. It does not mean you are not thankful to God or you are less holy.

Taking a legalistic view, judging others, holding an expectation of tithing at 10 percent, and praying in public by using flowery prayers extemporaneously are all similar traits of the Pharisees. During the time when Jesus walked the earth, the Pharisees were leaders of Judaism with the responsibility to teach the religious laws and enforce punishment on lawbreakers. The Pharisees also ensured religious taxes were paid. Pharisees were known to attend public events where they could be heard by many people saying flowery prayers. The Pharisees took pride in careful study of the laws so they would not break any of them. The Pharisees believed they were more holy than others because they sacrificed and followed all the strict laws. The Pharisees took comfort in being members of a small group who they believed to be more holy than most Jews and, therefore, more likely to enter heaven.

What Holiness Really Means

Many Fundamentalist Christians seem to believe Catholics and mainstream Protestants are less holy as a group because they do not sacrifice as much as Fundamentalists and follow fewer and less strict rules. But in one example after another in the Gospel, Jesus focused on how much faith a person had and how much love was in a person's heart, not on which laws a person followed. Jesus welcomed a prostitute into Christianity when he saw how much love was in her heart. Jesus healed a centurion's servant when he saw the centurion's level of faith. Jesus welcomed a tax collector into Christianity when he saw how much love was in his heart. Jesus did not look at what laws a person may have either followed or broken. He focused on how much love was in a person's heart and her or his level of faith.

Mother Teresa is a wonderful example of a holy person in more modern times. She chose to live a life of poverty and serve the poorest of the poor in Calcutta, India. She opened a home for lepers, another home for the dying and destitute, another for those with tuberculosis and with mental illness, and one for children. Mother Teresa and her followers chose to live no better than those they served. They ate sparingly, owned two sets of clothes, one pair of sandals, basic eating utensils, and minimal bedding. Mother Teresa attracted thousands of Catholic nuns, who followed her into a life of poverty to help the poorest of the poor in over a hundred countries across the world. They became the Missionaries of Charity.

Mother Teresa explained that the role of the Missionaries of Charity was to encourage Christians and non-Christians to do works of love. She believed every work of love brings people closer to God. She focused on acts of love, not direct conversion of people to Christianity.

Mother Teresa's personal goal was to properly balance time for prayer with time spent helping others. She began each morning with silence and patiently waited for God to speak with her through prayer. Prayer gave her the strength to labor through each day helping others. Just as silence would lead to prayer, she believed that prayer would lead to faith, faith would lead to love, love would lead to service, and service would bring peace. Mother Teresa taught her followers to love others as Jesus loved them. She gives us an excellent example of holiness through love.

Holiness can also be exemplified through faith. When Liz and I lived in Hampton, Virginia, for four years, we had the opportunity to gain a better understanding of members of military leadership and their families. Because of large Air Force, Navy, and Army bases in the area, there were many military families living in eastern Virginia. We lived in a neighborhood mostly comprised of military leaders and their families. We became friends with many of them. Like us, they were used to relocating to different cities. However, they were very adept at organizing neighborhood groups to support each other, like a babysitting co-op, children's play groups, a gourmet dinner club, a sewing and craft club, and others. Because of military outreach to the business community and my membership in civic organizations, I attended many meetings on military bases and met many two-star generals, other commissioned officers, jet fighter pilots, and noncommissioned officers.

Military leaders, like average Americans, primarily consisted of mainstream Protestants, Catholics, Orthodox, and Fundamentalists. I noticed that every military leadership meeting began with a prayer. I also noticed that military leaders showed great respect for soldiers who had fallen and for the families they left behind. It made me realize that death was part of their everyday job. They all had friends or family members who died at war.

Regardless of their individual Christian beliefs, military leaders and their families seemed to have a strong faith in God and were at peace with death and dying. They supported each other during good times and bad times. It did not matter what type of Christian group someone was in. Even those who were not Christian received support.

Military leaders were willing to make the ultimate sacrifice for their country. Each family accepted the idea that their husband or father may someday not return home. Because many of the wives were stay-at-home moms with young children, loss of a husband would also cause them to lose their house and quickly go into poverty. Even with that ever-present risk, they all seemed to joyfully cope with living a military family life by having a strong faith in God. They were normal people with human frailties and struggles. Yet I saw holiness, based on faith, in these military friends, neighbors, and acquaintances.

Many Fundamentalist Christians today seem to primarily use a single measurement of works to determine who are the stronger Christians. Leading a Bible study, singing in a church choir, serving on various church committees, following rules, praying out loud, and tithing are all good things. However, they can sometimes make you feel other Christians are less holy. Under legalism and the Jewish religion, those who are considered most holy comply with rules, tithe, sacrifice, and pray well in public. Under Christianity as taught by Jesus, the most holy also includes those who have strong faith and show the most love to other people. They do not judge others. They pray in the privacy of their home.

Faith, Love, and Works

Mother Teresa and her followers show us how to be holy by loving others as Christ loves them. Many military leaders show us how to be holy just by having a strong faith in God. These holy people are Catholic, mainstream Protestant, and Fundamentalist. God welcomes them all into heaven.

Fundamentalist Christians are very devout. They sacrifice and comply with many rules of behavior in order to live a holy life. God certainly welcomes them into heaven. However, they may be surprised at how many other Christians are also in heaven.

The Pharisees were responsible for killing Jesus for violation of religious laws, even though he showed the highest love for humankind. I wonder how Fundamentalist Christians would treat Jesus if he lived on earth today, under an assumed name. A fictional novel by Joseph F. Girzone, titled

Joshua: A Parable for Today, explores several of those possibilities. Some Fundamentalist Christians may very well view Jesus as being less holy if he came back anonymously in modern times.

When people sacrifice and follow stricter rules than other Christians in order to help ensure their entry into heaven, it's hard for them *not* to think of other Christian groups as being less holy. Believing many other Christian groups are less holy because they follow fewer rules and sacrifice less is a long-standing myth that was passed from one generation to the next. That myth continues through repetition, reinforcement, and control techniques, even though it is inconsistent with the Gospel teachings of Jesus and hinders further unity within the Christian religion.

CHAPTER 10

The Treadmill

After decades of not attending the Christian & Missionary Alliance denomination's Mahaffey Camp in western Pennsylvania, I went back with Liz to spend an entire day there. It was great to linger on different front porches and visit with family and friends. It was also fun to see a new children's building, a new playground, large bathrooms with indoor plumbing, and paved roads where dirt roads used to be. We attended both the morning service and evening service.

It's Like Being on a Treadmill That Goes Faster and Faster

In the morning service, the Fundamentalist Christian preacher referenced biblical verses from Leviticus and Deuteronomy, in the Old Testament. He seemed to feel more comfortable focusing on the Old Testament, where laws were taught, instead of the New Testament Gospels, where Jesus focused on love. He quoted God when he commanded the Israelites to imprint God's views on others, then jumped to the conclusion that God wanted Christians today to do the same. There was no explanation of why God's command to the Israelites of old should apply to today's Christians. Yet the underlying message was consistent with Fundamentalist expectations of always doing more. Regardless of how religious you may be, Christians should continue to work harder at meeting an even higher expectation. Christians always fall short and should do more.

The preacher in the morning service made a mistake that day. The same error is made by many Fundamentalist preachers and occasionally by mainstream Protestant preachers and Catholic priests. The preacher cited a law or something God said in the Old Testament and made a practical application to Christian living today, without any evidence or explanation of why a Jewish directive should apply to Christians.

The Old Testament is the Jewish Bible. Jewish rabbis correctly use it to teach Jewish history, prophecy, and how people of the Jewish faith should apply the Old Testament to their lives today. Christ came after the time of the Old Testament and made significant changes to begin the new religion of Christianity. Christians should use the Old Testament to learn about the history of Israel and the foretelling of the Messiah, but not to apply laws and God's commands under Judaism to Christian life today.

The New Testament should be used by Christians as the basis for practical applications of Christianity to the lives of Christians. The Old Testament is more of a reference document for Christians, not a source for practical ways of living. If Christians followed the laws and commands of the Old Testament, they would also comply with the Jewish dietary laws of being kosher. They would not be able to interact with other people who were not kosher. It is difficult to justify Christian compliance with a few arbitrarily selected Jewish rules and directives from the Old Testament and not comply with others.

It's fine for Christian preachers to reference Old Testament verses that coincide with similar New Testament verses and apply those New Testament verses to Christian expectations. It's also fine to correlate prophesies in the Old Testament and show how they came true in the New Testament. I listen very carefully and do not accept Christian expectations derived solely from the Old Testament under Judaism.

Because of myths learned in their youth, some Fundamentalist preachers set increasingly higher expectations, with more laws and higher levels of sacrifice. It's easy for them to reach back into the Old Testament and try to apply the many Jewish laws and commands of God to the everyday life of Christians today. But if Christians follow the laws of Judaism, there would be little difference between Judaism and Christianity. Paul tells us it would also mean Christ died quite unnecessarily.

The Treadmill Continues

The Fundamentalist Christian preacher who spoke in the evening service referenced biblical quotes from the New Testament Gospels but also conveyed the need to meet higher expectations. He quoted Jesus in asking, "What do you want?" He said he could tell what Christians want by looking at their checkbooks and asking them about their dreams and desires. The underlying message was that you should feel guilty if you dream about a nice vacation or a new car. It doesn't matter that you already tithe and help the poor. Even if you tithe 90 percent of your income, it seems to never be enough. Everyone is expected to sacrifice even more, to live the perfect Christian life. The ultimate expectation is that you should only think of Jesus and only do things that meet the highest Fundamentalist standards.

We were only at Mahaffey Camp for one day and may very well not have seen a fair representation of sermons normally preached there. However, many Fundamentalist preachers do seem to excel in finding new ways to make Christians feel guilty about not doing more. They often fail to see the similarities with the way the Pharisees and Sadducees of old made people feel guilty and depressed when they could not follow all the laws. Most people want to go to heaven after they die. When they are challenged to do more by a religious leader, they often feel compelled to comply. If their lives are already stressed and their finances are short, they can easily feel trapped, with no way out.

Some Fundamentalist Christian preachers unwittingly follow the myths they learned in their youth and are not as careful as they should be about the expectations they set for others. Jesus paid the price for our inability to meet those high expectations by dying on the cross. We are no longer required to comply with a long list of laws. Faith and love replaced laws.

Love the Lord with All Your Heart, Soul, and Mind

In the New Testament Gospels, Jesus said the greatest commandment in the law is to love the Lord your God with all of your heart, all of your soul, and all of your mind. The second greatest commandment is to love others as yourself. Fundamentalists often use this quote as a reminder that they should work harder at living a perfect Christian life.

However, Jesus made this statement in response to a Jewish scribe who asked a question. Scribes and Pharisees often tried to catch Jesus in a mistake to prove he was a lawbreaker. The question was, under the law, which is the greatest commandment? Jesus wisely recited the greatest law from Deuteronomy and the second greatest law from Leviticus in the Hebrew Bible or Old Testament. He was speaking to a Jewish scribe in response to a question about the Judaic law. He was not giving advice to Christians today on how to live their lives. Jesus came to change the law. But at this moment, he was not yet ready to publicly proclaim that compliance with the law is unnecessary after his death and resurrection.

Many Christians mistakenly interpret these two greatest commandments as a summary of Christianity. Instead, they are a summary of Judaism. The words about loving the Lord with all your heart, soul, and mind are part of the Jewish creed, called the Shema. They are recited at the beginning of every Jewish service.

Many Fundamentalist Christians reference these two greatest commandments to help justify the use of religious laws governing personal behavior. They also use it as motivation to live a perfect Christian life or to live like Jesus. Our knowledge of Jesus is available from the Bible, other historical documents, and tradition. Based on what is known, he never told Christians to love the Lord with all their heart, soul, and mind. However, he did tell Christians to love one another as he loves them.

Jews and Fundamentalist Christians emphasize our love for God. Conversely, Jesus emphasized God's love for us. Life as a Christian can be very different, in practical ways, with an emphasis on showing love for God versus an emphasis on God's love for us. With an emphasis on our love for God, Fundamentalists are more introspective. They focus on continuous self-improvement. With an emphasis on God's love for us, Catholics and mainstream Christians appear less constrained. They seem to celebrate their religion more.

Reflection and Reassessment

At times, it can be very beneficial to step back to regard your faith and assess how you personally show your love to others. But reviewing your insufficient progress every week by repeatedly setting higher expectations only results in a level of guilt and sacrifice that is unhealthy and un-Christian. Not everyone can live like Mother Teresa. They should not feel guilty about it. The world wouldn't work very well if everyone had full-time vocations in ministry. We need Christian plumbers, Christian doctors, Christian lawyers, Christian electricians, Christian tax preparers, and Christian carpenters. They can show Christian love in small ways to family, friends, co-workers, and those in need. We also need those Christians to show real joy in their lives, not guilt and fear.

In my experience with Fundamentalist Christian churches, there is an unusually high percentage of sermons that focus on personal reflection and reassessment of daily living, in order to set higher expectations in the way people live their daily lives. The attention and focus are mostly inward-looking. As a result, personal sacrifice increases, along with an increase in feelings of guilt. Some parishioners feel like they are on a treadmill that is going faster and faster, until they hopelessly give up.

In my experience with the Catholic Church and other mainstream Protestant churches, personal reflection and reassessment of daily living is reserved for the Lenten season each year. During much of the rest of the year, sermons focus on praising God, loving other people, celebrating Christianity, and other uplifting messages. The attention and focus are mostly outward-looking. As a result, members seem to be more joyful and less stressed in their daily living. There is no treadmill of ever-increasing expectations. They teach that Jesus made the sacrifice that was needed, for us. As Christians, we have no significant requirement for additional sacrifice. We no longer need to feel guilty.

Fundamentalist Christians generally live very devout lives. They sacrifice and work hard to comply with religious laws. They usually carry a lot of guilt for not doing more. I have no desire to add to their guilt. But other Christians, with a different perspective on Christian doctrine, can be just as holy as Fundamentalists. Christians can drink alcohol, smoke cigarettes, divorce, remarry, and be very holy. It's what's in their heart that matters. They may have a high level of faith or show tremendous amounts of love for Christ and other people. Only God knows what's in their heart.

CHAPTER 11

Myth 4: There Is One Correct Doctrine

"**M**y theology has as many holes in it as your theology." That is what my Presbyterian minister said from the pulpit one Sunday morning, six months before he retired. He enjoyed his work with people and the church, had a good sense of humor, and loved to play golf. He was not prone to outbursts of anger. But on this day, you could tell he was unusually agitated. The Presbyterian USA organization, to which our church belonged, recently voted on a stance regarding gay pastors. In response, a very prominent Fundamentalist Christian pastor publicly disparaged the Christianity of all Presbyterians. My minister, who normally does not take things personally, did take this comment personally. He was upset that a fellow Christian minister would disparage and question the legitimacy of all members of a large Christian denomination in such a public manner. He hoped to someday have a face-to-face conversation with that prominent Fundamentalist Christian pastor and tell him personally that "my theology has as many holes in it as your theology."

I believe that if my pastor disagreed with a decision by the Presbyterian USA organization, he would likely choose to remain publicly silent on the issue. At most, he might make a respectful statement of disagreement, without disparaging anyone. My pastor has a doctor of ministry degree in theological and ministerial studies. He spent his entire career as a senior pastor of various large churches on the East Coast. He firmly believes that although the Bible is sacred, our interpretation of the Bible is not sacred. Our interpretation is prone to error.

The prominent Fundamentalist Christian pastor who disparaged Presbyterians believes the same myth I once believed in my youth, that the

Fundamentalist Christian doctrine is the only correct doctrine. This myth is the most troublesome myth of all, because it is directly targeted against other Christians. It is needlessly divisive and hurtful to Christian unity, worldwide.

The Far Right

Fundamentalist Christians are part of the far right on the spectrum of Christianity. Similarly, Orthodox Jews are part of the far right of the Jewish religion. Believers of Sharia law are part of the far right of the Muslim spectrum. Hindus, Buddhists, and virtually every religion in the world have their own far-right group. A common perspective of religious people on the far right (fundamentalist) is to believe their views are the only correct views, and all views to the left of theirs are incorrect and less holy. Many Fundamentalist Christians hold that view, even though it is inconsistent with the commandment of Jesus to "love one another."

Some Fundamentalist Christians believe they are part of a small group of believers who are destined to go to heaven. Most mainstream Protestant groups, like Methodists and Presbyterians, are generally not considered holy enough to go to heaven. Most of those in the Christian faiths of Roman Catholicism, Orthodox, Anglican, and Lutheran are also not viewed to be Christ-like enough to go to heaven. I heard some Fundamentalist Christians occasionally refer to these mainline churches as *dead* churches. Of the more than six billion people in the world, less than one hundred million who believe some form of Fundamentalist Christianity may go to heaven. Everyone else appears to be destined for hell. Even though Jesus said only God can judge what is in a man's heart, somehow Fundamentalist Christians believe their narrowly defined path is the only path to heaven. They do not realize they may be judging billions of people to hell, in direct defiance to what Jesus taught against judging others. Fundamentalist Christians maintain these views only because of myths they were taught in their youth.

Some Fundamentalist Christians hold very specific interpretations of the Bible they fervently believe to be true. They believe in a more legalistic view of Christianity than most. They even have definite interpretations of the book of Revelation and the end times. If you do not share their views, you are typically considered to be less knowledgeable. Fundamentalist Christians are generally not open to other Christian views because it may raise doubts about their own beliefs, and that is unacceptable to them. Their Christian doctrine is viewed as sacred and the one correct doctrine. Consistent with the false narratives learned in their youth, all other Christian doctrine is considered simply wrong. Because Fundamentalist Christians were taught since they were young that their biblical interpretations were sacred, being open-minded about alternate interpretations does not come very easily.

Fundamentalist beliefs regarding the book of Revelation and end times are particularly telling. Many Fundamentalists have very specific interpretations of Revelation and convince themselves that end times are near. They tend to immerse themselves in details yet fail to place the story in proper perspective. They do not realize their specific interpretation of end times is relatively new. It was initially developed in the 1800s, less than three hundred years ago. This is a relatively recent interpretation compared to two thousand years of Christianity and five hundred years of Protestantism. In addition to fervently believing a relatively new interpretation, Fundamentalists conveniently ignore the words of Jesus when he said only the Father knows when the Second Coming and end times would occur. Fundamentalists also fail to consider the book of Revelation was the last book selected for inclusion in the Bible because it was considered very controversial due to its extreme use of symbolism and lack of clarity. Yet Fundamentalists believe their interpretation is correct and other interpretations are wrong.

Fundamentalist Christians are taught the false narrative that their interpretation of the Bible is right and others are wrong. They use the Bible as the sole authority for their interpretation. They rarely consult other religious writings. They rarely consult historical documents. They rarely consider culture and customs of past time periods. They rarely take into account language translation issues. They do not consult views of non-Fundamentalist Christians. They do not consider tradition. But somehow, they believe their interpretation is the one, right interpretation of Christian doctrine. Fundamentalist Christians believe Catholics and mainstream Protestants, who study the Bible along with other religious writings, historical documents, past cultures and customs, language translation, and other Christians' views and traditions, routinely reach the wrong conclusions and end up with incorrect Christian doctrine. Based on this perspective, the Fundamentalist narrative does not appear to reach a logical conclusion.

Catholics Also Believe Their Doctrine Is the Only Correct One

Roman Catholicism also has a strong tendency to believe their church doctrine is correct, and all other Christian church doctrines are wrong. History is on their side for being the first Christian church. History is on their side for being the only Christian church for the first fifteen hundred years. History is also on their side for having popes who were in an apostolic line of succession for those first fifteen hundred years. But at the time of the Protestant Reformation, when the Catholic Church leaders were unholy, it is difficult for me to agree that the apostolic line of popes remained unbroken.

During the time when unholy popes were at the head of the Catholic Church, I believe there was no apostolic, worldwide leader of the Christian religion. Yet Christianity did continue to exist, with regional leadership in Catholicism, Orthodoxy, Anglicanism, Lutheranism, Calvinism, and other reformed Christian churches. While Roman Catholicism has a very strong case for being the original Christian church, the case for remaining the only church with a correct doctrine is much weaker.

Worship Practice Changes in the Early Church

The early Christian church struggled with making changes to their worship practices in response to societal pressures. The apostle James was the head of the Christian church in Jerusalem, where the main Jewish temple and many of the Jewish leaders and enforcers of the law were located. James was very aware of the fact that Jewish leaders had Jesus killed and would kill other Christians who opposed their view of the law. Although James was a Christian, he still carefully followed all the Jewish laws. Because most of his parishioners also came from a Jewish background, they were not ready to risk their lives with a change away from the law to the new commandment of love.

However, Paul was in a very different situation from James. Paul started churches farther away from Jerusalem, with mixtures of Gentiles, pagans, and Jews. Outside of Jerusalem, it was much safer for Jews to practice Christianity without adherence to all the Jewish laws. But even outside of Jerusalem, many Jewish Christians still did not associate with Gentile Christians because of how they were raised under Jewish dietary laws. Jews were required to handle and prepare meat according to specific laws. They were not permitted to associate with other people, like Gentiles, who did not also follow Jewish dietary laws. It took time for Jewish Christians to grow enough in their Christian faith to move away from the Jewish laws under which they were raised.

Pagan Christians had a different issue with eating meat. Before becoming Christian, pagans worshiped idols and sacrificed animals to their idols. They were taught to never eat meat offered to idols. Other Christians, who were stronger in their Christian faith, ate meat offered to idols. This offended pagan Christians and caused controversy within the early Christian churches, until pagan Christians grew stronger in their Christian faith.

Many early Christian churches had divided congregations because some Jewish Christians would not associate with Gentile Christians, and because many pagan Christians were offended by their Christian brothers who ate meat offered to idols. When this developed into a larger controversy, the apostles and church leaders met in Jerusalem to determine church doctrine on these issues.

Any decision by church leaders on worship practice changes would be consequential. In Jerusalem, Christians could be imprisoned or killed for violating Jewish law. Outside of Jerusalem, the early Christian churches were in danger of falling apart and ending the spread of Christianity. Balance and compromise were required. Early church leaders also knew any decision on worship practices would necessarily change over time, as cultural conditions changed.

Paul saw no reason for Gentile Christians and pagan Christians to follow any of the Jewish laws. He strongly believed because Gentiles and pagans were never part of the Jewish religion, they should not be forced to first become Jewish before they became Christian. James had a different view, since he and his Christian church members in Jerusalem still followed all the rules of Judaism.

The book of Acts gives us a picture of how the meeting flowed. As leader of the church, Peter framed the question. Paul explained the problems he saw in churches mixed with Jewish Christians, Gentile Christians, and pagan Christians. James offered a potential compromise. Peter and the church leadership agreed to the compromise proposed by James, where all Christians were to comply with the following four laws: do not eat meat offered to idols; do not eat meat from animals that were strangled; any meat that is eaten must have the blood drained off first; and abstinence from fornication.

The apostles were aware of statements by Jesus saying, "Nothing that enters a man from outside can make him unclean.... What comes out of a man is what makes him unclean ... from within, out of men's hearts." In the church leadership's view at this early stage of Christianity, these four laws would allow Gentile Christians to be clean enough so Jewish Christians could interact with them. It also resolved the immediate concerns of pagan Christians.

Church leaders believed the culture at that time would stop growth of the Christian religion if they implemented all the views of Jesus too soon. They viewed it as a potential stumbling block for new Christians, until Jewish and pagan Christians grew stronger in their faith. The church leaders sent emissaries back with Paul to explain their decision, so Paul would not be accused of communicating an inaccurate interpretation. These four laws were temporary and later rescinded. But Christian churches with a legalistic view continued throughout history. They are manifested in modern times by the Fundamentalist Christian churches that still hold onto laws today.

Even with these differences among the early Christian churches, all Christians were unified on core beliefs and respect for each other. The Fundamentalist Christians in Jerusalem practiced Christianity in a manner that was consistent with their Jewish background. The Gentile Christians in Greece practiced Christianity in a manner that was consistent with their Greek upbringing. The apostles had to occasionally meet to resolve problems, but they exhibited an ability to compromise. No one believed other Christians were less holy. No one disparaged other Christians. All early Christians, Fundamentalist and mainstream, worked together toward the common goal of expanding Christianity to the rest of the world.

Politics in the Church

In today's Christian religion, many of the problems needing resolution in Protestant denominations seem to be associated with confusion between church doctrine and church political views. Members of the organizational hierarchy often vote to make changes on many issues. However, they fail to properly distinguish between doctrinal issues and political issues. When voting results are publicized, emotions usually run high. This often results in dissension among churches and causes further splitting within denominations.

The Catholic Church clearly distinguishes between church doctrine and church political views. Catholic doctrine is written in the Catechism of the Catholic Church and is available in book form or on the internet. Any change to church doctrine, which happens very rarely, must be approved by a majority of bishops and written in this book. All other views of the pope, cardinals, bishops, and priests are their own personal political views. Every Catholic is free to agree or disagree with political views, even if they are political views of the pope. This results in more unity within the Catholic Church.

The Story of the Second Cross

Fundamentalist Christians believe someone must first be saved by faith and then comply with many laws to meet the requirement of doing works to gain entry to heaven. Many Fundamentalists believe a Christian should be baptized, study the Bible, attend church regularly, participate in Communion, pray, tithe, not pray to Mary or other saints, comply with many behavioral rules, and strive to live a very holy life. However, this view seems to conflict with the story of the second cross.

Luke, a Gentile, is the only Gospel writer to tell the story of two criminals crucified along with Jesus. The cross of Jesus was in the middle, with a cross of a known criminal on each side. One of the criminals, named Dismas, was penitent and asked Jesus to remember him when Jesus comes into his kingdom. Jesus responded by telling Dismas that today, he would be with Jesus in Paradise. We do not know much about Dismas. We can assume he was never baptized, never attended church, never knew any Bible stories, never took Communion, never prayed, was unfamiliar with Christianity, never followed any religious rules governing personal behavior, and never strived to live a holy life. He did have faith, however, and because of that faith, he entered heaven. A narrow ideology, full of requirements, is inconsistent with what we learn from the story of the second cross.

It seems short-sighted to believe that only one, strict interpretation of the Bible is correct, and many other interpretations are wrong. Again, I wonder how Jesus would be treated if he lived on earth today, under an assumed name. Protestant Fundamentalists and Catholics may both tell Jesus that he is wrong in his views on Christian doctrine.

The two thieves crucified along with Jesus are not named in the Bible. From reading other historical books, we know their names were Dismas and Gestas. Dismas became a saint in the Catholic Church. Because Jesus assured Dismas, while he still lived on earth, that he would go to heaven, Saint Dismas became the church's first canonized saint.

Most mainstream Protestant denominations publish their positions on church doctrine, but with the understanding that it may not be correct. The tone is more of "Here is what we believe, to the best of our knowledge." They do not take the position that the doctrines of other denominations are wrong. They admit the simple truth that they don't know for sure. Mainstream Protestants understand Jesus spoke using metaphors and parables. Jesus lived a long time ago, in a different culture. The Bible was written in other languages. There appears to be conflicting viewpoints in the Bible. It is unreasonable to assume that any single interpretation is correct and everyone else is wrong.

Yet some Fundamentalist Christians believe the myth that their doctrine is the one correct doctrine. The myth, in addition to their false narratives, are passed on from generation to generation through repetition, reinforcement, and control. The myth is not true, and continued belief in this myth increases Christian disunity.

CHAPTER 12

Myth 5: Catholic Beliefs Are Wrong

The call came in at nine o'clock in the morning. My mother answered the phone. Ann, my mother's sister and closest friend, was calling from Philadelphia, where she lived. Aunt Ann had been distraught in recent weeks. She had a granddaughter, Amy, who was born with deafness in both ears. They just recently celebrated Amy's second birthday. When Amy was one year old, doctors diagnosed incurable nerve deafness and recommended that she begin attending a special school at age two to learn sign language. Aunt Ann always hoped the deafness was temporary. With Amy about to begin learning sign language, Aunt Ann had to face the reality that her granddaughter was permanently deaf, and she could not bear to accept that fact. Through her tears on the phone, Aunt Ann asked my mother to participate in a day of prayer for Amy's healing. She was asking family, friends, and church members all to pray for Amy on one specific day. My mother agreed to participate and to encourage her church members, extended family, and friends to participate too.

When the day of prayer for Amy arrived, there were hundreds of participants from Catholic churches, Fundamentalist Christian churches, and mainstream Protestant churches. There were also individual and family participants from various states throughout the country. Amy's mother, who is Catholic, held pieces of Sister Katharine Drexel's garment to Amy's ears and prayed for communication. Katharine Drexel was a Catholic nun who passed away decades earlier. The pieces of Katharine Drexel's garment are called *relics*, in Catholicism. The use of religious relics while praying for a miracle is intended only to help make a stronger spiritual connection.

Shortly after the day of prayer, Amy's preschool teacher noticed Amy was startled by loud sounds. Hospital tests later that month showed her hearing was completely normal. After learning of this news, the Vatican sent doctors and theologians to Philadelphia to investigate what they initially referred to as the "alleged cure." They interviewed the family, church members, and doctors. All pertinent medical records were examined. Five years later, the Vatican declared it a miracle. They flew Amy and her mother to the Vatican to participate in a celebration with Pope John Paul II that elevated Katharine Drexel to sainthood. Amy and both of her siblings were all given full college scholarships to Drexel University by the Vatican. Years later, after Amy graduated from Drexel University, Pope Francis visited Philadelphia. At the final Mass of his visit there, which was shown on national television, the Vatican arranged for Amy to be on stage with Pope Francis and read from the Bible.

This miracle was a wonderful Christian event. It should be widely celebrated by family, and the story should be repeated often. But there has been little or no acknowledgment by a few of my extended family members who are Fundamentalist Christians. Their silence is deafening. Some of them believe the miracle was due only to Fundamentalist Christian prayers. Even in the face of a modern-day miracle by God, a false narrative learned in their youth prevents an understanding and acceptance of the obvious facts. Though it is very limited, this Fundamentalist Christian response serves as an example of anti-Catholic sentiment that stems from a belief in myths.

Catholics Do Not Worship False Gods

The fifth and final myth I learned, growing up as a Fundamentalist Christian, is that Catholic beliefs are often wrong and sometimes sinful. Many Fundamentalist Christians believe Catholics worship Mary, worship saints and relics, and worship statues. They view worship of anyone or anything except God as breaking the Ten Commandments. Therefore, they conclude Catholics are sinners.

The Fundamentalist perspective that many Catholic beliefs are wrong is not overtly stated in Fundamentalist Christian churches as often as it used to be when I was growing up. However, this view remains widespread throughout the Fundamentalist Christian community and is still passed on through repetition and reinforcement from generation to generation.

It is now discussed more privately within their own community. However, it becomes obvious in the way some Fundamentalist Christians question Catholics about their beliefs.

After I became an adult and brought my Catholic wife home to visit my parents, we usually attended a Fundamentalist Christian church together on Sunday morning. On three different occasions, in two different Fundamentalist churches, we listened as the pastor explained why certain Catholic beliefs are sinful. Neither Liz nor I appreciated the comments. We wanted to walk out of the service. However, we chose not to make a scene. In more recent years, Fundamentalist Christian pastors stop short of saying Catholic beliefs are sinful. Yet they still occasionally comment disparagingly about what Catholics believe. Liz, who went to Catholic school from first grade through high school, said she never heard any disparaging comments about Protestants in any Catholic church or Catholic school class. Based on my experience in attending Catholic churches, Protestantism is never even mentioned at all. They simply focus on Jesus and proceed through the liturgical service.

From my non-Catholic and layman's perspective, I will try to explain what Catholics really believe concerning the worship of Mary, saints, relics, and statues. In doing so, I am not trying to convince anyone to become Catholic or to accept Catholic doctrine. Yet I do hope to show Catholic doctrine was developed by holy people and is very Christian.

The Catholic Marian Doctrine

The Gospel of Luke provides more information about Mary than any other Gospel. In Palestine during the time of Jesus, women were treated with very little respect. Each morning, Jewish men would typically recite a prayer thanking God they were not a Gentile, a slave, or a woman. Luke, a Gentile, was probably from Macedonia, where women were held in higher esteem. Luke writes about the birth of Jesus from Mary's point of view. He describes the roles of different women in the life of Jesus more vividly than other Gospels.

In the book of Luke, we learn Archangel Gabriel shows Mary great honor, first by saying she is "filled with the Holy Spirit," and second by twice calling her blessed. It is also prophesized in Luke that all generations will call her blessed. This is the biblical basis on which the Catholic Church honors the Blessed Virgin Mary. Christians believe Jesus is one divine person with two natures (divine and human). Because this one divine person was born of Mary, then Mary is not just the Mother of Jesus but also the Mother of God.

Many Fundamentalist Christians misunderstand the Catholic Marian doctrine. Catholics do not worship Mary, only God. However, they do honor Mary. Catholics believe that honoring Mary can lead Christians to a closer relationship with Jesus. The scriptures, through Luke, explain when Mary is honored, she in turn gives the honor to God. Any discomfort Fundamentalist Christians may have about showing a sacred respect for Mary is rooted in their belief in a false narrative about Catholicism learned in their youth.

Catholics also celebrate a holy day every year on December 8, in honor of Mary's Immaculate Conception. The holy day is called the Feast of the Immaculate Conception, or Immaculata, in Italian. My wife usually attends a Mass on that day. When our daughter happened to be born on December 8, my father-in-law recommended that we name her Immaculata, in honor of that holy day celebration. My wife has an aunt in Italy named Immaculata, who was also born on December 8. We appreciated the sentiment. However, we chose to name our daughter after another version of Mary's name, which is more commonly used in America. The initial recommendation of my father-in-law serves as an example of the respect many Catholics have for the Blessed Virgin Mary.

Praying to Saints

The Catholic practice of praying to saints is believed by many Fundamentalist Christians to be the same as worshipping a false god, which breaks one of the Ten Commandments. Catholics like to recognize Christians who have led exceptional lives by going through a canonization process to declare them saints, so they can serve as examples to all living Christians of how to live a holy life. There typically needs to be evidence of involvement by the saint in two miracles. Becoming a saint does not mean that person was perfect when they lived on earth. They were still human then, with human frailties. Mary, the Mother of Jesus, and all the original apostles were declared saints. More recently, Mother Teresa and Pope John Paul II were also declared saints.

Fundamentalist Christians and Catholics both believe when you die on earth, your soul goes to heaven, where you are still alive. Our heavenly Father and Jesus are in heaven. We can still talk to them there through prayer. Because saints are still alive in heaven, Catholics believe they can also talk to saints through prayer. Catholics often pray to saints to ask that they intercede with the heavenly Father for healing or to meet some other need. It is like asking other Christians in your church to pray for healing or some other need.

Many Fundamentalist Christians often make a leap to equate prayer with worship and condemn the practice of praying to saints as worshipping a false god. But at the same time, some Fundamentalist Christians take comfort in a visit to the gravesite of their deceased parents to talk with them. They believe their parents are alive in heaven and talking to them is not the same as worshipping them. However, there is little difference between talking to your parents, who are in heaven, and talking to saints, who are in heaven. Fundamentalist Christians who make the leap to equate Catholic prayer to saints with worship of false gods do so because of a belief in a false narrative they were taught in their youth.

While Mother Teresa worked with the poorest of the poor in India; she prayed to Jesus daily for strength. However, she also prayed to Mary. Mother Teresa wanted the Blessed Virgin Mary to intercede for her so she could serve Jesus fully and love him as Mary loved him.

"Hail Mary" is a famous prayer to Mary many Catholics recite from memory. It is based on Bible verses from the first chapter of the Gospel of Luke. A rosary, which is a beaded chain, is often held by hand and moved from bead to bead as each Hail Mary prayer is recited along with other prayers. The Hail Mary prayer was set to music, in the beautiful song known as "Ave Maria". The song is usually sung in Latin.

Statues and Relics

Another Catholic practice considered wrong by some Fundamentalist Christians is the use of statues in the Catholic church. There is at least one statue of Jesus hanging on a cross, which is normally called a Crucifix, in each Catholic church and cathedral. The stations of the cross are visible plaques in most sanctuaries that remind parishioners of the path Jesus walked on the way to the Crucifixion. A statue of Mary is common in many Catholic churches. Large basilicas may also have statues of some of the apostles. At Christmas time, a nativity scene is usually displayed.

There is a Catholic church near where I live that sets up an elaborate nativity scene, including a replica of the town of Bethlehem, each year in December. The priest, now retired, collected a set of hand-carved and hand-painted figurines and buildings as a personal hobby. With money earned from officiating at weddings and funerals, he purchased additional pieces for his collection every time he visited Italy. Upon his retirement, the priest donated his entire collection to the church.

Some Fundamentalist Christians believe Catholics worship statues, which breaks one of the Ten Commandments about having graven images. This is such a silly belief, I am unsure how to respond. I attended many Catholic services and never saw anyone worship any statues. Catholics can distinguish between a sculpture and the Almighty God. Fundamentalist Christians typically use an empty cross in their churches, but it does not mean they worship that cross. The Catholic statues, paintings, and symbols are reminders of real people. They are intended to visually tell the story of Jesus every time someone sees them.

After Liz and I had children, we began to display our own nativity scene at home during the Christmas season. With the hustle and bustle of Christmas, we felt it was important to have a visual reminder about the story of the birth of Jesus for our children, ourselves, extended family, and friends. We typically set up our nativity scene, which has twelve-inch-tall figurines, in a special place with some low lighting around it. In keeping with Italian tradition, we also added a small statue of a dog to the nativity set.

Historically, Fundamentalist Christians seemed to go out of their way to avoid having any statues. They found other ways to communicate the stories of Christ. Each year while I was growing up, there were several local Fundamentalist churches that would produce a live nativity scene. Church parishioners would dress up in appropriate costumes and stand outside in some very cold weather in a live nativity scene. Some churches would also host live scenes of Christ's Crucifixion during Easter. They would advertise the productions in the local newspaper so more people would attend.

In more recent years, I saw an increase in the use of small nativity sets in the homes of some Fundamentalist Christians. This may be a sign of a softening in their belief in the false narrative about Catholic use of statues. It may be the start of seeing more of the whole truth. The next step of acceptance would be to use more and larger nativity scenes inside Fundamentalist Christian churches.

I have yet to see any similar signs of progress about their belief in a false narrative concerning the Catholic use of relics. Similar to statues, religious relics are not worshipped by Catholics, either. Relics are only used in an attempt to make a stronger spiritual connection, as a way to show a higher level of faith, when praying for a miracle. It is like holding a Bible or a cross when you pray. Relics have no power in and of themselves. However, in many instances, the use of religious relics when praying for miracles has proven to be successful, as in the case of my second cousin, Amy.

Signs of the Holy Spirit

I shared the true story of my second cousin's healing in the Catholic church. I also have another personal story of a miracle of healing in a Fundamentalist Protestant church. Early in my mother's adult life, when she was expecting her second child, the pregnancy was not going well. She prayed for a miracle and asked the entire Christian and Missionary Alliance church to pray for a successful pregnancy. The pregnancy progressed, and the baby was born healthy. He was my older brother. No one thought much about those prayers at that time.

But one day, sixty-four years after that birth, my brother became short of breath while walking up a lot of steps in a Major League Baseball stadium. That spurred him to see a heart specialist. Following standard testing, the heart specialist found a complete blockage of the left anterior descending coronary artery that feeds the heart's left ventricle, which pumps blood to the body. This blockage is also known as the widow-maker.

The doctor initially told my brother that, based on the blockage, he should not be alive. After further testing, the heart specialist discovered that my brother had two large, parallel coronary arteries, which originated in the right coronary artery, came across and intersected the left anterior descending coronary artery below the blockage in two distinct locations, supplying the heart's left ventricle from the other side. The heart specialist indicated a naturally occurring double bypass of this kind is not known to exist in any other person.

Those two arteries bypassed a permanent blockage that had existed since birth. The blockage was really a missing segment of the left coronary artery, which never fully developed in utero. In some artery blockage cases, smaller arteries grow larger over time to replace the blocked artery pathway. That is not what happened here. These were two large arteries in existence since birth, where no arteries are normally located, with no other known human occurrences. The natural configuration of blood flow around the heart is different from any other person. Nothing like it is even noted in any medical textbooks. It was a miracle that occurred sixty-four years ago, displaying God's special handiwork, in answer to prayer.

No one knew God had performed this miracle until sixty-four years after it took place. Once the heart doctor figured out how the blood normally flowed in and around my brother's heart, he also eventually proceeded to diagnose the root cause of his shortness of breath. There were several other small blood vessels with partial blockages. Those partial blockages were then successfully corrected with the installation of stents.

Jesus told his disciples to look for signs and wonders of the Holy Spirit, like the miracle of healing, as evidence of a true Christian church. We know from reading the book of Acts, the apostles referred to signs and wonders when evaluating the effectiveness of early Christian churches. Miracles occur in both Fundamentalist Christian churches and Catholic churches. Despite any perceived shortcomings, there is evidence that both Fundamentalist Christians and Catholics have the power of the Holy Spirit active in their churches. That should be sufficient evidence for Fundamentalist Christians to accept Catholicism as a true Christian church. It should also be sufficient evidence for Catholics to accept Fundamentalist Christians as true Christians. Miracles also occur in many other mainstream Protestant, Anglican, and Orthodox churches.

Today, there may be many versions of Christianity, but there is only one Christian religion. All Christians are commanded to love one another. Understanding and supporting different versions of Christianity with varying beliefs is an expectation of being a Christian. Not supporting Christian churches that have the power of the Holy Spirit may very well be a stumbling block to new Christians and a deterrent to those in the world who currently claim no religious affiliation.

Catholics Celebrate Their Religion

Catholics seem to celebrate their religious beliefs more than Protestants. They perform special rituals during many holy days and festivals. They celebrate special Christian events in the life of each Catholic.

Because Holy Communion is so important to most Catholics, they celebrate each person's First Communion with a large gathering of family and friends. When Catholic children are in the second grade, they are deemed capable of understanding the importance of Communion. They are taught the meaning of Communion and the proper way to receive the sacrament. Extended family members and friends gather together to support the children as they receive their First Communion from a priest. Children usually receive a more formal outfit to wear to their First Communion. A celebration, like a small wedding, is held afterwards to commemorate this most important milestone.

On Palm Sunday, the local Catholic church gives a palm leaf to each person attending service. Many Catholics take the palm leaf home and keep it all year. Liz usually attaches it to a picture hanging on a wall in our home.

Many Catholics attend a special church service each year on Ash Wednesday. The church burns dried palm leaves into an ash. The blackened ashes are used to make the sign of the cross on their forehead. They usually wear the ash cross for the remainder of that day.

Liz has many relatives who live in southern Italy, where her parents were born. She visited them four times. I joined her on two of those visits. They live in a small town along the Mediterranean Sea. They faithfully attend a Catholic Mass every week, as do many of the people living there. A typical home displays a picture of the Last Supper, a Crucifix, a picture of Padre Pio, and a certificate or letter from a pope commemorating an important wedding anniversary in the family (Padre Pio was the Catholic priest with stigmata from southern Italy).

Every town in southern Italy usually has only one church, a Catholic church. It is not like the United States, where you can choose to attend a Catholic, Lutheran, Methodist, Presbyterian, Baptist, Anglican, Episcopal, or Independent church. The vast majority of Italy is Catholic. If you want to practice your Christian faith there, you have little choice except to be Catholic.

Each small-town church adopts a specific saint as their patron saint. The town where my wife's family lives has a patron saint named Saint Marziale. They have a statue of the saint in the church and know the saint's history. Every small town celebrates a patron-saint day each year. The townspeople celebrate their Christianity together on patron-saint day with a procession of church leaders who walk through the town, followed by a small festival. On one of our visits, we had the privilege of joining the townspeople in their patron-saint day festivities. It was wonderful to see an entire town unite to celebrate their Christian faith together.

While on another visit, with extended family members from America, to the cliffside resort town of Positano, along the Amalfi coast of western Italy, we again had an opportunity to attend a patron-saint day festival. When we first arrived in the town and began walking the last quarter-mile with our luggage down the steep and narrow streets to our seaside hotel, we happened to immediately follow the procession of church leaders. We recognized what was occurring because we had attended a patron-saint day several years earlier in southern Italy. Along the route, many people stood alongside the sidewalk to watch and cheer. That evening, there was a free concert on the beach of the Mediterranean Sea. It was followed by fireworks from barges out on the water.

World Youth Day

Every three years, the Catholic Church holds a World Youth Day. Pope John Paul II initiated this event in 1985. Catholic youth from around the world attend and usually hear an open-air Mass from the pope. It is held in a different city in the world each time. One of these events was attended by approximately 1.6 million people in Krakow, Poland, in 2016. Pope John Paul II appointed Saint Pier Giorgio Frassati to be the ongoing patron saint of World Youth Day.

I learned about Saint Pier Giorgio from a young Catholic priest in Alexandria, Virginia. Pier Giorgio was born into a wealthy family in Turin, Italy. His father owned a newspaper business, was an Italian senator, and an ambassador to Germany. He was also agnostic. Pier Giorgio was very religious and spent much of his spare time while in college helping the poor, the sick, and orphans. He would give his bus fare to charity and then run home. He skipped his family vacations at their summer home because somebody needed to be there to help feed the sick. Pier Giorgio loved mountain climbing, theater, opera, and museums, but he always made time to help the needy.

One day at age twenty-four, he caught poliomyelitis from his exposure to the sick. He died shortly after. At the funeral, his family expected elite and political figures to attend. They were surprised to see thousands of mourners lining the streets along the processional. They were the people Pier Giorgio directly helped during his brief life. His family was unaware of the extent of his works of charity until then. Pope John Paul II wanted Saint Pier Giorgio to be an example to the world youth of someone who lived a holy life.

Now I Understand

Once I began attending Catholic church services with Liz, I started to learn what Catholics really believed. As time passed, each of the false narratives I learned in my youth slowly fell by the wayside as I learned the truth about Catholic doctrine. Some Fundamentalist Christians believe Catholics are sinners because they worship Mary, worship saints and relics, and worship statues. The truth is Catholics worship God alone. They honor Mary in a way that also honors God. When Catholics pray to Mary and other saints, they are really praying to God through Mary and the saints. They are asking Mary and the saints to intercede and present their petitions to God, just as Fundamentalist Christians would ask prayer partners to pray on someone's behalf. Relics are only used in an attempt to make a stronger spiritual connection, as a way to show a higher level of faith, when praying for a miracle. They have no special power in and of themselves. Statues are used as visual storytelling about the life, death, and resurrection of Jesus.

Many Catholics are not as aware of the details of their own doctrinal interpretations as Fundamentalist Christians are of theirs. That does not make them less Christian or less holy. Information on Catholic doctrine is readily available in the extensively written Catholic Catechism. The majority of teaching in a Catholic service is focused more on the application of Christianity to everyday living. The majority of teaching in a Fundamentalist Christian service is more focused on the details of theology. Catholics attend church primarily for Communion. Fundamentalist Christians attend church primarily to learn doctrine. One approach is not better than the other. They are just different.

If a Fundamentalist Christian asks a Catholic a technical question about Catholic theology, they may receive an inaccurate answer. The details of theology are not that important to most Catholics. However, they are very important to most Fundamentalist Christians. When looking at this issue from a different paradigm, you could say a focus on the details of theology results in the highlighting of differences of beliefs, which leads to more splintering of Christianity. A focus on just the basic principles of Christianity and how they apply to daily living may result in more unity within the Christian religion. Again, one approach is not better than the other. They are just different.

For the first fifteen hundred years of Christianity, Catholicism was the only Christian religion. In my case, all four of my grandparents were raised Lutheran. My dad told me that his father's mother, my great-grandmother, was raised Catholic but later changed to Lutheran. It's safe to assume that all my ancestors were Catholic, if you go back far enough. The ancestors of most Fundamentalist Christians were Catholic at one time. A belief in Christianity and some amount of holiness was passed down through the generations. But somehow, a belief in false narratives developed and was also passed along. It is un-Christian for Fundamentalists to continue to view the religion of their ancestors through the lens of the false narratives they learned as youth. It may be difficult to change a belief in false narratives, but our ancestors would appreciate any effort in trying. Fundamentalist Christians can honor their ancestors by understanding their worship practices the way they understood them.

I am not trying to convince anyone to convert to Catholicism or to believe church doctrine according to Catholic interpretation. I am trying to show Catholic worship practices are very Christian and were important to the ancestors of many Fundamentalists. They are based on biblical interpretations and tradition, by holy leaders. We each have our own perspective of Christianity. It's only when we begin to learn the perspectives of other Christians that we begin to more fully understand our own Christian beliefs. I once believed false narratives and myths learned in my youth. Because I had the opportunity to experience Christian perspectives from many Protestant denominations and from the Catholic Church, I realized I held misguided beliefs that needed to be unlearned.

Simple indoctrination techniques are still being used today to continue passing on to the next generation the Fundamentalist Christian myth that Catholic beliefs are wrong and sometimes sinful. Once your mind is indoctrinated to a certain way of thinking, it is very difficult to change. By continuing to believe the myth, a Fundamentalist Christian either purposely or unknowingly passes it on to the next generation, both at church and at home. This keeps Christianity more splintered and fragmented. Understanding the whole truth about current Catholic doctrine is the best way to expose the myth that Catholic beliefs are often wrong and sometimes sinful. It is also a way to build another bridge toward Christian unity.

CHAPTER 13

Relics

The lance was approximately eighteen inches long. Its width was generally two inches but expanded to four inches at the wings. The middle third of its length was partially wrapped in a shiny, gold-colored sheath. The long wooden handle to which the lance was once attached was not there. Only the metal spear tip remains. It was made of steel, iron, brass, silver, gold, and leather. Parts of it were added in later years. The lance was kept behind protective glass in a secured area of the museum.

Liz and I saw the Holy Lance when we visited the Weltliches Schatzkammer Museum, or Imperial Treasury, at the Hofburg Palace in Vienna, Austria. The Holy Lance is believed by many to be the lance used by a Roman soldier to pierce Christ's side while he hung on the cross in Jerusalem. The lance is also known as the Lance of Longinus, named after the centurion who used it on Jesus.

Longinus is not mentioned by name in the Bible. However, he is probably the Roman centurion mentioned in the Gospels who suddenly knew Jesus was the Son of God immediately after Jesus drew his last breath. Longinus openly glorified God before his fellow soldiers with a spontaneous declaration of belief and outward conversion. Longinus was later named a saint in the Catholic Church. Within the dome of St. Peter's Basilica in Rome stands a large statue of Longinus holding his lance.

Adjacent to the Holy Lance in the museum were three pieces of the True Cross of Christ. Both the Holy Lance and the True Cross of Christ were displayed in the same glass enclosure. The wooden pieces of the True Cross were displayed in the shape of a small cross. It was about twelve inches long and laid in a brass-colored, cross-shaped holder. The metal holder made a noticeable border around the pieces of brown wood.

The Holy Crown of Thorns is housed in the Cathedral of Notre Dame in Paris, France. It can be seen on the first Friday afternoon of each month. King St. Louis came into possession of the Holy Crown of Thorns in the thirteenth century in Paris. St. Louis completed construction of the elaborate Sainte-Chapelle in 1248 to house the Holy Crown of Thorns. In 1806, The Holy Crown of Thorns was relocated a few blocks to the Cathedral of Notre Dame, where it remains today.

The Holy Lance, the True Cross of Christ, and the Holy Crown of Thorns are called relics by the Catholic Church. Relics can be items associated with Jesus. They can also be things associated with apostles and saints. First-class relics come from a saint's body, such as a sliver of bone or a wisp of hair. Second-class relics come from something belonging to a saint, such as clothing. The Catholic Church considers relics to be strong reminders of their faith. Relics do not have any special powers, yet many miracles occur in answer to prayer when relics are present.

Biblical Basis of Relics

While growing up in a Fundamentalist Protestant church, I was taught that relics were another form of idol worship by Catholics. It violated the Ten Commandments. There was no basis in the Bible for relics. I wish I knew then what I know now.

There is a clear biblical basis for the use of relics in prayer for miracle healings in the New Testament book of Acts, chapter 19, verses 11–12. The apostle Paul traveled extensively and often prayed to God to perform many miracles in healing the sick. The Bible says other early church leaders took sweatbands and aprons, clothing previously worn by Paul, and carried them to the sick. According to the book of Acts, early church leaders used those clothing relics of Paul to heal the sick while he traveled elsewhere.

The relics from Paul had no power in and of themselves. Healing miracles were performed through the power of the Holy Spirit. Early church leaders used their prayers and Paul's relics to help unleash the power of the Holy Spirit. Paul was not present for those healings. But pieces of clothing he previously wore were used to make a stronger spiritual connection. The clothing relics of Paul did not heal the sick. However, they did help support miracle healings.

A second example of a biblical use of relics is the story of the bleeding woman who touched the back of Jesus's cloak for healing. The bleeding woman was healed before Jesus knew what occurred. He felt some power leaving his body and turned to see why that power left him. After he saw the woman, he immediately understood why power left his body. A healing miracle occurred. The cloak of Jesus served as a relic in that miracle of healing. The story of this miracle is described in Luke 8:43–48.

The bleeding woman was healed by Jesus because of her strong faith. The cloak of Jesus acted as a relic to make a stronger spiritual connection. The cloak had no power in and of itself. The power of healing came from Jesus.

There is clear evidence in the Bible of the use of relics by early Christian church leaders to aid in miracles of healing. Articles of clothing worn by the apostle Paul are considered relics. Articles of clothing worn by Jesus are considered relics. Miracles also occur without the use of relics.

When I believed the false narrative about relics being part of idol worship, I was unable to fully understand those two stories in the New Testament. I could read over them multiple times, but they just would not register in my mind. The Bible clearly disproves the false narrative I was taught about relics. However, some Fundamentalists today still believe the use of relics is sinful and unsupported by the Bible. Many other Protestants are simply uncomfortable with relics.

Traveling Relics from the Vatican

Liz and I met a Catholic priest whose current assignment was to travel to Catholic churches, schools, and prisons throughout North America and display 166 relics from the Vatican. The exhibit is called *Treasures of the Church*. We saw the relics in a nearby Latin-based Catholic church.

Each relic was mounted in an ornate holder, called a reliquary, which was verified by the Vatican with official documentation and secured with a wax seal. Of the 166 relics, all but six were first-class relics. The church sanctuary had two tables in the front. The table on the left displayed a piece of the veil of the Virgin Mary, a fragment of Joseph's robe, and a piece of the Holy Crib of Jesus. The table on the right held small parts of the True Cross, part of a thorn from the Crown of Thorns, and a tiny piece of metal from the Holy Lance that pierced Jesus's side.

The remaining relics were displayed in the church auditorium and library. Those relics included bone fragments from each apostle. Among the many saints represented were Mary Magdalene, Thomas Aquinas, Ignatius of Loyola, Vincent de Paul, John the Baptist, Francis of Assisi, Pope John Paul II, and Mother Theresa.

Prior to venerating, or respectfully viewing, the relics, the traveling priest gave a sermon that was longer than a normal homily. He explained that miracles are done by the power of the Holy Spirit, not the relics. Relics can only help you make a stronger spiritual connection. They have no power in and of themselves.

The priest described how many of the older relics were initially gathered. In 315, the Roman emperor, Constantine, converted to Christianity. He then wanted everyone in his empire to also become Christian. To help convert the masses, Constantine sent his mother, Helen, to the Middle East to collect Christian relics. In a field just west of Jerusalem, Helen asked supporters to dig up many crosses and lay them on top of the ground. She arranged for a sickly man to lay next to each cross until he was healed. Helen then knew which cross was the True Cross and brought it back to Rome. Helen went on to collect and bring back many more relics that remain in Rome today.

Just as apparitions and old miracles cannot be proven beyond all doubt, relics from Christ also cannot be proven beyond all doubt. In addition to the Hofburg Palace in Vienna, the Vatican archives is rumored to house a Holy Lance. A few other sites also claim to own it. I asked the traveling priest about the Holy Lance and True Cross of Christ we saw in Vienna. He said he believed the items we saw in Vienna were the true relics of Christ. His relic of the Holy Lance is a small particle taken from the Holy Lance in Vienna. The wood for his relic of the True Cross of Christ and the wood in the relic of the True Cross we saw in Vienna came from the same True Cross of Christ. He also believed the Holy Crown of Thorns in the Cathedral of Notre Dame in Paris was the true Holy Crown of Thorns. Another one of his relics on display was part of a thorn taken from the Holy Crown of Thorns located in Paris.

Saint Maria Goretti

The traveling priest told a story about his favorite saint, Saint Maria Goretti. At eleven years old, Maria was the youngest saint ever canonized by the Postulate of the Catholic Church. The Postulate is the Catholic organization in the Vatican charged with investigating and determining whether someone should be named a saint.

Maria Goretti's father was married with six children. He worked hard on his farm to feed his family. One day, Maria's father passed away suddenly. Her mother then had to work the farm. That left Maria to cook, clean, and care for her five younger siblings.

An older man named Alessandro came to court Maria. Maria turned him down because she was needed at home. Alessandro became angry and stabbed Maria fourteen times. Within twenty-four hours, she died. Before she passed, Maria told a priest she forgave Alessandro and wanted him with her someday in heaven. Following Maria's death, Maria's mother had to give up her five remaining children to adoption in order for them all to survive.

Alessandro was later sentenced to thirty years in prison. That is where he became very angry with Maria. One day, Maria came to Alessandro in an apparition and handed him fourteen white lilies, one for each stabbing. Alessandro became contrite, confessed to his sins, and evangelized others. After an early release from prison, Alessandro visited Maria's mother and asked for forgiveness. Maria's mother forgave Alessandro and adopted him as a son.

When Maria was canonized as a saint, it was the first time a mother witnessed the canonization ceremony of her own child. It drew the largest gathering ever at the Vatican for a canonization. The crowd filled St. Peter's church. Many had to stand outside. The Christian message learned from Saint Maria Goretti is to forgive others even if they do not want forgiveness. Oftentimes you may need to forgive yourself before you can forgive others.

By sharing 166 relics all over North America, the priest learned of many miracles of healing associated with those relics. He encouraged each person in attendance to let the saints speak to them. There could be one particular saint, now alive in heaven, who has a special message to share. He also asked that he be kept informed of any future miracles of healing that may be associated with saints linked to the relics on display.

CHAPTER 14

Different Catholic Worship Practices

There are several Catholic worship practices that seem to disturb some Fundamentalist Christians. While not necessarily considered wrong, they appear to be bothersome. These practices include the following: confessing sins to a priest, the pope's infallibility, ornate churches, personal use of the sign of the cross, and holy water.

Confession of Sins

An issue that causes many Fundamentalist Christians the most distress is the Catholic practice of confessing sins to a priest. Fundamentalist Christians strongly believe in a personal relationship with Jesus, which allows everyone to speak directly to God without an intermediary, like a priest. It's an emotional issue for Fundamentalist Christians because it was related to the unholy abuses by the Catholic Church that led to the Protestant Reformation. However, what is not widely known in the Fundamentalist Christian community is that Catholics also believe in a personal relationship with Jesus. They can speak directly to God without an intermediary priest. While Catholics are encouraged to occasionally confess their sins to God through a priest, they also confess sins directly to God without a priest. I never confessed my sins through an intermediary. It must be a very humbling experience. My guess is that it is also very good for the soul.

Private confession of sins directly to God allows each sin to be forgiven. However, any restitution or making amends for those sins is largely forgotten. Occasionally, Protestants may voluntarily pay for damages or stolen property following private confession to God. Most of the time, making amends or making some form of restitution never occurs to them. Confession of sins to God through a Catholic priest often results in making amends.

A common form of restitution recommended by a Catholic priest following confession of sins is to pray the rosary a specific number of times. Praying the rosary is a lengthy Catholic prayer using standard prayers based on the Bible. The rosary begins with the Apostle's Creed, followed by the Lord's Prayer. The standard Catholic prayers of Hail Mary and Glory Be are recited multiple times. The Lord's Prayer is repeated and followed by additional Hail Mary and Glory Be prayers. This sequence is repeated a total of six times. Other standard Catholic prayers are included throughout the rosary prayer. When praying a complete rosary, the Lord's Prayer is repeated six different times. It may take fifteen to twenty minutes to pray the rosary properly.

A necklace-type rosary is usually held in your hand when praying the rosary. It consists of fifty-nine beads, a Crucifix, and a medal. Praying the rosary begins by making the sign of the cross. Next, the cross on the necklace-type rosary is held between your fingers while saying the Apostle's Creed. Your fingers then move to the first bead on the rosary to pray the Lord's Prayer. Your fingers move from bead to bead along the rosary when praying each prayer or set of prayers. Because of the number of repetitions of prayers, the rosary beads help keep count to insure a complete rosary prayer is made. The rosary prayer is concluded by making the sign of the cross a second time.

I like the Presbyterian practice of having the congregation jointly read aloud a different prayer of confession every Sunday morning. I remember one particular group confession that said something like the following: "The Christian church is not united, as Jesus had asked. As Christians, we isolated ourselves from each other and failed to listen to each other. We misunderstood, ridiculed, and even attacked other Christians. Forgive us, O God, and make us fully one." Presbyterian prayers of confession are typically written to align with the sermon each Sunday. They teach parishioners about common shortcomings. However, restitution or making amends is not mentioned.

The closest thing to confession through a priest, for Fundamentalist

Christians, is the opportunity to go to their pastor for private counseling. Confidential indiscretions are often disclosed to the pastor during counseling. The pastor usually encourages a change in behavior but without making amends for past bad behavior.

Infallibility

Some Fundamentalist Christians are also distressed about the pope's infallibility. Catholics believe that the pope, when in unity with the bishops as a whole, can teach church doctrine as true. In modern times, this means if the pope wants to revise church doctrine, he will need the majority of bishops worldwide to agree with him.

Pope Francis wanted to revise church doctrine to make it easier for divorced Catholics to fully participate in Communion. Yet he was unable to gather enough votes among the bishops to gain approval. The numerous conservative bishops from Africa voted as a block against the pope's proposal. A pope is not authorized to change church doctrine on his own.

Catholics base their infallibility belief on two Bible verses that both quote Jesus when speaking to early church leaders. The first one is "The one who listens to you listens to me" from Luke 10:16. The second is "Whatever you shall bind on earth shall have been bound in heaven" from Matthew 18:18. In addition to those two verses, there is a story in the book of Acts where Peter, the apostles, and other church leaders meet in Jerusalem to make a decision on church rules about whether Gentiles must follow Jewish laws before becoming Christians. However, Catholics do believe the pope can easily be wrong when expressing personal views. Catholics also believe the pope can sin, because he is still human like the rest of us.

I heard a sermon by a highly educated Baptist minister who stated that when Protestants broke from the Catholic Church in 1517, they attempted to change many things from their Catholic past, over and above the original religious grievances. Because the Catholic church was ornate, the Protestant church would be unadorned. Because the Catholic Church used a statue of Jesus on a cross, the Protestant church would use a simple cross. Because the Catholic Church canonized saints, the Protestant church would not. Over the years, false narratives likely developed to explain those differences based on religious reasons, which led to additional accusations of breaking the Ten

Commandments by worshipping idols and false gods. These false narratives were then passed on from generation to generation using the techniques of repetition and reinforcement.

Many Catholics Are Very Religious

Fundamentalist Christians often believe Catholic practices are wrong, yet they make exceptions for specific Catholics. If asked about someone like Mother Teresa, Fundamentalist Christians often agree she is in heaven. Pope John Paul II also gets an exception. If they meet an everyday Catholic who seems especially holy, that also qualifies for an exception. What Fundamentalist Christians don't realize is how many Catholics would get an exception if they had an opportunity to know them better. It seems that Catholics, as a group, are considered to engage in sinful practices because it is consistent with the myth some Fundamentalist Christians learned in their youth. When Fundamentalist Christians meet Catholics individually, there may be a better outcome.

There are over seven hundred thousand Catholic nuns in the world today who voluntarily give up having a family of their own and choose to live very frugally in service to others. There are over four hundred thousand Catholic priests who elect to live a celibate life, with no spouse or children of their own, so they can focus full-time on serving God. There are many verified miracles among Catholics. There are over ten thousand named saints, now deceased, who each did something extraordinary for God. There are many Catholics who attend church each week, along with attending weekly Bible study groups and weekly prayer groups. Including these people in a group considered as sinful just because they are Catholic is simply wrong.

I happened to marry a Catholic who is also very religious. That was one of the things that attracted me to her. Over the years, I came to appreciate how reverent Catholics can be. Upon entering a Catholic sanctuary, Catholics touch a small pool of holy water (blessed by a priest) and make the sign of the cross. Touching the forehead represents the Father. Touching the middle of the chest represents the Son. Touching the left and right shoulder represent the Holy Spirit. They say the Trinity names either quietly or silently as they make the sign of the cross. When Catholics walk up to a pew, they genuflect, or bow, and make the sign of the cross again. Upon entering the pew, they typically say a silent prayer while either kneeling or sitting. The entire Catholic service is centered around Jesus.

There are usually three Bible readings. The first two readings are read by laypeople. The third reading is always from one of the four Gospels. It is typically read by the priest. Everyone stands for the Gospel reading, out of respect for the increased importance of the Gospels over the rest of the Bible. The prayers, songs, and cantor are all focused on leading up to the highlight of the service, which is Communion. During the Communion part of the service, everyone kneels in prayer. After receiving Communion, Catholics typically make the sign of the cross, again remembering the Father, Son, and Holy Spirit.

A Catholic church altar.

Because the bread and wine are consecrated by the priest to become the body and blood of Christ, both must be fully consumed. The unused bread wafers are stored in a small ornate box, called a tabernacle, in the church for use in the next Communion service. But none of the excess can be discarded, not even the crumbs of bread or drops of wine. The bread crumbs are brushed into the cup of remaining wine. The priest drinks the remaining wine, then rinses the cup with water and drinks the water.

There are reminders of Christ in the sanctuary. There is usually a statue of Jesus on a cross, to remind everyone that he died for our sins. There are fourteen markers on the walls, to remind everyone of the fourteen stations of the cross where Jesus walked on the way to his Crucifixion. Some churches have other stories of Christ displayed on stained glass windows or in paintings. The service, rituals, Communion, and reminders are all focused on telling the story of Jesus.

Three of fourteen stations of the cross.

The Importance of Sermons and Communion

In Fundamentalist Christian churches, the highlight of the service is the sermon. Fundamentalist Christian preachers usually present a sermon that contains a lot of Bible teaching and instruction. The sermon may also have encouragement, admonishment, and an application to everyday life. In Catholic churches, the sermon is called a homily. A homily is shorter than an educational sermon and usually focuses on Christian principles as applied to everyday life. The Catholic Church provides teaching and instruction primarily through Catechism training for their youth, prayers and rituals during religious holidays and holy observances, Communion, and the visual messages expressed by statues and stations of the cross. Catholics view receiving Communion as a higher priority over listening to a homily.

When I first attended Catholic services with Liz, I misunderstood the service, focused on the homily, and came away disappointed. My perspective was that of a Fundamentalist Christian, expecting the sermon to be the main part of the service. The filter on my brain made me believe every sermon should contain a lot of Bible teaching and education. As I attended more Catholic services, I began to understand and appreciate the teaching, instruction, and messaging throughout the entire service. If Fundamentalist Christians attend one or two Catholic services, I would expect them to leave thinking they know why Catholics are weak Christians, at best. But if Fundamentalist Christians can see beyond the filters and myths they have about Catholics and attend with an open mind, they may find a Catholic church service to be spiritually uplifting.

Conversely, when Catholics attend a Protestant church service, they often walk away feeling spiritually unfulfilled. Catholics look forward to Holy Communion, which is the highlight of their service, and are usually disappointed when Communion is not part of the Protestant service. Even when Communion is served at Fundamentalist Christian churches, Catholics still miss having what they consider to be a real Communion where the elements are consecrated to become the body and blood of Christ. In addition, Catholics are not used to the lengthy sermons included in most Protestant church services.

The *Didache*, written by the original apostles, discusses four kinds of early church preaching. *Kerugma* is an announcement or plain statement of fact. This type of preaching is used to announce that Jesus died on the cross to save us from sin. *Didache* is instructional teaching. It is educational in nature and allows for a deeper and fuller understanding. *Paraklesis* is exhortation. This type of preaching is used to inspire and encourage. The *Homilia* type of preaching is an application of the scriptures to everyday life. The Catholic homily used in a Catholic Mass comes from *Homilia*. Most

Fundamentalist Christian sermons use *Didache*, or instructional teaching. A sermon can use one, two, three, or all four of these types of preaching. A well-rounded sermon would use all four.

Holy Water and Incense

Holy water is simply water that is blessed by a priest. There is usually a small font of holy water near the entrance of the sanctuary of every Catholic church. Most Catholics touch the holy water upon entering and exiting the church. Then they make the sign of the cross.

During special services on some Catholic holidays, the priest may use a small branch of leaves dipped in holy water to spray the holy water onto parishioners as he walks through the church aisles. I often end up with water droplets on my glasses, which I then need to wipe off to see clearly again. The ritual of using holy water is symbolic of purification. Holy water is used as a sign of repentance of sin, for protection from evil, and as a reminder of Baptism.

In a similar fashion, on special occasions, Catholic priests may walk through the church aisles with a container of burning incense, motioning smoke from the burning incense toward the parishioners. This ritual is symbolic of sanctification, purification, and prayers of the faithful. The rising smoke reminds parishioners that prayers rise to God in heaven. Prayer helps purify the worship of God, allowing the Holy Spirit to work to make parishioners holy.

The use of holy water and burning incense are simply worship practices that are intended to remind Christians of specific Christian concepts. I view them more as a celebration of my Christian faith. They also make me feel that I am in a holy place of worship and closer to God.

Lighting Votive Candles

Jesus said, "I am the light of the world." As a reminder of Jesus as light of the world, Catholic churches use many candles in the sanctuary. Altar candles are lighted for every Mass. Additional candles are used for special occasions and religious holidays.

Parishioners can light small votive candles as a prayer for a loved one.

They often pay for the cost of the candle. The light symbolizes prayer offered in faith that comes into the light of God. The lighted candle shows their desire to remain present in prayer even though they depart from the church to go about their daily activities.

The Monstrance

The thin round wafer used as bread during Communion by Catholics is usually called a host. Once a host is consecrated by a priest, it becomes the body of Christ. To Catholics, the real presence of Christ is in the host. In addition to eating the bread, or host, during Communion, some Catholic churches may also display a consecrated host.

A displayed host is usually placed in an ornate holder called a monstrance. A typical monstrance is about two feet tall and made of brass, gold, or silver. Some are in the shape of a cross with a hole in the center of the cross to hold the host. Others may be in the shape of a sunburst, with a host in the center of the circular sunburst.

In the Catholic church where Liz is a member, a monstrance holding a sacred host is displayed every Friday in a side chapel, just off the main sanctuary. The monstrance is in the front center portion of the chapel and serves as a focal point of religious devotion to Christ. Parishioners are free to enter the chapel to pray in the presence of Christ.

A neighboring Catholic church displays a sacred host in a monstrance in their chapel only on one Friday each month. At other Catholic churches, a monstrance may be carried in a procession by a priest during a religious celebration. Anglican and Orthodox churches also use a monstrance, like Catholics, as a worship practice.

Using a Pyx

Near the end of Communion in a Catholic service, the priest typically walks to the front of the congregation holding a tray of pyxes. A pyx is a small round container that holds a Communion host or bread wafer. Volunteer Eucharistic ministers from the congregation drop off their pyxes just prior to the service, usually in a side chapel. The hosts are consecrated by the priest to become the body of Christ during the Communion service. Near the end of Communion, a consecrated host is placed in each pyx and placed on a tray. Each Eucharistic minister retrieves their pyx from the priest's tray and delivers Communion to parishioners who are homebound due to sickness or injury.

The Lord's Prayer

One last item of difference between Catholics and Fundamentalist Protestants is the length of the Lord's Prayer. The last phrase, "For thine is the kingdom and the power and the glory," is not included in the Catholic Bible. The longer version of the Lord's Prayer, which does include this phrase, is typically included in the Protestant Bible. The last phrase was not included in the earliest known Greek manuscripts of the Gospels. Because the Catholic Bible is based on the older manuscripts, it does not have the longer version of the Lord's Prayer.

However, the last phrase was included in the *Didache* and in later manuscripts of the Gospels. Because the Catholic Mass is based on the Catholic Bible, it does not include the last phrase directly with the congregation's recital of the Lord's Prayer, but adds it following a separate prayer by the priest. My Protestant Bible, which is written in the New American Standard version, does include that last phrase but places it in brackets.

It is very appropriate for Christians to say, "For thine is the kingdom and the power and the glory." However, it does not seem to be a particularly appropriate prayer for the Son of God to say to his Father. While the Catholic Church does not believe Jesus really spoke the last phrase, they do believe it is theologically correct and perfectly fine for Christians to use the longer version of the Lord's Prayer.

Caricature-Like Images of Catholics

The Catholic religion was in existence for about two thousand years, since the time of Christ. They continue to have the same core Christian beliefs they held since the early church began. Catholics consistently believed Christ died so we can have eternal life. It is through faith that they believe in Christ. They love others as Christ loves them.

Because tradition is very important to Catholics, little has changed in their main worship practices over those thousands of years. They continue to focus on Holy Communion with the presence of Christ in the bread and wine. They continue to pray to God directly and indirectly through saints. They continue to honor Mary and pray to God through her. They continue to have statues, relics, paintings, and stained glass windows in their churches. They continue to confess their sins through a priest and directly to God without a priest. Burning incense and lighting candles are not new. Catholics have been doing that for centuries. They continue to use rituals and ceremonies with significant religious meaning. Not much has changed.

About five hundred years ago, Protestants broke away from the Catholic Church and started their own versions of Christianity. They made many changes from how they used to worship as previous Catholics. Hundreds of years later, after numerous generational changes, many Protestants look at Catholics now and think their worship practices are very strange. It is almost as though Protestants have caricature-like images in their minds of how they think Catholics worship. These images likely grew out of false narratives they learned in their youth. Catholics, unsurprisingly, do not understand why their worship practices are viewed as strange, because they have not changed their core worship practices in any meaningful way for two thousand years.

A Different Language

The Catholic Church is much more liturgical than most Protestant churches. They use many symbols and rituals as reminders of Christ. Much like Judaism, the Catholic Church successfully uses rituals to pass on their religious beliefs in a consistent manner from one generation to the next, and they have done so over thousands of years.

Along with the liturgy comes many new words and phrases that are unfamiliar to most Protestants. Fundamentalist Protestants use the simplest form of worship service and are the least familiar with Christian liturgy. As a Fundamentalist Protestant who attended many Catholic services, it took me a long time, and required much repetition, to understand the symbolism and the language.

When I first attended a Catholic church, so many of the words they used were new to me. Some commonly used Catholic terms that were unfamiliar to me include Eucharist, the host, the Blessed Sacrament, holy water, Crucifix, relic, stations of the cross, genuflect, patron saint, chalice, the mystery of faith, homily, missal, encyclical, vigil, beatification, canonization, sacrament, catechism, ordinary time, rosary, apparition, sacristy, the Great Amen, tabernacle, vestments, lectionary, font, Kyrie eleison, and indulgences. Other less commonly used Catholic terms that were also unfamiliar to me include monstrance, holy days of obligation, requiem, apologetics, *Didache*, Madonna, novena, pyx, veneration, stigmata, reliquary, Postulate, theca, incorruptible, Cursillo, mitre, bishop's staff, curia, tribunal, Memorare, Hail Holy Queen, Magnificat, ciborium, chrism, alb, cincture, conclave, Tridentine Mass, and triduum. Many other Catholic terms were also new to me. In addition, a few of the choruses are sometimes sung in Latin.

For a long time, it seemed like Catholics spoke a completely different language. Not only did I fail to understand, I had difficulty asking questions to even begin an understanding. When I inquired about the meaning behind certain rituals or ceremonies, I heard explanations using words I could not comprehend. But over time, with repetition and assistance from my patient wife, I slowly began to understand the new language and unravel the meaning behind many of the rituals and celebrations. With this new understanding came acceptance. As more time passed, acceptance grew into appreciation.

Sharing the Same Core Beliefs

Once I gained some clarity with many of the Catholic worship practices, I eventually learned that Catholics and Protestants share the same core beliefs. They believe Christ died so we can have eternal life. It is through faith that Christians believe in Jesus. They also love others as Christ loves them. These are the core beliefs of all Christians, both Catholic and Protestant. However, the worship practices of Catholics are very different from Protestants.

I am not trying to convince anyone to convert to Catholicism or to believe church doctrine according to Catholic interpretation. I am trying to make a case that Catholic worship practices are neither sinful nor weak.

They were developed by holy leaders based on biblical interpretations and tradition. We each have our own perspective of Christianity. It's only when we begin to learn the perspectives of other Christians that we begin to more fully understand our own Christian beliefs.

I believed false narratives and myths that were learned in my youth. Because I had the opportunity to experience Christian perspectives from many Protestant denominations and from the Catholic Church, I realized I held misguided beliefs that needed to be unlearned. I no longer believe Fundamentalist Christians interpret the Bible literally. I no longer believe the Bible is the sole authority for Christian doctrine. I no longer believe the Bible can be correctly interpreted by the average person. I no longer believe other Christian groups are less holy than Fundamentalist Christians. I no longer believe there is only one correct doctrine. I no longer believe Catholic worship practices are wrong.

I did not necessarily adopt new worship practices. I just came to the realization there were many ways to honor Christ. There are many different roads to heaven, not just the narrow path I learned in my youth. I now believe there are a lot more Christians in heaven than I previously imagined, including many Fundamentalist Protestants and many Catholics.

CHAPTER 15

Indulgences

Many of the false narratives about Catholics originated around the time of the Protestant Reformation. In order to better understand the Protestant Reformation, it is helpful to first understand the concept of indulgences. There are two consequences of sin: they are guilt and punishment. Guilt is removed once your sins are forgiven. But as punishment, amends may still be needed, even though you have been forgiven. The making of these amends is called indulgences. Depending on the type of sin, indulgences can include doing good works, making a confession, paying restitution, praying, or reading the Bible.

The Catholic Church believes they have the authority to forgive sins. This authority is based on the words of Jesus after his resurrection when speaking to the disciples in John 20:23, saying, "If you forgive the sins of any, their sins have been forgiven them; if you retain the sins of any, they have been retained." With this power to forgive sins, the church believes they also have the lesser power to administer indulgences.

Pope Leo X was the Catholic pope at the time of the Protestant Reformation. Pope Leo X accelerated a project to rebuild Saint Peter's Basilica. Because there were insufficient funds to rebuild the basilica, Leo sold indulgences to raise money. Making restitution by paying money to the church could potentially be an acceptable practice for indulgences. But the degree to which it was done and the motives behind it were rightly challenged by Martin Luther.

The Medici Family

Pope Leo X was a member of the Medici family. Liz and I visited Memphis, Tennessee, with friends one weekend and discovered an art exhibit from Florence, Italy, on display there. The exhibit contained artwork commissioned by the Medici family. The Medicis were a powerful family who governed the city-state of Florence beginning in the thirteenth century. They made their money in the banking industry. The Medicis loved artwork and commissioned many famous artists to work in Florence. Michelangelo, Leonardo da Vinci, Botticelli, and Donatello were some of the artists who worked for the Medicis. Many of the world's young artists also moved to Florence to learn from the master artists.

Florence Cathedral.

The most famous piece of art in Florence is Michelangelo's sculpture of David, who is remembered for slaying Goliath with a sling. Most artists sculpted David accurately as a small shepherd boy. Because David slayed a giant, Michelangelo pictured David in his mind as someone who was strong. Using his artistic genius, Michelangelo depicted David as a tall, muscular man. Michelangelo's statue of David and the extensive amount of artwork commissioned by the Medici family still make Florence a major tourist attraction today.

In Memphis, I learned about the Medici family history from the art historian. The Medici family had power and money, but they also had a strong desire to become royalty and to gain control of the church. I saw paintings of people from one time period who were shown with other people from a different time period. For example, some members of the Medici family were purposely shown in paintings with members of royalty who lived hundreds of years earlier. In other paintings, members of the Medici family were shown sitting with the original apostles of Jesus. With the first set of paintings, the Medicis were using art to convince the public of the false narrative that they were members of royalty. With the second set of paintings, the Medicis were using art to convince the public of the false narrative that they were very religious.

Over time, their schemes were very successful. Members of the Medici family did marry into royalty. In addition, Pope Leo X was the first of four Medici family members to be elected pope of the Catholic Church. Remember that during this time, the leader of the Catholic Church was also the government leader of the Papal States, which later became known as central Italy. Because the Medici family governed one of the neighboring city-states just to the north of the Papal States, they aspired to have a family member become pope in order to govern a larger territory. They had no real interest in religion. However, the Medici family was successful in taking control of the church. As pope of the Catholic Church, Medici influence extended across the entire Holy Roman Empire. The election of Pope Leo X continued the line of unholy popes from city-states in Italy who controlled the Catholic Church for 100 years.

The timing of Pope Leo X becoming pope in 1513 worked well for the Medicis. After spending so much money on artwork in Florence, their family treasury was nearly gone. Now, the artists all moved to Rome, where they were paid commissions from the Vatican treasury. Pope Leo X led a lavish lifestyle. He continued with the family practice of having significant amounts of artwork created, including paintings, sculptures, ornate doors, and adorned buildings. He also planned for his largest project yet, rebuilding Saint Peter's Basilica. In order to pay for the new basilica, he decided to raise money by selling indulgences.

Poorly trained Catholic priests universally followed the unholy pope's directive by collecting money for indulgences during confession. Martin Luther believed strongly that helping the poor was a much better indulgence than paying cash. He posted his objections on the door of the Wittenberg Castle Church in 1517.

The Catholic Counter-Reformation

Many of the false narratives believed by Fundamentalist Christians about the Catholic Church were true at the time of the Protestant Reformation. However, they are no longer true in the modern-day Catholic Church. During the time of the Reformation, the leadership of the Catholic Church lost its way and became unholy. Bishops were appointed to their position for political reasons and through nepotism. During a sixty-year period leading up to the Protestant Reformation, a number of those politically appointed bishops were also elected to be popes. Their unholy leadership led to corruption, like charging church members to pay for indulgences under Pope Leo X. Because of these unholy acts in the Catholic Church, Protestant groups in different countries organized and left the Catholic Church.

Several decades after the Protestant Reformation, holy leaders regained control of the Catholic Church from the unholy city-state leaders. They quickly started to work on a Counter-Reformation at the Council of Trent during twenty-five separate meetings from 1545 to 1563. Under new and more holy Catholic leadership, these meetings resulted in changes away from the unholy practices of the past. The Catholic Church no longer permitted the charging of money for indulgences. The pope's authority was limited. A new initiative started to better train all priests. Nepotism in appointing new cardinals was severely limited. Adequate controls were in place to ensure their religion would never again be hijacked by immoral leaders. Additional councils were held in later years to further refine Catholic Church organizational rules to maintain control.

The Bible was printed in German and a few other languages by Protestants shortly after the Protestant Reformation. In 1582, the Church of Rome agreed to embrace printing the Bible in English so many more church members could read it for themselves. Within fifty years of the Protestant Reformation, the Catholic Church corrected its unholy practices.

However, it was not until 1946, when Italy was unified into one nation, that the Vatican gave up sovereign state control of the Papal States. Today, a pope's only control over government is limited to a tiny city called Vatican City, with fewer than nine hundred citizens. The Vatican government does not maintain its own protection personnel but outsources protection services to the Swiss Guard, Italian police, and the Italian military. After experiencing three schisms, the Catholic Church also learned that a proper separation between church and state is necessary for the long-term success of Christianity.

After fifteen hundred years in existence, the Catholic Church lost control of its leadership for a hundred-year period before regaining control. It has now been four hundred years since holy leaders regained proper control. I am not suggesting the Catholic Church has been perfect since the Counter-Reformation. It was not until 1964 that the Catholic Church changed worship services from Latin to each country's own language. The church incurred a child abuse scandal beginning in the 1970s. However, there has not been recent widespread abuse by the church directly due to doctrinal issues.

Recent Catholic Problems

Widespread abuse of children by priests and a subsequent cover-up by church leaders was well publicized. The Catholic Church has four hundred ten thousand priests in any given year, but nearly three thousand known priests were accused of child molestation over a forty-year period beginning in the 1970s. Protestant churches also experienced their share of unholy ministers. These problems have terrible consequences, but they were not doctrinal in nature.

I personally encountered several priests and preachers who exhibited deviant sexual behavior during the 1980s and 1990s. The Catholic Church required Liz and I to attend a Pre-Cana Conference prior to being married in the church. The name Cana is taken from the town of Cana in Galilee where Jesus miraculously turned water into wine during a wedding celebration. The conference entailed two Saturdays of marriage counseling and required reading of five books on marriage for discussion at the conference. The conference was led by a married couple from the Catholic Church and was taught at a diocesan or regional level.

After completing the Pre-Cana Conference, we returned to the Catholic church where we planned to be married to submit our marriage license and Pre-Cana certificate of completion to the priest. Final marriage counseling by the priest was also scheduled to be completed at that meeting. Because the main priest who married us was not available, a substitute priest handled our final marriage counseling. This was my first experience with a priest who was rumored to be sexually abusing young boys. After receiving many complaints in Tennessee, this priest was transferred to Pennsylvania. We could immediately see he was very uncomfortable in providing any marriage counseling. After asking if we thought the Pre-Cana Conference was worthwhile, our counseling session abruptly ended. It lasted two minutes instead of the scheduled two hours.

This priest took young boys bowling. He bought them T-shirts and other small items. He took some young boys on overnight trips. He displayed little interest in anything religious. It became clear that the priesthood was a great vocation where he could hide and maintain access to young boys. Years later, this priest was removed from having any contact with parishioners.

A decade later, another priest with rumors of sexual deviancy with young boys was brought in as the main priest. He was a very arrogant man who immediately replaced the choir director and other leaders in the church. He also ordered the sanctuary to be repainted in a different color and replaced the altar with a different one. Later, he was removed from the priesthood altogether.

During this same time, an acquaintance of mine who served as pastor of a small, independent Protestant church was removed from the church after complaints of improper behavior with females in the church. Following an investigation, it was discovered that he used his position to have affairs with multiple married ladies and single women in the church. His wife filed for divorce. Later, this preacher accepted a pastoral position in another independent Protestant church. The leaders of the new church failed to perform a background check prior to hiring him as their pastor.

There are ongoing problems in both Catholic and Protestant churches. However, the Catholic Church did not engage in the widespread, unholy practices that caused the Protestant Reformation for over four hundred years. Still, many Fundamentalist Christians believe the unholy practices continue to occur in today's Catholic Church. While growing up in the

1960s and 1970s, I was taught by my Fundamentalist Christian church that Catholic practices were wrong and sometimes sinful. This was reinforced by my parents. I believed it, even though it has not been true for hundreds of years.

When I first began unraveling the false narratives and learning the truth about today's Catholic doctrine, I thought the Fundamentalist Christian view of Catholics was just a misunderstanding. The Catholic service is very different from a Fundamentalist Christian service. Because Catholics still have saints, that all could be misunderstood. It wasn't until after I met the expert on cults that I realized there could be a different explanation. The false narratives about Catholics were too consistent across different Fundamentalist Christian denominations to be the result of current misunderstandings. The false narratives began in the 1500s. Even though the Catholic Church reformed itself, the myths lived on. The myths were repeated and reinforced. They were passed on from one generation to the next, for hundreds of years.

CHAPTER 16

Early Protestantism

If I no longer like my pastor or my current church, I can easily attend another neighboring church. There are many from which to choose. With religious freedom, changing from one denomination to another, or changing between Protestantism and Catholicism, has little consequence. However, it was not always that way. During the time of early Protestantism, a change in denomination or type of Christian church often resulted in imprisonment or death.

The Protestant schism with Roman Catholicism was very different from the other two schisms. Extensive changes were made to church doctrine and worship practices immediately following the Protestant schism. Wars broke out between Catholics and Protestants causing the loss of many lives. Today, Catholic and Protestant Christians keep a distance between each other. Misunderstanding and a lack of trust remain evident even now.

How It Began

Most people credit Martin Luther, an Augustinian monk who was also a Catholic professor of theology at the University of Wittenberg in Saxony, Germany, with starting the Protestant Reformation in 1517. It was the posting of his Ninety-Five Theses on the front door of the All Saints' Church (more commonly known as the Castle Church) in Wittenberg that began the schism. Wittenberg is approximately seventy miles southwest of Berlin, on the Elbe River.

Luther's theses attacked the Catholic practice of an indiscriminate sale of indulgences to finance construction of Saint Peter's Basilica in

Rome. Luther was personally searching to find assurance of salvation in traditional Catholic teaching. He believed such assurance was included in the doctrine of justification by grace through faith. However, the Catholic Church obscured this assurance of salvation by giving equal weight to good works in order to raise funds. The sale of indulgences was an abuse that was based upon a new emphasis on works, instead of faith.

Three Early Protestant Groups

At first, Martin Luther only wanted to reform the Catholic Church. The pope took a strong stance against Luther and demanded he recant his views publicly. After Luther refused to back down, he was excommunicated from the Catholic Church. Luther had little choice except to start a separate and competing church. Protestantism began with Lutheran reforms to the Catholic Church.

The Lutheran tradition, also known as Evangelical in Europe, became one of three early Protestant traditions to emerge from the Protestant Reformation. The second Protestant tradition, Zwingli's reforms, began in Zurich, Switzerland, under the leadership of Pastor Huldrych Zwingli. The third tradition, called Anabaptist, was a more radical form of Protestantism in Europe that encompassed many smaller sects of varying beliefs.

Lutheran Reforms

Lutheranism retained much of the Roman Catholic liturgy. However, there were a few doctrinal differences. The primary change from Catholic doctrine is a belief that our salvation is by faith alone, not works. A faith in Christ is all one needs to gain everlasting life in heaven. Lutherans believe good works follow from faith, just as a good tree produces good fruit.

The Bible is central to Lutheran worship. The seven sacraments of the Catholic Church were reduced to two sacraments: baptism and Communion. Lutherans removed the remaining five Catholic sacraments because they found no biblical evidence indicating they were instituted by Christ. Like Catholics, Lutherans affirm both the baptism of infants and the presence of Christ in the Communion elements.

Lutherans adopted a doctrine of the priesthood of all believers.

Under this new doctrine, all Christians elect their vocations, with equal opportunity for discipleship. One member from laity in each church is trained to serve in the vocation of priesthood. This doctrine places priests on a similar level to parishioners. Unlike Catholic priests, Lutheran clergy may marry and raise a family.

During the sixteenth century, religion and government were significantly intertwined. The government of Holy Roman Empire, along with governments of many countries, heavily regulated religion. Governments selected one religion as the only lawful religion. Religious leaders were approved by government officials and removed by government officials. Government leaders served as judges over those who violated religious norms.

In January of 1521, Pope Leo X excommunicated Luther from the Catholic Church. Charles V, emperor of the Holy Roman Empire, summoned Luther to appear before secular authorities in the town of Worms, Germany, in April of 1521. After Luther again refused to recant his beliefs, he was condemned by the emperor.

Luther was declared an outlaw. The emperor ordered his arrest and punishment as a heretic. His literature was banned. It was also a crime for anyone in Germany to give Luther food or shelter. Anyone could kill Martin Luther without legal consequence. Lutheran parishioners were placed under an imperial ban.

The Prince of Saxony took Luther away and placed him safely in hiding at Wartburg Castle. There Luther began translating the New Testament into a standard German language. Outside of Wartburg Castle, Lutheranism spread. However, intermittent religious wars also followed.

Extreme followers of Luther created disturbances in Wittenberg. They taught revolutionary doctrines, including adult baptism and Christ's imminent return. When the town council asked Luther to return, he secretly left Wartburg Castle. After preaching his sixth sermon in Wittenberg, calm was once again restored.

Radical Protestant reformers took social unrest and violence to other places in Europe. Luther continued to teach and write in Wittenberg. He now understood there were two fronts in the religious battle: one with the Holy Roman Empire and Catholic Church, and a second with radical Protestant reformers.

Radical reformers gained support from peasants across Germany. Soon there was widespread plundering and destruction. It evolved into the Peasants' War from 1524 to 1526. Peasants justified their violence and demands somewhat illegitimately from Luther's writings. Luther angrily denounced them and supported the government's effort to successfully restore order.

At age forty-one, Martin Luther married Katharina von Bora, a former nun who was fifteen years younger. She supported Luther during the busiest part of his life. Luther's marriage placed a seal of approval on clerical marriages. The marriage was happy and successful. Katharina bore six children.

Lutheranism developed in separate national and territorial churches. It spread from Germany to Scandinavia. Because Lutheranism was tied to its respective governments, a uniform system of internal church governance was never developed.

Zwingli's Reforms

Huldrych Zwingli was a Swiss theologian and Catholic pastor who led the Protestant Reformation in Zurich, Switzerland. He was educated at the University of Vienna in Austria and the University of Basel in Switzerland. He could read and interpret the Greek and Hebrew writings of the Bible. Zwingli's reforms were more radical and more far-reaching than Luther's.

Zwingli concluded that only what was specifically authorized by the scriptures should be retained in church practices and doctrine. While Lutherans retained many of the Catholic rituals in their services, Zwingli implemented a very simple church service. This practice was in direct opposition to both Catholicism and Lutheranism.

Zwingli cited as unscriptural the practices of adoration of saints and relics, promises of miraculous cures, and required payments for indulgences. He no longer accepted the presence of Christ in the Eucharist. Holy Communion used elements that were only symbols of Christ. However, Zwingli did agree with Luther on a limited power of government over the church. Because Zurich previously adopted a limited government power over religion, Zwingli successfully gained approval of his reforms by the town council.

The Catholic pope removed Zwingli from the pulpit and asked the Zurich town council to repudiate him as a heretic. In January of 1523, the town council held a hearing in which Zwingli defended himself. After deliberation, the town council upheld Zwingli by withdrawing the Zurich region from the jurisdiction of the Catholic Church. They affirmed their previous ban against any preaching not based on the scriptures.

Zwingli then married Anna Reinhard, a widow with whom he lived openly. Zurich became a theocracy under rule by Zwingli and a magistrate. Monasteries were converted into hospitals. Religious images and confessionals were removed from all church buildings.

When a town or regional government converted from Catholicism to Protestantism by decree, all Catholic churches and Catholic property immediately came under ownership of Protestants. Any remaining Catholics were in violation of the law. They were subject to imprisonment or death. Catholic monks living in monasteries needed to leave immediately, under cover of darkness. Catholic nuns living in convents were forced into hiding until they could relocate to a Catholic territory. Catholic priests with a desire to remain Catholic moved to a Catholic town or region. Anyone offering assistance to nuns, monks, or other Catholics was subject to arrest.

Friends of both Luther and Zwingli arranged a meeting between the two Protestant Reformation leaders, with the hope they could reach agreement on church practice and doctrine. With a goal of unifying the two major Protestant groups, the meeting was held in Marburg, Germany, in 1529. Because neither Luther nor Zwingli could change their personal belief concerning Holy Communion, the meeting ended in failure.

With assistance from a printing press, Zwingli's ideas spread throughout Switzerland. In addition to Zurich, approximately half of the remaining parts of Switzerland converted to Zwingli's version of Protestantism. The rest of Switzerland remained staunchly Catholic.

In 1529, relations between the Swiss Catholics and Swiss Protestants worsened, and a civil war broke out. Zwingli served as chaplain for the army of the Reformed movement. On October 10, 1531, Zwingli was wounded in battle and later put to death by Catholic soldiers. Growth of the Reformed movement in Switzerland ended. Today, Switzerland remains half-Protestant and half-Catholic.

Anabaptist Reforms

The word *anabaptist* means "one who baptizes again." Anabaptists, or rebaptizers, consisted of radical sects of Protestants with disparate doctrines in Europe during the Reformation. They were located primarily in Germany, the Netherlands, and Switzerland. Generally, Anabaptist sects practiced adult baptism, even if the person was previously baptized as an infant. They called it a "believer's baptism," since only an adult can understand enough to make a conscious decision to follow Christ.

Some people use the term *Anabaptist* in a narrow reference to a smaller number of Protestant Reformation sects with similar beliefs and a nonviolent approach. Others use the term in a broader reference to all Protestant Reformation sects outside of the established churches that followed either Luther or Zwingli. Some of these sects used violence to force their beliefs on others. Consistent with Luther and Zwingli, the broader definition is used here.

Anabaptists believed in the supreme importance of personal faith in God. They opposed any use of religious symbols, rituals, and ornate items. They believed followers of Luther and Zwingli did not go far enough in the direction of a simplified, biblical Christianity. Anabaptists opposed any government control or regulation of religion. Some Anabaptists wished to establish communal groups who lived apart from others, with no government interference. They also opposed the taking of oaths. Many early Anabaptist Protestants expected the imminent return of Christ based on their interpretation of the book of Revelation.

Anabaptists largely consisted of the poor, uneducated peasants, and artisans. Many radical Anabaptist leaders believed religious reformation must include social reformation through political violence and war. Some Anabaptist sects physically attacked established Protestant churches and Catholic churches with equal vengeance. They invaded churches and destroyed stained glass windows, statues, and organs. Because Anabaptists rejected civil authorities, rejected the hierarchy of the Catholic Church, and rejected the hierarchy of established Protestant churches, many were persecuted, imprisoned, and martyred.

Other Anabaptist sects renounced all use of force. Three of the pacifist Anabaptist sects were known as the Mennonites, the Brethren, and the

Quakers. One of the more radical Anabaptist sects practiced polygamy. This entire sect died out after a year's siege and the execution of its leader. Many other Anabaptist sects continued to arise throughout Europe.

Second-Generation Calvinism

Immediately following Luther's and Zwingli's generation, John Calvin became the most influential reformer of Protestantism. Calvin was a French theologian, pastor, and author. He was educated at the College de la Marche and the College de Montaigu, branches of the University of Paris. He also studied law and the Greek Bible at the universities of Orleans and Bourges in France.

Calvin settled in Geneva, Switzerland, and began reforming the church there. He implemented a democratic form of church administration, which is governed by representative assemblies of church elders. Calvin wrote the first systematic explanation of Protestant theology. He founded influential educational institutions to train future Protestant leaders. Calvin also wrote many hymns and encouraged others to do so.

Although Calvin advocated separation between church and state, he wielded great political power in Geneva, where church and state were one. The walled city was often threatened by Catholic armies. With limited commerce and surrounded by farmland, citizens lived a harsh life. Dissenting Christians were often expelled. With Calvin's personal approval, one Unitarian was captured in the city and executed for religious heresy.

Calvinism spread to Scotland, where it was known as the Presbyterian church. It spread to France, where followers were known as Huguenots. Calvinism also spread to Holland.

Wars of the Protestant Reformation

There were many religious wars following the Protestant Reformation. In Germany, the Peasants' War resulted in nearly one hundred thousand peasants killed in battle, largely against Lutheran armies. Germany also incurred other religious wars during the sixteenth century. The Thirty Years' War between Catholics and Protestants in the seventeenth century resulted in the loss of millions of people.

In Switzerland, the civil war between Swiss Catholics and Swiss Protestants resulted in the deaths of Zwingli and many other Christians. In France, the Calvinist Huguenots fought a bloody civil war with French Catholics. That war ended with a massacre of many Huguenot leaders in 1572. In England, a civil war was fought between the Puritans and the Anglicans.

Protestant Schism Conclusions

Immoral Catholic popes and their complicit priests caused the Protestant Reformation. The pope ordered all Catholic priests to collect mandatory payments from Catholic parishioners as restitution for minor sins. The priests blindly followed orders from their immoral pope. At that time in history, Catholic priests were not well trained in church doctrine. Parishioners did not tolerate the new collections for very long. They lost all trust in the Catholic Church and in Catholic priests.

From the history of the Protestant Reformation, we can draw some important conclusions that may provide insight into the variety of worship practices experienced across the various Christian groups and denominations today. The first conclusion I reached is that many of the Protestant reforms were made in order to displace the need for untrustworthy priests. The doctrine of salvation through faith alone eliminated the need for any restitution previously made to priests during confession of failures to complete good works.

The "priesthood of all believers" treated the priesthood vocation as equal to the other vocations of parishioners. One member of laity in each church would receive training to become a priest. Because parishioners and the priest were on similar religious levels, confession to a priest was no longer required. The number of sacraments involving a priest was greatly reduced. A new interpretation of the Communion elements as symbols no longer required a priest to consecrate the bread and wine into the real presence of Christ.

These new reforms, which greatly reduced the authority of untrustworthy priests, were adopted in various forms and to varying degrees among the early Protestant denominations. While Luther and Zwingli were educated sufficiently to make their own biblical translations, it appears a common goal was to reduce the religious authority of priests. Because Catholic priests abused their power, Protestants revised church doctrine to greatly reduce the religious control new Protestant priests held over parishioners.

The second conclusion I reached is many Catholic worship practices were changed for nondoctrinal and non-biblical reasons. In particular, Zwingli and many of the Anabaptist sects greatly simplified worship services. Catholic rituals were eliminated. Ornate windows were removed from churches. Statues and paintings were removed from sanctuaries. Saints and relics were no longer venerated. The practice of honoring Mary was eliminated. The crucifix was replaced by a simple cross. While the early Lutheran church retained most of these worship practices, significant changes toward simplification were made in varying degrees among the majority of other Protestant denominations. It seems the underlying message of most Protestants became "We do not need your priests, your rituals, your saints, your devotion to Mary, your statues, your stained glass windows, or your church buildings to worship our God; the only thing we need is the Bible."

Once reforms to the church were made by Luther and Zwingli, many other church leaders felt free to make different reforms for their own group of followers. Numerous Anabaptist sects were unleashed to each develop their own set of doctrines. When Martin Luther was in hiding, two radical Lutheran doctrines developed in Zurich when parishioners disagreed over the meaning of Luther's writings. Luther quickly returned to Zurich to explain the true meaning of his writings in order to temporarily end the unrest.

Luther implemented the *sola scriptura* concept as he originally designed it. The Bible and church tradition would both help determine church doctrine, not just the Bible. His intention was only that tradition not take priority over the Bible. Luther retained many of the Catholic traditions like honoring the Blessed Virgin Mary and personal participation in Confession to a priest.

Zwingli's view of *sola scriptura* went further than Luther's. Additional church traditions not explicitly included in the Bible were also eliminated. Anabaptists implemented a more radical version of *sola scriptura*, which resulted in the simplest form of worship possible. The vast majority of previous traditions were either removed or changed.

Early Protestant reforms do not appear to be the result of guidance from the Holy Spirit under *sola scriptura*. If the reforms were guided by the Holy Spirit, it is doubtful there would be some doctrines in conflict with other doctrines, and so many variations in worship practices. However, the core beliefs of all Christians do appear to be the same.

Christians believe Christ died so we can have eternal life. It is through faith that Christians believe in Christ. They also love others as Christ loves them. These are the core beliefs of all Christians. Unfortunately, during the Reformation, many Christians failed to love other Christians when they took up arms against them.

Following years of war between Protestants and Catholics, animosity remained between the two groups. The death and imprisonment of family members left scars in the minds of many Christians. Protestants, in particular, bore the brunt of the persecution. Because of the level of hostility and its personal nature, many Protestants passed their hatred of Catholics on to their children. Their children passed it to the grandchildren. Even after many families relocated to America for religious freedom and a better life, the hostility and distrust of Catholics remained with them and continued to pass from generation to generation. The reason for distrust between Protestants and Catholics today is rooted in the Protestant Reformation from five hundred years ago.

Catholics Lost Control of Their Own Religion

Paying money as restitution for minor sins to raise funds for the construction of St. Peter's Basilica was the external cause of the Protestant Reformation. The real cause was holy leaders in the Catholic Church lost control of their religion to immoral government leaders for a hundred-year period. The Protestant Reformation occurred during that time. Decades after the Protestant Reformation, holy leaders then regained control of the Catholic Church. However, it was too late to reunite Protestants and Catholics.

Understandably, early Protestantism was anti-Catholic. Under the direction of immoral leaders, untrained Catholic clergy violated their parishioners. However, when you understand how those immoral leaders came to power in the Catholic Church, you begin to realize that Catholics were victims too. Their religion was stolen from them by immoral, city-state government leaders.

Holy Catholic leaders, like Luther and Zwingli, started Protestantism with good intentions. They attempted to institute religious reforms from outside of the Catholic Church. However, they quickly lost control of the populist revolt, and religious wars ensued. Other holy Catholic leaders worked within the church to regain control of the leadership and institute corrective controls. Fifty years passed before they were successful.

The many lives that were lost during the Reformation cannot be recovered. Unity within the Christian religion was broken and remains elusive today. Anti-Catholic sentiment among some Protestants continues to pass from one generation to the next.

CHAPTER 17

Post-Reformation Report Card

At the time of the Protestant Reformation, four related violations were cited by Martin Luther as abuses by church leaders. First, parishioners were forced to pay large amounts of money to the church. Second, church leaders accumulated wealth and lived lavish lifestyles. Third, one church leader unilaterally changed church doctrine. Fourth, the church had too many untrained leaders.

The first and primary violation was a new doctrinal requirement for church parishioners to pay money to the church for restitution of sins. Due to that new practice, unholy popes and other church leaders became wealthy and lived lavish lifestyles. The unholy popes unilaterally developed this new church doctrine in order to enrich themselves personally, even though it violated the scriptures. Unholy popes also took advantage of untrained priests by forcing them to implement a new church doctrine that placed tradition in a priority position over the Bible.

Protestants made immediate reforms to reverse the sacred violations of the unholy popes. It required more time for holy Catholics to remove immoral church leaders and make internal reforms. However, within fifty years of the Reformation, control of the Catholic Church was regained by holy leaders. With valid leaders back in control of the Catholic Church, they quickly made the needed changes to reverse the sacred violations.

Now, five hundred years passed since the Protestant Reformation occurred. It is beneficial to review whether the changes made by both Protestants and Catholics were successful. Let's review the four original violations, one at a time.

Violation 1: Forcing Parishioners to Pay Large Amounts of Money to the Church

Within fifty years of the Reformation, Catholics changed church doctrine so restitution of sins no longer required payment of money to the church. That doctrine remains in force today. In addition, there is no tithing requirement or tithing recommendation communicated by church leaders to parishioners. Although there is wide variability, Catholic parishioners worldwide donate an average of 1 percent of their income.

Protestants changed church doctrine so restitution of sins does not require payment of money to the church. That doctrine remains in force today among most of the Protestant denominations. However, many church leaders strongly communicate that tithing 10 percent of income is an expectation. Although the average Protestant donation is slightly above 2 percent worldwide, church leaders in the United States often make parishioners feel guilty if they give less than 10 percent. In some Protestant denominations, church leaders communicate that parishioners who give more than 10 percent of their income to the church will receive more rewards from God in return.

Violation 2: Church Leaders Are Wealthy and Have Lavish Lifestyles

Within fifty years of the Reformation, the unholy popes who lived lavish lifestyles were removed from power. Holy popes took control of the church and lived more modest lifestyles. Today, most priests live in small houses or together with other priests in a rectory. Some priests take vows of poverty and live very frugally. However, there are a few cardinals who live in large houses and routinely travel in limousines.

The majority of Protestant pastors live in modest houses. However, there are some (but not all) pastors of independent mega-churches who live very comfortably in large mansions. They also tend to accumulate wealth. There are also some televangelists who became multimillionaires. They own multiple large houses and sometimes fly in private jets.

Violation 3: One Church Leader Can Change Church Doctrine

Within fifty years of the Reformation, Catholics changed church doctrine so the pope no longer had the authority to unilaterally change church doctrine. To change church doctrine today, a pope needs to have a majority of all bishops around the world in agreement with the change. A recorded vote of the bishops on each proposal to change church doctrine is required. As a result of these changes, there is seldom any change to church doctrine.

Most large Protestant denominations have annual meetings of church leaders and representative church members. They typically vote on doctrinal changes at these meetings. As a result of this process, changes to church doctrine occur often and typically follow changing political views in the country. In small denominations, a handful of church leaders can control church doctrine. In each of the many independent churches, an individual pastor typically has enough respect among the parishioners to interpret church doctrine unilaterally.

Violation 4: Untrained Church Leaders

Within fifty years of the Reformation, Catholics began a training program for all priests so they would be more knowledgeable about the Bible, church doctrine, and leadership. Today, it takes an undergraduate college degree and training in a seminary for someone to become a Catholic priest. Many priests also have additional graduate degrees.

Most large Protestant denominations require an undergraduate college degree and training in a seminary to become a pastor. Many of those pastors also have additional graduate degrees. Smaller Protestant denominations usually require an undergraduate college degree. Some independent churches have no educational requirements.

Learning from History

It is always helpful to understand history so we can avoid repeating the mistakes of the past. A good example of repeating a mistake by not learning from history is the invasion of Russia during winter. In 1812, Napoleon Bonaparte assembled an army in June and invaded Russia. They successfully reached Moscow to claim victory and then returned during the winter months. The army was unprepared for the freezing temperatures on the long march back. Only a small portion of the army made it back home alive.

Then, in 1941, Adolph Hitler assembled an army in June and invaded

Russia. After some success, the army tried to return in the winter months. Without coats or other winter provisions during the long march back, most of the soldiers were lost. Unfortunately, they did not learn from the first failure, and history was repeated.

Early Warning Signs in Protestantism

Religious leaders with a desire to accumulate wealth and live a lavish lifestyle caused irreparable harm to Christianity in the past. Today, in a limited number of cases involving independent mega-churches and Protestant televangelists, the growth of personal wealth at the expense of parishioners is once again starting. Too much control is placed in one individual instead of a group of church deacons or trustees. In these limited situations, parishioners should vote with their feet by leaving the church and refusing to support it financially.

In the past, poorly trained priests caused irreparable harm to the Christian religion by blindly following immoral orders from the pope. Today, many smaller independent churches have poorly trained pastors. They often have autonomous control of the church. In these instances, parishioners should encourage the pastor to attend a seminary for proper training.

The Jewish Pharisees enacted thousands religious laws that parishioners were required to follow. Jesus came to correct the injustice of having so many laws. He created the new Christian religion based on love. Following the Reformation, Protestants gained a newfound freedom to reimplement the Christian religion in thousands of different ways. In an attempt to lead a perfect Christian life, some Fundamentalist groups chose to revert back to the use of numerous religious laws, like the Pharisees.

History is at risk of repeating itself again, this time on the Protestant side. All three of these risks are in the early stages. There is still time to take corrective action before any of them spiral out of control.

Early Warning Signs in Catholicism

The Catholic Church is the largest Christian organization in the world. Compared to other Christian organizations, Catholicism retains the highest degree of control over local congregations. The church, not the parishioners, determines who can receive Holy Communion. The church decides who may or may not have their marriage annulled. This decision can also result in a lifetime ban from participation in Holy Communion. The church decides which parishioners may have a Catholic wedding.

Church buildings are owned by the diocese, not the local members. Priests are appointed to specific churches by the bishop, without input from local congregations. Because priests are not directly accountable to local parishioners, they are free to unilaterally replace key personnel, banish long-standing church volunteers, change the music normally sung each week, replace the altar and artwork with a different décor, and repaint the sanctuary with their personal choice of color. Most priests do consult the parishioners, but they are not required to do so.

The Catholic hierarchy should rethink the amount of control they wield over sacraments and local parishes. A noteworthy portion of the leadership of the church is proven to be untrustworthy with child molestation, unethical transfers of known child molesters, and a cover-up that reached the highest levels in the Vatican. It is time to relinquish some control to the parishioners. Done correctly, it can better protect both the church and the parishioners.

Obstacles to Bridge Building

Over the years, I heard many older Catholics say they believe in God, but they do not attend church because they don't trust the priests. It is obvious that comments like these are just excuses for not going to church. Church attendance is to worship God. It should not be affected by what you think of the priests.

However, those comments do point to a much larger issue. When the Catholic Church lost control of their religion to unholy popes, there was an egregious violation of people's trust that went right to the core of who they were. The emotional scars of having your religion abuse you run deep. They remain with you always. They are passed on from you to your children. Your children pass them on to their children. The emotional scars live on, well past the lifetime of the original victims.

Even after five hundred years, the root of Protestant misunderstanding about Catholic worship practices goes back to the Reformation. Mistrust from the Reformation, when coupled with uncertainty about a different worship practice, resulted in an emotional response, not a logical conclusion. It's hard to be open to understanding a new worship practice when you don't trust the worship leaders. This is part of the reason Catholics and Protestants have difficulty in rebuilding the bridge over the schism between them.

The mistrust from the Reformation was exacerbated again during the time when several thousand Catholic priests sexually abused children. Compared to Protestantism, the Catholic Church places a lot of religious authority in the hands of priests, bishops, and the pope. When control of some Catholic leadership was lost a second time, the mistrust became magnified for Protestants who watch from the outside.

It also doesn't help when a Catholic pope publicly takes a political stand on nonreligious issues. With the public evenly divided between conservative and liberal views, half of the public feels undermined by the pope when told they are wrong in taking a political stand. Mistrust of Catholicism by Protestants in that undermined group further increases. To them, the pope is once again exceeding his authority as a religious leader.

Some popes, bishops, and priests are aware of Protestant concern about Catholic religious control and authority. They are careful about what they say and how they say it. Other Catholic leaders remain unaware of this Protestant concern with religious authority and say things that unwittingly increase mistrust.

Some Catholic leaders may believe the abuses occurred long ago, were corrected, and are no longer relevant today. Catholic misunderstanding of this issue contributes to the inability of Christians to cross the schism of understanding between Catholicism and Protestantism. This is another part of the reason Catholics and Protestants have difficulty communicating.

At times, Catholics and Protestants both celebrate conversions of Christians from one group to the other. However, this is divisive. When one group tries to convert parishioners from the other group to their side, there will be little progress toward Christian unity between Catholics and Protestants. Both sides are already Christian. They need to learn to first accept each other as fellow Christians, just as they are, with no changes. Acceptance rebuilds trust. Then, and only then, can meaningful communications begin in earnest.

The Trade-Off

When selecting a Christian place to worship, there is no perfect choice. However, there are many great options. It really comes down to a personal preference of how you want to worship and where you feel most comfortable. Options to consider include ornate sanctuaries versus plain sanctuaries; symbolic rituals and religious ceremony versus educational sermons; a large organization with religious scholars versus a small organization with few or no religious scholars; and whether you want more control to remain with the pastor or with the congregation.

Catholicism generally provides the ability to worship God in ornate churches that are rich in history, symbolic ritual, and religious ceremony. Faith in Christ is often celebrated. Religious scholars in such a large organization provide adequate checks and balances on proper interpretation of church doctrine. But with Catholicism also comes a high degree of direct religious authority placed in their religious leaders. Although the majority of popes, bishops, and priests are very holy men, history has shown that leaders cannot always be trusted with increased authority.

Protestantism generally provides little history, ritual, or religious ceremony. The religious leaders have indirect authority yet can still make parishioners feel obligations that are not necessarily based in Christianity. Although the majority of pastors and denominational leaders are very holy, occasionally there are unholy leaders. Depending on the size of the denomination, there may or may not be adequate checks and balances on proper interpretation of church doctrine. Larger denominations have religious scholars who can properly interpret scripture. Small denominations and independent churches often do not have adequate religious scholars in their organization.

There are exceptions to these generalities. When visiting Dresden, Germany, Liz and I toured a large baroque Lutheran church. Constructed in the eighteenth century, the Frauenkirche of Dresden is an example of Protestant sacred architecture. It has one of the largest domes in Europe. The altar is ornate, using white and gold colors, with a few statues. The interior of the dome has paintings using white, gold, and red colors. The church seemed much like a Catholic cathedral, except for more pastel colors and no stained glass windows. In the city square just to the right of the church stands a statue of Martin Luther.

Another exception to these generalities is a large Baptist church near Richmond, Virginia. Inside, there are two large stained glass windows, one on each side of the pulpit area in the sanctuary. Each window portrays Jesus in a different setting. While these are exceptions to the rule, they may also be indicators of a future trend in Protestant churches to become more ornate over time.

Anglican and Orthodox options are also excellent choices for a place of Christian worship. They both tend to have more liturgical worship practices like Catholicism. Their organizations are large. They each have religious scholars to accurately interpret scripture.

Because I was raised in a Protestant Fundamentalist church, I learned Fundamentalism firsthand early in life. Throughout my adult life, I attended many Catholic church services and many Protestant church services from a variety of Protestant denominations. I am comfortable worshipping in a plain church with a simple service and a lengthy educational sermon. I am also comfortable worshipping in an ornate church with a high degree of liturgy using symbolic rituals and ceremonial practices. Over the years, as a layman, I learned more about the meaning and intent of many Catholic worship practices. I now understand that each symbolic ritual and ceremonial practice is executed to honor Christ.

Although I only have a layman's understanding, I feel very fortunate to be able to cross the schism between Catholics and Protestants. While remaining Protestant, I learned to speak both languages. I learned to respect both Catholicism and Protestantism as true Christian religions. The core Christian beliefs of Catholics are the same as the core Christian beliefs of Protestants. Only the worship practices differ.

Christians believe Christ died so we can have eternal life. It is through faith that Christians believe in Christ. They also love others as Christ loves them. These are the core Christian beliefs of Catholics. These are the core Christian beliefs of Protestants.

Looking back, the early Christian religion was imperfect. There were many differences of opinion, especially on whether to comply with Jewish laws. Looking at circumstances now, the modern Christian religion is imperfect. There are many differences of opinion on worship practices. However, the core Christian beliefs remain unchanged throughout history and across different types and different denominations of the Christian religion.

CHAPTER 18

Unum versus Requiem

E Pluribus Unum is permanently stamped on every standard coin minted in the United States. It is the Latin phrase for "Out of many, one." Our founding fathers used this phrase to recognize the achievement of thirteen colonies unified as one country, even though they had many differences of opinion. The thirteen colonies held significant disagreements on many issues, such as a priority in the North for industry versus a priority in the South for agriculture, war with England versus peaceful occupation, slavery to support agriculture in the South versus freedom for all, a strong federal government versus strong state governments, and federal tax authority versus state tax authority. Out of these many, strongly held and divergent views came one unified country.

Unification into one country was not easy. It not only required acceptance of other points of view but also respect for those you disagreed with. It required compromise on principles and ethics. It required innovative solutions. It required surrender of control to someone else. It required a trust in people you disagreed with. It required the courage to ask a slave owner from the South to write the Declaration of Independence. It required the courage of that slave owner to voluntarily write that "all men are created equal." It required a lot of soul-searching. However, the result was certainly worth the effort. That one country is now the greatest country in the world. Because of our individual freedoms and sustained economic strength, many world leaders look to the United States to provide moral leadership worldwide.

The Fragmentation of Christianity

While the United States transitioned out of many, to one, Christianity appears to have gone in the opposite direction. Jesus created one Christian religion, with one set of leaders, and directed those leaders to expand the religion worldwide. That one Christian religion grew successfully and remained unified for the first fifteen hundred years, but then it splintered into many organizations, with many different beliefs and different leaders. Today's worldwide Christian religion consists of Catholics, Orthodox, Anglican, Lutheran, Baptist, Presbyterian, Methodist, and many other denominations. Most denominations split again into multiple organizations after internal disagreements grew too great. Some of those splintered denominations went on to fragment even further. More splits are planned. Many independent, or nondenominational, churches started on their own, with no organizational support or guidance. There are now over thirty thousand different Christian denominations and organizations worldwide.

Unfortunately, Christian cults, which include Christian Scientists, the Moonies, Jehovah's Witnesses, the Unification Church, Unitarian Universalism, Unity, the Mormons, and numerous offshoots, continue to grow in number and size. Christian cults distort the true meaning of Christianity and pose a serious threat to the success of the Christian religion over the long term. There are many different types of Christian cults, some of which include Doomsday cults, communal cults, cults that proselytize, authoritarian cults, and polygamist cults. Over the last five hundred years, Christianity fragmented out of one faith into many religious organizations.

Christianity could be more widely accepted in the world, if it had not splintered into so many different and competing versions. Christianity could expand in number worldwide if the fragmented groups would work together, understand each other's point of view, trust each other, and respect each other. Out of the many types and denominations of Christianity around the world, there could be one great, unified religion. I am not suggesting all of Christianity should be in one organization or one church, but only that all Christians have a unified perspective of their religion and support each other. To accomplish that, it would take a lot of work. All Christians worldwide united in their core beliefs, and respectful of each other, is one potential destination of the Christian religion. However, there is also a second potential destination.

Liz and I learned more about this second potential destination when we went to New Orleans and attended an outdoor jazz festival in a city park alongside a bayou. We were in town for an extended weekend to visit a friend. The first band on the main stage played New Orleans jazz. There were six band members, all in black sport coats and wearing black fedora hats. The leader of the band played a trumpet. Their music was lively and entertaining, just the experience we wanted while in New Orleans. The sun was out. The park was crowded. Some people listened from their canoes and kayaks in the bayou.

Near the end of the last set, the bandleader announced they would play a dirge they first played at a funeral for a musician friend who passed away a year earlier. Once they began to play, it took me a little while, but I finally recognized the song as an old Gospel hymn. A dirge is a type of requiem, which is religious music played for the dead. However, a dirge is typically short, played at a much slower speed than normal, and in a New Orleans jazz style. The extremely slow speed is the reason it took me so long to recognize the song.

I asked our friend about the dirge. He explained that during a funeral procession for a jazz musician, it was customary for a jazz band to walk behind the casket while playing a dirge to lament the loss of the musician. Once the dirge ended, the band would immediately play upbeat jazz music to celebrate the life of the musician, while other people danced to the music in a line behind the band. It is a requiem custom unique to New Orleans. But whether sad or happy, a requiem is still a symbol of death.

My friend's explanation of the dirge prompted my thinking about the second potential destination of the Christian religion: for it to die in failure and have its own requiem. The fragmentation of Christianity is increased by the recruitment of believers away from one Christian organization to another, misconceptions by some people about the beliefs of other Christian organizations, a disparagement by some Christians of what other believers hold sacred, and an escalation in mistrust and conflict within denominations. Because there are so many denominations and independent churches, Christian cults can develop and expand unnoticed. It is easy to see Christianity may someday lose control, which leads toward its own requiem.

So there seems to be two possible destinations for Christianity: It can move toward unification with one set of core beliefs and mutual respect for all Christians, or it can become so splintered and out of control that it moves toward its own requiem. Christianity is unlikely to reach either destination. There is natural momentum against complete success, and there is natural momentum against total failure. However, there is an entire spectrum of possibilities between unity on one end and requiem on the other. The Christian religion remains somewhere between the two destinations. But knowledge of the two potential destinations gives us a clearer picture of where Christianity is located on the spectrum and in which direction it currently travels.

An Example of a Religion Traveling toward Requiem

The religion of Islam, over the last couple of decades, is an example of a large religion on a death march toward the requiem end of the spectrum. Although Islam is currently the world's fastest-growing major religion, its growth is due to Muslims having larger families than non-Muslims. The religion of Islam first splintered into many different factions with many different leaders. Then, additional groups formed that were only partially based on Islam but still identified themselves as Islamic.

Sunni Muslims make up the largest number of Muslims worldwide. Shia Muslims make up the second-largest group. Countries consisting of a majority of Sunnis include Syria, Turkey, Afghanistan, Pakistan, Saudi Arabia, Egypt, and Indonesia. Saudi Arabia practices an extremely conservative or fundamentalist version of Sunni Islam called Wahhabism. Shia Muslims dominate the countries of Iran, Iraq, and Lebanon.

Many Islamic countries, with a majority of Muslim citizens, have leaders who serve in dual roles as both religious leaders and government leaders. Islamic control of governments has led to religious intolerance. Sunni Muslim government leaders have little tolerance for Shiite Muslim citizens. Shiite Muslim government leaders have little tolerance for Sunni Muslim citizens. Although Muslims claim Islam is a peaceful religion, Sunni and Shiite Muslims are at war with each other in multiple countries in the Middle East. This results in tyranny and significant bloodshed within the Muslim community.

In addition, there are some Muslim groups who want to kill all Israeli Jews, while many other Muslim groups are quietly supportive of this view. Some Muslims practice Sharia law, which includes honor killings of family members. Islamic cult extremist groups, like Hamas, Hezbollah, al-Qaeda, ISIS, Boko Haram, Taliban, Houthi Rebels, Haqqani Network, Al-shabaab, and Ansar-al-Sharia, advocate violence and murder in order to expand an Islamic revolution. ISIS wants to indiscriminately kill everyone in the Western culture and other Muslims who do not agree with their narrow ideology.

For a religion that is supposed to be peaceful, it is ironic that so many Muslims are involved in murder, suicide, and warfare. With this needless loss of life in the name of Islam, the world does not know what to think of that religion. There are numerous Islamic leaders, many with very different perspectives. There is no central leadership group to offer guidance to the 1.8 billion Muslims worldwide or to explain the true beliefs of the Islamic religion. With such widespread religious fragmentation, there is a lack of leadership and a dangerous loss of control. These are all signs of a religion on a path toward its own requiem.

An Example of a Religion Traveling toward Unity

Roman Catholicism, in isolation from the rest of Christianity over the last five hundred years and after three schisms, is an example of a large religious organization near the unity end of the spectrum. Catholicism contains many groups with diverse views on worship practices. Some of the different Catholic groups that hold a wide variety of beliefs include fundamental; evangelical; charismatic; ethnic; modern; and traditional members. They all coexist harmoniously under one set of leaders. Their core beliefs are the same. Differences in views, styles of worship, and worship practices are accepted by Catholic leadership. Each group may worship separately, but they respect the other groups.

Liz and I once attended a Latin-speaking Catholic church. The conservative congregation at that church uses the Latin language in every service. Only the Bible readings and homily are spoken in English. Women wear a lacey veil on their heads when in the sanctuary. When speaking with local members, I learned the church building is under the regional mainstream bishop, but their Latin-based priests report to a different bishop. That bishop is Latin-based. This organizational structure allows them to retain their conservative worship practices without interference from mainstream Catholicism.

Roman Catholicism is as large as the Orthodox groups and the Protestant denominations combined. Yet there is one centralized leadership group that speaks on behalf of all 1.1 billion Catholics worldwide. This global leadership provides moral guidance and effective control. These are all signs of a large religion nearing unity.

Religious Unity within One Country

Poland is an example of a country that has one unified religion. Before World War II, much of Central Europe was Christian. Approximately 95 percent of the population was Catholic. Like Italy, the country of Poland is still predominantly Catholic. When touring through Poland, our tour guide pointed out the only Protestant church in Warsaw. When questioned, the tour guide did not know the denomination of that lone Protestant church. With only one Protestant church in the area, the locals are mostly unfamiliar with the various types of Protestant denominations that exist elsewhere in the world.

Following the war, countries like Slovakia, the Czech Republic, Hungary, Bulgaria, Romania, East Germany, and Poland were placed under Soviet control. Under the Soviet style of communism, children learned the Russian language in public schools. The Soviets built simple apartment buildings, in and around existing ornate buildings, where much of the urban population lived. The buildings were very basic and made from cinder blocks. There was no paint, no adornment, and no balconies on those buildings. Most people refer to them now as commie condos. Millennials currently buy them as starter homes.

Under Soviet communism, an elite government group of people responsible for centralized planning assigned each adult to a specific job, a set wage, a specific apartment, and a set amount of food rations for their family. Cars were very small, made from recycled garbage, and required a five-year notice to purchase one. Members of the Soviet Secret Service police lived in single-family houses in areas previously owned by the wealthy class.

While on a tour through the capital cities of Central Europe with Liz, I learned firsthand how the Soviet communist regime discriminated against religion. The local guides in each country all told a very similar story. The Secret Service watched those who attended church and reported their names to the government. The churchgoing fathers, along with their immediate families, were then transferred from a larger family apartment in a city, near their extended family, to a smaller family apartment in a rural area, away from their extended family. The father's job was changed from a professional job with higher wages to a mining job with lower wages. Their assigned family food rations were smaller. When their children became old enough to begin high school, they were no longer eligible to attend. For those who wanted to continue some religious practices without discrimination, a priest came to their apartment in the middle of the night to baptize a newborn baby. One of our local guides was baptized that way.

Because this religious discrimination lasted over multiple generations, society in Central Europe lost its religion altogether. According to local tour guides who lived through the Soviet era in Slovakia, the Czech Republic, Bulgaria, Romania, East Germany, and Hungary, the population in their countries mostly discontinued the practice of any religion. Today, less than 15 percent of the population claims to be religious.

However, Poland was different. With guidance from leaders of the Catholic Church in Poland, the country's forty million people believed if they all continued to attend church, the Soviets would not be able to punish them. The Polish people knew the Soviets needed workers to make a communist economy work. They could not punish everyone. So the vast majority of Polish people under Soviet control continued to attend church weekly. Their plan succeeded.

Years later, when Pope John Paul II was elected pope of the Catholic Church, the confidence of the Polish people increased significantly. Pope John Paul II came from a Catholic leadership position in Krakow, Poland. He then used his global influence to visit Poland multiple times and to encourage regime change through patience and nonviolence.

In coordination with the pope, US President Ronald Reagan placed additional pressure on the Soviet economy with the announcement of plans to build a Star Wars missile defense system. The Soviet Union could not afford to maintain control over Central Europe and invest in an arms race with the United States. Within ten years of Pope John Paul II's first visit to Poland, communism fell in Central Europe. To memorialize their success over Soviet communism in a peaceful manner, the new democratic Poland constructed multiple statues of Pope John Paul II and President Ronald Reagan. Today, 97 percent of the Polish population is Catholic, and the vast majority of those attend church regularly. Due to an oversupply of young priests who graduate from Catholic seminaries in Poland, shortages of priests in other countries are filled. Poland remains an example of a country with one unified religion.

Core Beliefs of Christians

Christians believe Jesus died so we can have eternal life. It is through faith that Christians believe in Jesus. They also love others as Christ loves them. These are the core beliefs of all Christians.

Separate from the common core beliefs, there are many other beliefs among Christians about doctrine, sacraments, and worship practices. There are groups of Christians who place different priorities on specific topics, like adherence to rules of behavior to live a holy life, inner peace through strong faith in God, works of love to those in need, participation in Holy Communion, the study of scripture, prayer, worship, baptism, sanctification, efforts to evangelize, and mission work. All of these can be good things. However, they can also become problematic when one group of Christians believes their priorities and worship practices are the only right ones and other Christians are wrong when they do not agree. When Christians lose sight of their core beliefs and focus solely on their own priorities and worship practices, they are in danger of religious fragmentation, which leads to mistrust of other Christians.

What Jesus Wanted

I wonder what Jesus intended when he first began the Christian religion. Did he intend for a worldwide Christian religion to always be unified and respectful toward all believers? Or did he know the Christian religion two thousand years later would split into numerous factions, many with distrust and ongoing divisiveness among themselves? When Jesus gave us the commandment to love one another, maybe Christians simply failed to follow it.

During early Christianity, the original apostles held different doctrinal beliefs among themselves. Some apostles followed more Jewish laws than others. Yet the apostles remained unified on core beliefs and respected each other. A few early Christian churches retained all the laws of Judaism. Other early Christian churches did not retain any Jewish laws. A third group of early Christian churches retained a limited number of Jewish laws. Yet early Christian churches remained unified on core beliefs and respect for one another.

Jesus prayed to his Father for the unity of his disciples. In John 17, we are told Jesus prayed for his disciples to be one, just as Jesus and his Father are one. We cannot know for sure exactly what Jesus meant. Many people interpret this passage to mean Jesus prayed for unity among all Christian churches. Competition between Christian churches harms Christianity and inhibits the rest of the world from being evangelized. Others interpret this Bible passage to mean each individual Christian should be one with the Father, just as Jesus is one with the Father; they claim Jesus did not necessarily pray for unity among all Christian churches.

Regardless of what Jesus really prayed for, today we certainly have significant disunity within Christianity. If we looked at the Christian religion now, through the eyes of someone who is religiously unaffiliated, we would see confusion, discontent, disagreement, fragmentation, and so many choices that our heads would spin. Christianity may not look very appealing to those who do not currently follow any religion. Christianity may not look very appealing to the newest Christian converts, either. It seems ironic that a religion based on love has become so fragmented, with many groups distrustful of each other.

Steps to Unify Christianity

Our religion would grow in number if all believers would strive to make Christianity less fragmented and more tolerant of different viewpoints. Jesus gave us this wonderful gift. We should not squander it. Christianity's long-term vision for the future should be to have a worldwide Christian religion unified on core beliefs and mutually respectful of each other.

This would allow Christianity to grow in number and maintain proper control. I'm not suggesting all Christians should belong to one church or one organization. I'm not even suggesting all Christians should have the same doctrine, sacraments, or worship practices. However, I am suggesting all Christians should understand they have the same core beliefs, despite their differences, and they should learn to respect each other because of those differences. Increased unification would help Christians make better decisions that are all directionally aligned. Based on my experience, the largest gap in trust and harmony seems to be between Fundamentalist Protestants and Catholics.

Further evidence of disunity is also shown in the sheer number of denominations and independent churches. For example, there are eighty Methodist or Methodist-related denominations in the world. There are eighty Presbyterian denominations, thirty of which are in the United States. Lutherans have over 250 denominations worldwide. Baptists have over three hundred different organizations. There are twenty-two thousand independent denominations. After taking five hundred years to reach the current level of disunity, it may take a long time to increase unity in any meaningful way. With such a large undertaking of significant cultural change, a transition that takes one step at a time may provide the best opportunity for success.

There are steps we can take today to better align with the vision of further Christian unity. The first step would be for Christians everywhere to maintain a positive tone toward all other believers, even when there are differences in specific beliefs. Increasing knowledge of each other's beliefs, out of love instead of suspicion, should be actively pursued. Respect for each other as fellow Christians complies with the commandment to love one another. Many mainstream Protestant denominations are already very respectful toward each other. An expansion of that respect and harmony among Catholics, Evangelicals, and Fundamentalists would add immediate benefits.

A respectful tone toward all other Christians would help reduce recruitment from one sect to another, so recruitment can focus more on the one billion people in the world who identify themselves as religiously unaffiliated. We should learn to think of ourselves as Christians first and as Baptists, Catholics, Evangelicals, Lutherans, or any other group last. We should develop the common identity of being Christian, regardless of which denomination we belong to. Maybe we could start with a new standard reference that uses the names Christian Baptists, Christian Catholics, Christian Lutherans, and so on.

A second step we could take today is to limit further splitting of denominations, except in extraordinary circumstances. If we do not agree with our religious leaders, we should be patient and wait for change. As Christians, we must remain in ongoing prayer and fully trust the Holy Spirit to guide and direct the church toward unity so that in time, the church will grow together, not apart. We should not be so quick to jump ship to a new organization. There should be fewer Christian organizations, not more.

One example of many past denominational splits in Protestant history is the Christian & Missionary Alliance, the denomination I was raised in. This group originated as a movement in Canada in the 1880s, under the leadership of a prominent Presbyterian minister from New York City. The group expanded over many decades and became a separate denomination in 1974.

Then, just seven years later, in 1981, the Christian & Missionary Alliance in Canada and the Christian & Missionary Alliance in the United States decided to separate into two denominations, each with their own president and leadership organization. Combined, the two denominations have only six million members. The two denominations have very similar doctrinal beliefs. They continue to cooperate on many initiatives. Yet something is wrong when, out of 2.2 billion Christians in the world, the governing board of six million Christians with similar beliefs decides to split into two separate denominations, each with their own set of leaders. It is inconsistent with loving one another. It does not show Christian unity.

Some intermediate goals to help unify Christianity could include the reunification of some of the past denominational splits. Methodists already experienced success in the reunification of several denominations that were once separate. They began the reunification process with a joint conference open to all Methodist denominations. They should continue to build upon their success.

The Baptist organizations could also work toward a significant decrease in the large number of their existing organizations. The eighty Presbyterian denominations could work toward reunification of their denominations. Orthodox, Anglican, and others could do the same. In order to accomplish this, political viewpoints may need to be clearly identified as separate from decisions on church doctrine. Christian views on political issues are still important, but church doctrine should remain separate and change much more slowly.

Like Catholicism, distinct groups of parishioners, each with similar political views or similar areas of focus, could still worship separately but remain part of the same larger organization. Christian unity could be further enhanced by independent churches and smaller Christian denominations joined with larger Christian organizations that have similar beliefs. While Protestant groups work to increase unity among their organizations, Catholicism should consider how to transition their Communion practices to be more open and welcoming to other Christians.

Christians Need to Speak with One Strong Voice

The Islamic religion is splintered and fragmented so severely, there is not even a small group of Muslim leaders who can speak clearly on behalf of most Muslims. With numerous Muslim groups at war with each other, and at war with Western civilization, it is difficult to make any distinction between destructive terrorist Muslim cults and mainstream Muslim groups. To the non-Muslim world, Islamic terrorist murderers look a lot like warring mainstream Muslims. Their death and destruction seem to be done in the name of Allah. The muddled voices of Islamic leaders attempt to communicate different messages to the world, but none are understood.

As Christianity continues down a path of increased fragmentation, the world becomes more confused about any distinction between Christian cults and mainstream Christian groups. With thirty thousand Christian organizations in the world, there are thirty thousand Christian leaders who can speak on behalf of Christianity (some with a larger microphone than others). The Catholic pope can now speak for about half of the world's Christians. But with a lack of unity among so many Christian organizations in the world, any message would likely be confused with clarifications and disagreements from other Christian leaders. Unification of more Christian groups helps clarify Christian messages to the world.

A small group of leaders who can speak together with one strong voice on behalf of Christianity, against harmful Christian cults, and in support of Christian love for the world, is necessary for the long-term success of the Christian religion.

It may be time for today's Christians to begin to look for similarities among Christian groups, instead of differences. It may be time for today's Christians, with an open mind and an open heart, to better understand their Christian brothers and sisters who have different worship practices and different doctrinal views from theirs. It may be time to address impediments to Christian unity, which may include fear of losing control, political differences, and misconceptions of other Christian groups.

If we are unable to limit the ongoing fragmentation and do nothing else to help unify our religion, Christians should at least increase their love and respect for each other. Based on my personal experiences in Christian Catholic churches and in many types of Christian Protestant churches, we have much more in common with each other than most believers imagine. I hope that an increased exposure to some of these experiences creates harmony and clears up misconceptions among Christian organizations. Each insight that is gained about the beliefs and practices of other Christians serves as one small bridge to Christian unity.

CHAPTER 19

The Worldwide Church

The directive Jesus gave to his disciples in the Great Commission was to expand Christianity worldwide. The disciples were largely successful in meeting this expectation. Christianity is now the largest religion in the world, comprised of 2.2 billion people, almost one-third of the world's population.

An American Perspective versus a Worldwide Perspective

The Roman Catholic Church has the largest reach across the world, compared to any Protestant or Orthodox group. There are 1.1 billion Catholics. They are located on every continent in the world. Having a worldwide reach requires coexisting with a variety of governments, including communism, socialism, dictatorships, and democracies. Having a worldwide reach requires communicating with people who speak many different languages. Having a worldwide reach requires an understanding and acceptance of many different cultures. Having a worldwide reach sometimes requires the support of Christians in different countries who are at war with each other.

Fundamentalist Christians are primarily located in America. Their perspective on many issues is typically viewed through an American lens. When looking at decisions made by a worldwide church through an American lens, misunderstandings often result. A statue of Jesus hanging on a cross communicates the story of Christ dying for our sins in every language used in the world, without words, and is understood in every culture. A nativity scene visually communicates the story of the birth of Jesus in every language. A statue honoring Mary sends the message to people in all cultures that women are to be honored and respected. There are some cultures in the world today where women are still treated with little or no respect.

Mother Teresa was elevated to sainthood because she lived a holy life. That message is understood in all languages and all cultures. Kneeling to pray before taking Communion at every service communicates a message in every language of the importance of Jesus willingly sacrificing his body and blood for us. Standing when the priest reads from the Gospel at each service communicates in every language and in every culture that the four Gospels are the most important books in the Bible. Having the responsibility of a worldwide church causes leaders to view religious practices through a new lens.

At times, church doctrine of mainstream Protestant denominations varies according to changing perspectives in American politics. Current political thinking in the United States moves into mainstream church doctrine through the votes of denominational representatives at annual meetings. Even among some Fundamentalist and Evangelical Christians, political narratives about women's rights occasionally take precedence over the life of an unborn child.

The annual March for Life, a public stand against abortion rights, began after the *Roe v. Wade* Supreme Court decision in 1974, with considerable support from Catholic leaders. Catholics provide strong support for the march every year, even when it is not popular to do so. The Southern Baptist Convention and other Evangelical organizations belatedly increased their support for it in 2016, after public sentiment in the United States shifted in support of the right to life. With the broader perspective of a worldwide church, like Catholicism, the lives of unborn children are always given the higher priority. When others are quiet, the Catholic Church speaks up publicly to support life and to protect those who cannot speak for themselves.

Recent Catholic Popes

The leadership of the Catholic Church did not always properly seize on its worldwide reach. Over the past few centuries, almost all elected popes were from Italy. That changed in 1978, when Pope John Paul II was elected to the papacy. John Paul was of Polish descent. With his election, the Catholic Church could no longer be accused of being a church only for Italy, instead of the world. John Paul was a religious conservative who spoke in multiple languages. Because of his personal experience with communism in Poland, John Paul understood how capitalism could benefit the poor worldwide.

With much energy, Pope John Paul II traveled extensively and communicated with many people in their own language. He changed the Vatican canonization process to allow many more saints to be named, so people everywhere would have examples of someone nearby who tried to live a holy life. Pope John Paul II canonized more saints than all the popes over the previous five hundred years combined, dating back to the Protestant Reformation.

Liz visited a new Holocaust museum in Richmond, Virginia, and was surprised to see an exhibit on Pope John Paul II. From it, she learned that John Paul's best friend was a Jewish man from his hometown in Poland. This friend was also the first person to officially visit John Paul after his election to pope. When they were younger, they both experienced the horrors of the Holocaust. Despite having different religious views, they formed a bond of friendship that lasted their entire lives.

My son was in St. Peter's Square at the Vatican on the day Pope John Paul II died. He saw the square full of thousands of people who came to hold a vigil during John Paul's last hours alive and to show their respect for a great religious leader. John Paul was also respected by many Protestants all over the world, in addition to most Catholics. He came the closest to being a leader for all of Christianity than anyone had in a very long time. He spoke for and represented Christianity at appropriate times during world crises. His leadership is rare and is certainly missed.

The next pope was Benedict XVI, a scholar who came from Germany. His election would continue the message that Catholicism represented the church worldwide. Pope Benedict was the first pope to voluntarily step down from the position in modern times. Previous popes remained in their role until death.

The part of the world with the most Catholics is Latin America. In 2013, Pope Francis was elected as the 266th pope of the Catholic Church. He was born in Argentina and lived there most of his life. With his election, Catholicism claimed its first leader from outside of Europe since the year

741. Pope Francis also brought his personal strengths of humility and concern for the poor. Those strengths are what the church needed most at that point in time. He chose to live less lavishly than other popes, in a smaller apartment in the Vatican.

However, because of his experience in Argentina with socialism, Pope Francis does not like capitalism. He views capitalism as driven by greed and sees little to gain from it. Pope Francis also holds strong political views on the environment, which are his own personal views, not church doctrine. Unfortunately, he often publicly states his personal views about capitalism without being fully aware of the benefits capitalism has brought to the poor of the world. He also publicly communicates his views on the environment without being fully aware of the negative impact on the poor from the high cost of some environmental regulations that are not effective.

Pope Francis is the first pope to come from the Society of Jesus, also known as the Jesuit order in Catholicism. Jesuits take vows of poverty, chastity, and obedience. They also have a reputation for their love of the poor. Historically, Jesuits disagree with Vatican teaching on issues including abortion, birth control, and homosexuality. Differences in views often result in a tense relationship between Jesuits and the Vatican hierarchy. Unfortunately, it appears a lifetime of servanthood to the poor and challenge to church hierarchy in the Jesuit order did not adequately prepare Pope Francis to successfully lead a worldwide organization of one billion people.

Saintly Protestant Leaders

Pat Robertson and Franklin Graham are both Protestant Christians from America who extended their reach worldwide to help the poor. Through Operation Blessing International, Pat Robertson helped invest several billion dollars in over a hundred countries to assist the disadvantaged and disaster victims. Similarly, Franklin Graham leads Samaritan's Purse, which provides relief and assistance to the poor, sick, and suffering in over a hundred countries.

If Protestantism used saints as examples of people who tried to live holy lives by helping others, these two individuals would be prime candidates. They may not necessarily be recognized for their many accomplishments in America, but more for their compassionate works of love for others in the rest of the world. There are many other Protestant leaders also deserving to be held up as examples of Christians who are holy, like Billy Graham, Robert Jeffress, Rick Warren, and James Dobson. They tirelessly communicate Christian principles to millions of people in a manner that common people understand.

Billy Graham actively encouraged unity among all Christians. When his team came to a city to prepare for a crusade, where he preached to a large audience, Billy Graham included a requirement for all Christians in that city to be represented. He wanted Fundamentalists, Catholics, Baptists, Orthodox, Evangelicals, mainstream Protestants, Pentecostals, and groups of all color and ethnicities. In Billy Graham's view, they were all Christians. One Christian group was no less holy than any other. Billy Graham, an Evangelical Southern Baptist, was a friend of Catholics. He was a friend of Pope John Paul II. They met on three different occasions and treated each other as brothers in Christ.

Efforts toward Christian Unity

If Christians really want to fulfill the Great Commission directive of Jesus to expand Christianity worldwide, they need to focus on the similarities between Protestants and Catholics, not the differences. The myths learned in youth need to be unlearned in adulthood. The whole truth should be clearly seen and understood. One group of Christians should not feel more holy than another. They are commanded to love one another. One group of Christians should not feel other groups of Christians engage in sinful practices. They are commanded to love one another.

There are active signs and wonders, gifts of the Holy Spirit, in most Protestant denominations and in Catholicism. Protestants and Catholics should accept each other as Christian brothers and sisters, then work together to accomplish the single goal of expanding Christianity worldwide. There are over one billion people in the world who describe themselves as religiously unaffiliated. Expanding Christianity to those individuals should be the united focus of Christians everywhere.

Just as the thirteen American colonies overcame many strong differences in beliefs to become more united, Christianity has similar challenges.

There are many different perspectives among Christians in doctrine, sacraments, and worship practices. Many Christians believe in adherence to numerous religious laws, while other Christians believe in few or none. Many Christians believe in giving control to a centralized organization, while other Christians believe in keeping local control at the individual church level. Many Christians believe in organized membership in a church, while other Christians believe in no earthly church membership. There are many Christian churches where the wealthy congregate, and others where the poor prefer to worship. Some Christian churches excel in the use of music and musical instruments. Other Christian churches have little or no music. There are ethnic differences, geographical differences, and political differences. There are differences in symbolic rituals and religious ceremonies. There are numerous differences in the details of Biblical interpretation and areas of focus.

Christians are free to express their faith in different ways. But the core beliefs of all Christians everywhere are the same. With God's help, the differences in worship practices can be accepted in a way that all Christians love and respect each other again.

Christians believe Jesus died so we can have eternal life. It is through faith that Christians believe in Jesus. They also love others as Christ loves them. These are the core beliefs of all Christians.

The World Methodist Council is an ecumenical organization that promotes unity among Christian churches. They work to unify eighty Methodist or Methodist-related denominations, representing eighty million Christians worldwide. The organization is headquartered in Lake Junaluska, North Carolina, and has an ecumenical office in Rome, Italy. Every five years, they hold a world conference for all Methodist-related denominations to promote discussion and understanding of Christian unity. They were successful in reuniting several Methodist denominations that were once separate. The World Methodist Council also coordinates bilateral dialogues with other Christian churches. The earliest bilateral dialogue was held with Roman Catholics in 1947. They also hold dialogues with the Orthodox Church. More recently, initial bilateral dialogues were held with Lutheran, Reformed, Anglican, and Baptist churches.

The Global Christian Forum fosters mutual respect and unity among diverse Christian churches who were not in conversations with each other previously. In 2002, initial organizing participants included Catholic, Orthodox, Anglican, Evangelical, Pentecostal, Holiness, and African Instituted churches. When they held their first official Global Christian Forum meeting in 2007, more Protestant denominations attended. Additional participants included Baptist, Church of Christ, Disciples of Christ, Society of Friends, Mennonite, Methodist, Moravian, Seventh Day Adventist, and United and Uniting churches.

There are Christian people and organizations working to help unify the Christian religion from its many splintered groups. Worldwide ecumenical discussions recently started, but they only take place every four or five years. Progress is slow. In the end, success or failure will depend on what Christians in each denomination are willing to accept.

While we wait for further reunification, Christians should learn to love and respect other believers, regardless of differences in doctrine and religious practices. With an open mind and an open heart, they should strive to increase their understanding of other Christian beliefs. While we all have our own perspective of Christianity, it's only when we begin to learn about the perspectives of other Christians that we begin to more fully understand our own beliefs. All Christians can grow stronger in their faith by seeing their religion from new and different perspectives. They should think of themselves as Christians first and work toward common objectives. Through loving one another, Christians can move the Christian religion further away from the requiem end of the spectrum and actively build bridges toward worldwide Christian unity.

previously. In 2002, initial organizing participants included Catholic, Orthodox, Anglican, Evangelical, Pentecostal, Holiness, and African Instituted churches. When they held their first official Global Christian Forum meeting in 2007, more Protestant denominations attended. Additional participants included Baptist, Church of Christ, Disciples of Christ, Society of Friends, Mennonite, Methodist, Moravian, Seventh Day Adventist, and United and Uniting churches.

There are Christian people and organizations working to help unify the Christian religion from its many splintered groups. Worldwide ecumenical discussions recently started, but they only take place every four or five years. Progress is slow. In the end, success or failure will depend on what Christians in each denomination are willing to accept.

While we wait for further reunification, Christians should learn to love and respect other believers, regardless of differences in doctrine and religious practices. With an open mind and an open heart, they should strive to increase their understanding of other Christian beliefs. While we all have our own perspective of Christianity, it's only when we begin to learn about the perspectives of other Christians that we begin to more fully understand our own beliefs. All Christians can grow stronger in their faith by seeing their religion from new and different perspectives. They should think of themselves as Christians first and work toward common objectives. Through loving one another, Christians can move the Christian religion further away from the requiem end of the spectrum and actively build bridges toward worldwide Christian unity.

CHAPTER 20

A Long Crossing

We all experience many crossings in life. Some crossings are longer or more difficult than others. It depends on where and when you begin, where you end, and how you choose to travel across. The benefits of making a crossing often outweigh the risks.

Years ago, while my family and I were on vacation in San Francisco, we walked across the Golden Gate Bridge on a windy day during rush hour. We used a sidewalk along the side of the roadway that was protected from traffic by a steel cage and constructed as part of the bridge. Most sightseers who walk on this bridge stop in the middle of the bridge, then return to their starting point. We chose to walk across the entire length of the bridge, to the other side, and back. Even with a steady stream of speeding cars traveling on the bridge, the views of the San Francisco skyline and San Francisco Bay were stunning. Compared to those who only went halfway across and back, we saw the city and bay from twice as many angles and perspectives. It made the lengthy crossing worthwhile.

I have experienced other rewarding crossings. My son and I crossed large swaths of Virginia on foot while hiking sections of the Appalachian Trail with his Boy Scout troop. Walking all day and sleeping on the hard ground at night took its toll on me, but the mountain views of God's creation were well worth the effort. After previously driving through these mountains and seeing them from the air, the experience of hiking them added a different texture and granularity of understanding and enjoyment.

My daughter and I walked across the Brooklyn Bridge in New York City. While enjoying the beautiful views of New York City, the East River, and the Hudson River, a man on a bicycle accidently ran into me.

It seemed many people there were in a hurry and only used the crossing as transportation to the other side. They had no interest in the views and showed little tolerance for those looking to gain a different benefit from the crossing.

While in Arizona, my family and I crossed the Grand Canyon in a helicopter, flying from south to north. After takeoff, it was a steady climb the entire way because the north rim of the Grand Canyon is one thousand feet higher than the south rim, where we began. Even with headphones over our ears, the ride was very loud. It was also scary to look down at the bottom of the canyon from that height and barely make out the Colorado River. But seeing the broader view of some of God's best handiwork on earth from the air, compared to seeing smaller parts of the canyon when standing on the rim, gave us greater clarity of the vastness of the canyon.

Each of these crossings varied in length and difficulty. They offered both impediments and benefits. In each case, the benefits of making the crossing greatly outweighed any risk. They all added perspective and new understanding.

Crossing the Schism

By far, the longest crossing experience in my life was crossing the schism from Protestantism to Catholicism. Because I grew up in a Fundamentalist Protestant church, my crossing began a long distance away from Catholicism. It took most of my lifetime to successfully cross this schism. Those who begin their crossing in a mainstream Protestant denomination have a shorter crossing than those who begin in a Fundamentalist church. However, many people choose to never make the crossing at all.

By starting in a Fundamentalist Protestant church, there were additional impediments to overcome, which made the crossing longer. Because I was indoctrinated at an early age to believe in many false narratives and myths, I first needed to unravel those myths in order to see the truth. Because I was unfamiliar with the histories of Christianity, the Bible, and Protestantism, I also needed to gain a better perspective of my religion by first understanding its history.

Over several decades, extensive exposure to many Protestant denominations clarified my understanding of differences in worship practices and doctrinal interpretations. It also clarified my understanding of the core principles of Christianity, which are common to all believers. Finally, attending countless Catholic services for many years gave me the opportunity to learn and appreciate the extensive rituals, symbolism, organizational hierarchy, and terminology used in Catholicism.

For me, crossing the schism was a four-step process. However, some of the steps did overlap. The first step was to unlearn false narratives and myths I learned in my youth. The second step was to learn the histories of Christianity, the Bible, and Protestantism. The third step was to gain exposure to worship practices and doctrinal beliefs in many types of Christian churches. The fourth step was to learn about Catholic rituals, symbolism, doctrine, and terminology.

Step 1: Unlearn False Narratives

My greatest difficulty in crossing the schism between Protestants and Catholics was in the first step. To gain the capability of being open to other Christian viewpoints, I needed to first overcome mental roadblocks that were planted in my mind beginning at an early age. Once I became indoctrinated to myths and false narratives in my youth, it was very difficult to reset my own thought process as an adult to unlearn those false narratives and know the truth. Mental barriers are often more difficult to overcome than physical barriers.

Some of the false narratives were easier for me to overcome than others. Easier ones include drinking alcohol is a sin; smoking cigarettes is a sin; you must tithe 10 percent of your income to the church; Catholic beliefs are wrong; and you must live differently than others in the world. Reading the Bible on my own and meeting other Christian people who did not believe in those false narratives allowed me to reason through these independently, to uncover the truth.

Other false narratives were more difficult for me to overcome. They include you must love the Lord with all your heart, mind, and soul; everything you need is in the Bible; every word in the Bible is true; and we interpret the Bible literally. I was taught at a young age that not believing even one of these myths meant I would go to hell when I die.

This message was communicated differently and less directly. Still, I understood the intent. It was stated more like, I must believe these things in order to be saved. To be saved meant I would go to heaven when I died. Not believing one of these false narratives meant I was not saved and would not go to heaven.

Denying one of these myths also meant I would never see my family again after I died. They would be in heaven for eternity, and I would not. At times, Fundamentalist Christians used fear in place of the faith and love taught by Jesus. The use of fear-driven false narratives is the same tactic used by cults. They can have a powerful control over your mind.

Because of the grave consequences, it is much harder to break away from these types of myths. Far-right religious groups, like the Islamic sects who practice Sharia law, also use this form of indoctrination. They can immediately excommunicate someone from their family for breaking a law that brings embarrassment to the family. Their punishment does not necessarily wait for the afterlife.

Step 2: Learn the Histories of Christianity, the Bible, and Protestantism

For me, learning about the histories of Christianity, the Bible, and Protestantism helped greatly in unlearning the more problematic false narratives. Reading history books about Christianity clarified the origins of the Catholic religion, which went back to the time of Jesus. It also made clear many of the practices, rituals, and symbolism in Catholicism began in the early church with the original apostles.

Learning about the history of the Bible clarified the potential for misunderstanding what I read in the Bible due to translation issues and cultural differences from long ago. I also learned controversial books were included in the Bible, even though religious scholars at that time disagreed with some of the writings in those books. This increased my confidence to no longer believe every word in the Bible is true. It is still a very holy book, which I treasure dearly. However, the absolutism with which I was raised concerning every word was replaced with a desire to place the Bible in a greater context, for a more accurate understanding.

Learning about the history of Protestantism explained the reason for many of the differences in worship practices today between Catholics and Protestants. The more simplistic type of Christian worship began fifteen hundred years after the time of Christ, during the Protestant Reformation. The hundred-year period of the Catholic Church being led by immoral government leaders and subsequent wars between Catholics and Protestants also explained the lingering lack of trust between the two groups.

All combined, the histories of Christianity, the Bible, and Protestantism gave me a much better framework on which to more fully understand my religion. Only then could I see similarities in the false narratives that were easy to overcome and the false narratives that were more difficult to overcome. Over time, I successfully replaced the fear of disbelieving the more difficult false narratives with an understanding of the truth based on faith. This was only possible after independently gaining more knowledge about the histories of my religion.

Step 3: Learn about Other Christian Worship Practices

With the false narrative hurdle mostly gone, I began working on additional steps to make the schism crossing. I met other strong Christians from a variety of churches, including many from Catholic churches. I found it reassuring that people of strong faith, with a belief in miracles, came from all types of Christian denominations. I began to distinguish between core beliefs of Christians and differences in doctrinal views and worship practices.

To gain a broader perspective, I continued to read nonfundamentalist books about Christianity. I also read a seventeen-volume Bible commentary on the New Testament written by a professor who taught at a Presbyterian seminary in Scotland. I actually read the entire Bible commentary twice and referred back to it often. Over many years, I regularly worshipped at churches, including Christian & Missionary Alliance, Church of God, United Church of Christ, Disciples of Christ, Catholic, Baptist, Methodist, and Presbyterian. At some point, it became very clear to me that all Christians shared the same core beliefs.

Step 4: Learn about Catholic Liturgy

Although I believed Catholics shared the same core beliefs as Protestants, I still had lingering doubts about some of their worship practices. In particular, I needed to learn more about praying to Mary, the naming of saints, and the use of relics. Although these worship practices did not seem biblical to me at first, I kept an open mind as I learned more about them.

Like most Protestants, the first time I attended a Catholic worship service, I was unable to follow or understand the Mass. Without some prior training, there was no possible way for me to know when to pray or sing along with the congregation. I assumed few people would notice whether I participated responsively or not.

However, I was also unable to cross myself at the same time the rest of the congregation crossed themselves. It seemed like everyone knew when to make the sign of the cross except me. They all finished making the sign of the cross before I knew what happened. I think a few people seated around me may have noticed my lack of participation, but not the majority.

To avoid any real embarrassment, I focused my attention on when to sit, stand, or kneel at the proper times by following others. Standing when others were sitting, or sitting when others were kneeling, attracts a lot of attention. That was the last thing I wanted. So I watched others carefully and did my best to react seamlessly.

When it came time for Communion, I remained in my pew when everyone else walked to the front of the sanctuary. I knew I was not permitted to take Communion since I was not Catholic. While I continued kneeling, I soon figured out I blocked others in my pew from exiting the pew to receive Communion. I quickly sat back up on the pew and lifted my kneeler out of the way as they crawled around me. Then I felt embarrassed because I was sitting and everyone else was kneeling. So I knelt again. In a few minutes, the people from my pew returned, and I realized I was blocking their path one more time.

I tried my best to follow the multipage order-of-service bulletin. Because some parts were in the wrong order, I needed to flip pages back and forth. Also, some parts of the service seemed to be missing from the bulletin. As a result, I often could not find in the bulletin where we were currently in the service. While some occasions when people knelt were noted in the bulletin, many other occasions when people knelt or stood were not noted. At first, I felt the order-of-service bulletin was designed specifically to confuse Protestants like me.

Over time, I attended many Catholic services with my Catholic wife.

As I attended more worship services, I began to better understand the flow of the service. I discovered the congregation would cross themselves at the same points in the service consistently every week. Responsive prayers and responsive singing were also consistently done at the same points in the Mass. I learned the cantor would often sing a chorus alone, then raise their arm as a signal to the congregation to sing the chorus along with the cantor. During Communion, I realized it was a fairly common practice for those not participating to remain seated in their pew until others in their row returned from taking Communion. With these seemingly simple understandings in place, I could then begin to focus more on the meaning of some of their worship practices.

After listening carefully, I learned the practice of honoring Mary was based in the Bible's book of Luke. It was not worship of another god, as I learned in my youth. I heard stories about wonderful Christians who lived their entire adult lives to help the poor and were honored as Catholic saints after they died. I also discovered that relics were used by early church leaders and are based in the Bible's books of Acts and Luke. My early concerns about some Catholic worship practices possibly conflicting with core Christian beliefs were answered. There were no conflicts.

Liz explained details about different aspects of the Mass and holy days. I read several books on Catholic theology, miracles, saints, and organizational rules. I learned much, but not all, of the Catholic terminology from a layman's perspective. We visited the Vatican and other holy Catholic sites in various places throughout the world. Through these experiences, I gained enough knowledge about the Catholic faith, rituals, symbolism, and terminology to feel comfortable in any Catholic setting.

The Same Core Christian Beliefs

After completing all four steps in my long crossing of the schism between Protestants and Catholics, I easily reached the conclusion that Catholics and Protestants share the same core Christian beliefs. They believe Christ died so we can have eternal life. It is through faith that Christians believe in Jesus. They also love others as Christ loves them. These core beliefs are what define us as Christians. The use of different worship practices, rituals, symbols, and terminology to worship the same Christ does not matter.

Whether someone is Orthodox, Anglican, Catholic, or Protestant is of little consequence. What does matter is they are all Christian. Jesus told us to love others as he loves us. This directive applies to all Christians. Fundamentalist Protestants are directed to love and respect Catholics. Catholics are directed to love and respect Fundamentalists. Believing that a narrow ideology is the only correct Christian ideology fails to show love to other Christians.

My crossing of the schism between Protestants and Catholics is complete. I remain Protestant. However, I have tremendous respect and appreciation for the Catholic Church.

CHAPTER 21

A Short Crossing

Contrary to my lengthy experience of crossing the schism between Protestants and Catholics, Liz experienced a much simpler crossing. One major difference is that she crossed the schism in the opposite direction. She grew up as a Catholic and learned about Protestants as an adult.

Raised Catholic

Liz attended Catholic school for twelve years, from first grade through twelfth grade. During the first eight years of school, she attended religion class every day and went to Mass each week. From ninth through twelfth grade, she attended religion class three times per week, due to block scheduling, and attended Mass once each month. She also attended Mass outside of school, with her family, each week. They attended additional services together on high, holy days.

With all this training and exposure to Catholicism, Liz learned about Catholic rituals, symbolism, and terminology at an early age. It all seems normal to her. She also understood at an early age that Catholics worship God alone, not saints, nor Mary.

Protestantism is purposely very simple. It has very little in rituals, symbolism, or complex terminology. So when Liz began attending Protestant churches with me, there was very little for her to learn. This helped make her crossing of the schism between Catholicism and Protestantism much easier and much shorter than my experience.

Liz was raised in mainstream Catholicism, not Fundamentalist

Catholicism. Mainstream Catholics focus on their own beliefs and typically never even mention Protestantism. Unlike my early views of Catholicism, she had no preconceived notions about Protestantism. There were no false narratives planted in her mind at an early age that needed to be unlearned. This greatly shortened her crossing of the schism.

Liz grew up in the original Christian church, the one founded by Jesus and his disciples. It is also the largest Christian religion, with 1.1 billion members. For two thousand years, the Catholic Church retained many of the same traditions, rituals, symbolism, and terminology used in the early church. In stark contrast to her church, Fundamentalist Protestant churches had simple buildings, a simple cross, a simple altar, no stained glass windows, no statues of Jesus or Mary or the disciples, no paintings, no rituals, no symbolism, and little religious terminology. Protestantism was only five hundred years old and had none of the traditions of the early church of Jesus.

Of the four steps I needed for my crossing, she was able to skip steps 1 and 4: unlearning false narratives and learning Catholic liturgy. She only needed steps 2 and 3. The second step is to learn the histories of Christianity, the Bible, and Protestantism. The third step is to gain exposure to worship practices and doctrinal beliefs in many types of Christian churches.

Protestantism through Catholic Eyes

Liz's lifelong experience in the Catholic Church was very different from a Protestant experience. In the beginning steps of her crossing, she made some early observations. Her initial views about Fundamentalist Protestants would surprise most Christians.

At first, Liz thought Fundamentalist Protestants seemed to worship the Bible as much as they worshiped Jesus. Fundamentalists said everything you need to know is in the Bible. Every word in the Bible is true. The Holy Spirit will guide each person to interpret the Bible correctly. Many Fundamentalists carried their Bible with them and studied it often. Liz has great respect for the Holy Bible and holds it in the highest regard. She also has great respect for other Christian writings and other Christian traditions. Treating the Bible with such extreme reverence by Fundamentalist Protestants and with such a large investment of time, at the exclusion of all other Christian writings and traditions, at first appeared to look a lot like worshiping the Bible.

Liz also had the initial impression that Fundamentalist Protestants placed Paul on a pedestal equal to Jesus. Many of the sermons were based on required rules of behavior from Paul's letters to the early Christian churches. Fundamentalists applied those many rules governing personal behavior to their current everyday lives. It seemed they lived their lives according to Paul's laws, not necessarily according to the message of Christ.

Unlike Catholic cathedrals and basilicas, many Protestant churches have unadorned sanctuaries. The lack of Christian adornment fails to encourage reverence upon entering a church. Catholics enter their sanctuary, touch the holy water, then quietly enter a pew to pray on their knees. Protestant congregations greeted each other loudly and engaged in nonreligious, personal conversations. They seemed much less reverent than Catholic congregations. From Liz's early perspective, they appeared to be at a social gathering instead of preparing for a religious worship service.

Liz was accustomed to a seven-minute sermon in a Catholic church. The twenty-minute Protestant sermons seemed to be extremely long. She initially thought many of the Protestant sermons required ideas to be repeated multiple times in order to fill the twenty minutes. Unlike Catholics, Protestants appeared to treat the sermon as the highlight of the church service.

The main reason Liz attended a Catholic church each week was to participate in Communion. Holy Communion was the highlight of every Catholic service. In most Fundamentalist Protestant churches, Communion is rarely served. When it is served, the elements are not consecrated to become the body and blood of Christ. Without a real Communion of consecrated elements at every service, Liz initially did not feel Protestant churches were very Christian. Being unable to participate in a real Communion, she saw little reason to attend a Protestant church.

Because there are over thirty thousand different Protestant denominations and organizations worldwide, all with different doctrinal beliefs, she also thought Protestants believe whatever they want to believe. With so many differing interpretations of the Bible, there appeared to be little or no guidance from biblical scholars. Without proper guidance from knowledgeable religious scholars, many Protestant beliefs directly conflict with other Protestant beliefs. There often appears to be no basis from which to provide proper rationale in determining what to believe.

Catholics Need to be Saved

When Liz initially interacted with Fundamentalist Protestants, she was treated as though she needed to be saved from Catholicism. They thought she needed to be re-baptized. She stood silently accused of worshiping idols, worshiping Mary, not understanding the Bible, and failing to be Christian. This would be her greatest challenge in crossing the schism to accept Protestantism as Christian.

In response, Liz began to study. She read religious books. She attended Catholic Bible study classes. She attended Protestant Bible study classes. She participated in Catholic women's prayer groups. She participated in Protestant women's prayer groups. She went to Catholic religion training classes. She learned more about Catholic symbolism and the meanings behind it. She learned how Catholics interpret the Bible. She learned how Protestants interpret the Bible. She watched Pat Robertson's *700 Club* on television. She attended both Catholic and Protestant churches each week. She went to different types of Protestant churches with me and learned differences in Protestant worship practices. She researched the histories of Christianity, the Bible, and Protestantism. She became informed on how Protestant doctrinal views and worship practices developed and changed over time. She learned of miracles that occurred in the Catholic Church. She discovered miracles that occurred in Protestant churches.

The Crossing is Complete

Eventually, Liz learned Fundamentalist Protestants did not really worship the Bible or place Paul on a pedestal equal to Jesus. She also realized how many Fundamentalists were devoted to living holy lives. She gained enough knowledge to defend and explain Catholic perspectives to Fundamentalist Protestants using non-Catholic terminology in order to be understood.

Liz knew many Catholics who were strong in their faith. By attending different Protestant churches, she also met many Protestants who were strong in their faith. Most importantly, she learned that Catholics and

Protestants share the same core Christian beliefs. The use of different worship practices, rituals, symbols, and terminology to worship the same Christ does not matter.

Liz's crossing of the schism between Catholics and Protestants is complete. We met halfway across and walked both directions together. She remains Catholic. Yet she respects the faith of Protestants.

CHAPTER 22

My Antenna Went Up

I was walking alone through Manhattan one night. Suddenly, I noticed fewer people around. The area was not as well lighted as the last few blocks. Some of the buildings were vacant and in disrepair. My antenna went up. I became much more aware of my surroundings. I felt unsafe. As two people walked toward me from the opposite direction of my travel, I became nervous. I walked to the other side of the street well before our paths crossed in order to maintain some distance between us. I looked in front, behind, to the left, and to the right for the closest area with more people and more lighting. I turned left, walked one block, and was back in a lighted area with more people. I felt safe again. My antenna went back down. I could enjoy the rest of my stroll through New York without nervousness and without an increased focus on my surroundings.

My Church Antenna

I was raised in a very conservative Christian church, where I was taught to believe in some false narratives and other myths about the Christian religion. This experience spurred me to study Christianity on my own and experience different denominations of the Christian religion. I read about the beginnings of the Bible and learned religious scholars disagreed over which books to include in it. I learned about the history of the religion and visited significant Christian sites around the world. I learned about different worship practices among the various Christian denominations and Catholicism. After gaining a broader perspective of Christ and the Christian religion, my belief in those old false narratives is now gone.

However, when I attend a church service today, my antenna goes up. I listen carefully to each sermon or homily for common mistakes made by preachers and priests. Just as I took precautions when walking in an unsafe neighborhood in Manhattan, I continue to take precautions while attending Christian church services. I do not want to add any new false narrative into my belief system. I learned that repeated reinforcement of any false narrative can lead to that falsity being accepted by a normal human mind. So I am cautious about what sermons I hear and which preachers or priests present them.

Filtering the Sermon

As part of my protective antenna system, I also use filters to help gauge the general accuracy of a sermon. It helps me feel more in control of Christian ideas that enter my mind. I am also less likely to be led astray by inaccurate preaching.

The first filter I use when listening to a sermon or homily is whether the preacher or priest is speaking about a reference from the Old Testament or the New Testament. The Old Testament is the Jewish Bible, and the New Testament is the Christian Bible. Christians use the Old Testament for historical reference, to learn about prophesies of the future Messiah, and for reading religious poetry. My antenna goes up when a preacher uses an Old Testament reference and applies it to how Christians should live their lives today.

Jewish rabbis correctly use Old Testament references to make an application to daily living for their Jewish congregations. Christian preachers should use New Testament references when they intend to make practical applications to how Christians should live their lives. Jesus started the new Christian religion after the Old Testament was already written. Christ's changes about how Christians should live are documented in the New Testament.

The second filter I use on sermons concerns quotes of Jesus from the four Gospels. I place quotes from Jesus into two categories: One is Judaism; the other is Christianity. You should not mix quotes between the two categories. Jesus often answered verbal questions from Jewish scribes and Pharisees about the laws of Judaism. He also spoke to his disciples and the public about the new Christian religion. Keeping the proper context among the various quotes of Jesus is very important. My antenna goes up when a preacher uses quotes by Jesus. Using a quote by Jesus about Jewish law and applying it to Christian life today is a common mistake.

One of the most oft-repeated quotes of Jesus I hear is the one about loving God with all your heart, mind, and soul. My antenna goes way up when a preacher applies this quote to Christian life today. Jesus used this response when answering a question by Jewish leaders about the laws of Judaism. The context of this quote was not about Christianity. Jesus was not speaking to Christians or about Christians at the time of this quote.

Another useful filter is whether biblical quotes come from the apostle James or the apostle Paul. James and Paul held opposing views on whether Jewish laws applied to Christians. Paul believed the imposition of any law on Christians meant Jesus died needlessly. James, on the other hand, believed Christians need to comply with many Judaic laws. James also continued to attend services in the Jewish temple in addition to meeting separately with the Christian church.

When I hear preachers speak about the views of James, I discount those views as either suspect or incorrect. Martin Luther, an educated biblical scholar, called the book of James a "book of straw." He felt James disagreed with Paul, Peter, the other apostles, and the rest of the New Testament.

The final filter I find beneficial is with any mention of Paul's letters to early Christian churches. These include letters to the Corinthians, Galatians, Ephesians, Philippians, Colossians, and Thessalonians. Paul's letter to the Romans was different because he had not met the Roman church leaders yet and wrote about his Christian views in more general terms. Paul wrote letters to the other early church leaders to offer guidance on how to handle some immediate and specific problems they faced in their new Christian church. Paul did not intend for his advice on specific problems at that time to be interpreted as laws for all future Christians to follow. If a preacher misinterprets Paul's guidance in these letters as laws for required Christian compliance today, I consider the sermon to be inaccurate.

Other Antenna Topics

My antenna goes up when I hear "every word in the Bible is true." I learned a long time ago that using absolute words like *every* or *never* is usually proven inaccurate. Religious scholars disagreed over which books and letters to include in the Bible. They compromised by including some books they believed to contain errors. There are also translation errors in the English versions of the Bible. In addition, the apostles James and Paul disagreed about whether any laws or rules apply to Christians. The two opposing views cannot both be correct.

My antenna also goes up when I hear Christians have an obligation to tithe 10 percent of their income to the church. That is a Jewish law from the Old Testament. Jesus instructed Christians to help the poor and support Christian preachers. The poor can be helped either outside of the local church directly or through the local church.

I have concerns when I receive significant pressure from a local church to become more involved in church committee work. To me, a church should operate more like a religious institution and less like a business or a government. I also have concerns when I hear the goal of a local church is to grow their congregation or their denomination. My view is that Christians should focus more on growing the Christian religion worldwide, regardless of denomination.

My antenna goes up when I hear a preacher denigrate Catholicism or some other Christian denomination. It is usually done out of ignorance and an unwillingness to learn about other worship practices. It also fails to meet Christ's primary directive to love others.

I become very uncomfortable when I hear political positions represented as Christian positions from the pulpit. When one political party is supported by the church significantly more than another political party, it is time for me to change churches. A church should be more like a religious institution and less of a political machine.

When a preacher focuses too much on introspection and self-improvement, my antenna goes up. The primary purpose of attending church is to worship and praise God. We are also reminded to love and help others. Jesus instituted a change from the Jewish religion of following many laws to the Christian religion, which is based on faith and love. He died to pay the price for our failure to comply with so many laws. Too much focus on self-improvement after inventing many new laws and obligations is a reversion back to Judaism and is inconsistent with Christianity.

My Antenna Goes Down

When the theme of a sermon is one of worship, praise, or inspiration, my antenna goes down. I relax. If the topic celebrates Christianity and God's love for us, my antenna stays down. If a sermon is purely educational, with no treadmill expectations, my antenna is down. I listen and learn. When the message is one of reverence for God, joy and appreciation, or miracles, my antenna goes down. I enjoy the service.

Who Is at Fault?

A friend of mine from New York City visited my home for a weekend. Upon his arrival, I noticed two black eyes and several cuts on his face. He explained how he was mugged by two guys when walking alone at night in Manhattan. His money and wallet were stolen. He claimed it was his fault. He drank too much alcohol. He failed to pay attention when he entered a block with less lighting and few people around. When two people walked toward him, he did not cross the street or run in another direction.

The real fault of the mugging lies with the muggers, not with my friend. The muggers behaved badly. They broke the law. From this experience, my friend learned he should take additional precautions in order to avoid this situation. His antenna should go up when he enters an unsafe area while walking alone at night.

Similarly, Christians who believe false narratives are not at fault. The individual or group who initiated the false narrative is at fault. Many false narratives began five hundred years ago, during the Protestant Reformation. Some began in the late 1800s, after the American Civil War. Other false narratives are relatively recent.

In any case, Christians should take precautions. One precaution is to read about the histories of Christianity, Protestantism, Catholicism, and the Bible from sources other than your own church or denomination. If you only read Christian literature written by other Christians who believe the same false narratives, you will not discover truth.

Another precaution is to learn about other Christian worship practices with an open mind. Learning more about the many Christian miracles throughout the world is a great starting point. It may be best to begin with those miracles that attract millions of visiting Christians each year. After securing your personal religious beliefs over decades, you may feel some risk in stepping out to search other viewpoints. Only faith can help overcome any discomfort you may have when learning how other types of Christians practice their religious beliefs.

I once believed many false narratives. Beginning with a leap of faith, I exercised many precautions, learned much about Christianity, and worked my way through the false narratives to see truth. Now, after gaining new insights into my personal Christian beliefs, my antenna goes up quickly in order to keep from adopting any new false narratives.

CHAPTER 23

From Tiny Seeds

I heard a Presbyterian minister say it's a Christian's job to plant mustard seeds. It's God's job to help them grow. He used this explanation in reference to mission work for Christians. If Christians simply share their core beliefs with non-Christians, God would help make those ideas and the personal faith of those non-Christians grow.

The minister used the parable of the mustard seed from the Gospels as his Bible reference. Jesus said the kingdom of God is like a mustard seed, which is the smallest of all seeds. Yet when planted, it grows to become a large plant with strong branches where birds can perch in the shade.

I believe many of the ideas presented in this book can serve as the planting of small mustard seeds within the Christian community. There is a need for Christians today to better understand and accept other Christians. There is a need for Christians today to show love to Christians everywhere, despite their differences in worship practices and doctrinal views.

Overcoming the Language Barrier

The language barrier between Catholics and Protestants remains a significant impediment to Christian unity. Catholics grow up in a high-liturgical environment and absorb the extensive religious terminology, symbolism, and rituals. Because it becomes a normal way of life as they reach adulthood, they do not realize how much information they gained or how little of the religious language Protestants know concerning liturgy and Christian rituals.

Protestants purposely keep their church and services very simple.

They use little to no religious terminology, symbolism, or rituals. Many Protestants are generally unaware of this whole world of Christian liturgy within Catholicism and the religious terms associated with it.

When most Catholics and Protestants first attempt to discuss different worship practices, they typically use different terminology and cannot understand each other. It takes time, patience, and repetition in order to communicate effectively. Yet it all begins with having an open heart and being willing to learn.

Protestants can benefit by reading literature from Catholic sources. Catholics can also benefit by reading literature from Protestant sources. Reading literature from sources other than your own denomination or group helps avoid tunnel vision. There are some excellent Catholic books about Mother Theresa and other saints. In addition, reading more about the histories of Christianity, the Bible, and Protestantism can benefit both Catholics and Protestants. Reconciling your faith with historical facts adds much needed perspective and a greater understanding.

Most importantly, Catholics and Protestants should understand they share the same core Christian beliefs. Many Catholic and Protestant churches use the same creed (or a very similar one) to identify and communicate their core beliefs. Commonly used creeds include versions of the Apostles' Creed and the Nicene Creed. Some versions of these creeds refer to the universal church and the communion of saints. This means that past and present Christians throughout history share the same core beliefs. All Christians throughout time are united with Christ in one Christian religion.

The Christian religion is practiced in both high-liturgical environments and low-liturgical environments. Examples of high-liturgical Christians include mainstream Catholic, Orthodox, and Anglican churches. Examples of low-liturgical Christians include Fundamentalist, Baptist, mainstream Protestants, and some Catholic monasteries. If you practice Christianity in a low-liturgical environment, learning about the symbolism and rituals of high-liturgical Christians serves as a multiplier of Christian knowledge. If you practice Christianity in a high-liturgical environment, learning about the simplicity and power of personal faith of low-liturgical Christians will also expand your Christian knowledge.

The goal is not to convert anyone to a different type of Christianity. The goal is for Christians to gain a better understanding of their own Christian beliefs and to become aware of any false narratives they may believe. By learning about the history of Christianity, the Bible, and other Christian worship practices, all believers can increase their understanding of their own view of Christianity with a richness they cannot imagine today.

An Example of the Richness of Understanding

Liz met a Baptist minister who came to speak at a weekly Catholic adult education class she attends. The minister was asked if he ever benefited from a Catholic relationship. After thinking about the question for a moment, he said that while at Yale working on his PhD, a Catholic professor recommended he attend a weekend retreat at a nearby monastery. The Baptist minister saw little benefit in visiting a monastery. He felt preaching was the most important skill for pastors to hone, not separation from the world. Preaching was also the area in which he exceled.

However, he attended the retreat anyway. At the monastery retreat, the monks taught and practiced silence. After the first day, the Baptist minister realized his external Christianity was strong, but his internal Christianity was too hollow. It needed strengthening. He continued to practice silence until his internal Christianity recovered. The Baptist minister was grateful to the Catholic professor for teaching him there is much more substance to being a pastor than preaching.

All Christians have their own view of Christianity. It's only when they add the views of other Christians that they more fully understand their own views. If they only read Christian literature written by Christians who have similar beliefs and similar worship practices, they will not fully understand their own beliefs. Learning more about the perspectives and worship practices of other Christians adds texture and dimension to their own understanding.

Jesus used miracles in his ministry to start and expand the new Christian religion. After Jesus ascended into heaven, the Holy Spirit came to continue the use of miracles. Jesus told his apostles to look for signs of the Holy Spirit as evidence a church is working well.

Do you believe in miracles? Do you believe in Protestant miracles? Do you believe in Catholic miracles? Do you believe God is powerful enough to perform miracles for both Catholics and Protestants? Do you believe

God can perform any miracle humans can imagine, including those with apparitions and a dancing sun? Do you believe God can perform miracles humans cannot even imagine?

Because of my experiences with different worship practices in churches from many different Protestant denominations and Catholicism, I believe. After reading different Protestant and Catholic literature over many years, I believe. After learning about the histories of Christianity, Protestantism, and the Bible, I believe. Because of my visits to personally see and experience holy sites around the world, I believe. It all started from tiny seeds.

Epilogue

I am not attempting to persuade anyone to change from one Christian church to another. There are good churches in every type of Christianity I experienced. However, I do hope all Christians find the church that best meets their own spiritual needs.

With a new understanding about false narratives and myths, I hope Fundamentalist Christians can begin a journey to unravel any myths they may still hold. Reading Christian books from outside of the Evangelical circle provides a new perspective that helps to clarify individual Christian beliefs. Occasional attendance at Catholic services and mainstream Protestant services also provides a new perspective that helps to clarify individual Christian beliefs. I especially hope Fundamentalist Christians learn to accept and appreciate the Catholic religion as a true Christian faith. This leads to Christian unity.

I trust this book helps Catholics better understand their Fundamentalist Christian friends. Although some Fundamentalist beliefs and questions about the Catholic Church are misguided, there may be confusion created by myths learned in their youth. I also hope Catholics can accept Fundamentalist Christian denominations as a true Christian faith. They proved themselves with miracles of the Holy Spirit. By occasionally attending a Fundamentalist Protestant church service, Catholics can gain a new perspective by learning firsthand how devoutly many Fundamentalists live.

My desire for all Christians is that they come closer together in an ecumenical way, once all the false narratives and myths are unlearned. The differences among most Christians are insignificant in God's eyes. Acceptance and respect for other Christians lead to unity.

My prayer for everyone, whether they are Christian or not, is that they be more aware of false narratives in all areas of life, including religion, politics, education, and government. I hope they take actions to first understand different and opposing views, then verify relevant facts, in order to uncover the whole truth before developing a strong belief on any issue. This would make the world a much better place.

Those Feeling Disenfranchised

Most importantly, I have a special concern for those people who were Fundamentalist Christians at one time, then left the Christian religion altogether. I know of some who were so frustrated and depressed when they failed to live up to all the sacrifice and legalism expectations, they left the church and lost all faith in God. I hope these former Fundamentalist Christians give Christianity another chance, by visiting a more mainstream Christian Protestant church or a Catholic church. They should try a variety of these types of churches until they find one where they feel comfortable. If they perceive that a preacher or congregation has a narrow ideology, they should leave quickly. Once they find a church that seems right, they should feel free to attend services without any pressure to join as a member. They can just enjoy the religious experiences without any personal obligations.

I know of other Fundamentalist Christians who were so angry and embarrassed when they discovered their own beliefs in myths were false, they stopped believing everything they learned in church and turned away from God. I hope they now understand that a belief in false narratives is very common in the world. It is no cause for shame. Their parents and church leaders were also unwittingly taught to believe in false narratives. No one tried to fool anyone else on purpose. I hope these former Fundamentalist Christians also give Christianity another chance.

Understanding Other Christian Perspectives

By better understanding the perspectives of those in other Christian denominations and in the Catholic Church, I more fully understand my own Christian beliefs. I hope every Christian takes the opportunity to learn more about the perspectives of other Christians, so they can also grow and develop in their faith. I remain thankful for being raised in a Christian home. Even though Fundamentalist Christians may believe in some myths, they typically are devout and willing to sacrifice for others. I feel blessed to have gained a strong foundation in a Fundamentalist Christian home, and to have escaped from the myths I learned in my youth.

Now that our children are grown, Liz and I try to attend both a Catholic Mass and a Presbyterian church service together on most Sundays. We noticed that except for religious holidays like Ascension Day and Feast of the Immaculate Conception, the Sunday morning Bible readings in Catholic and Protestant churches are usually the same. We often hear two sermons on the same subject, but with different approaches. At Easter and Christmas, when our children visit, we attend a Catholic Mass together as a family.

Liz is a long-standing member of the local Catholic church, where she also carries out the duties of being a Eucharistic minister by helping to serve Communion. Our children are members of the Presbyterian church. At this time, I do not feel the need to officially join any particular church organization. While I was raised in a Fundamentalist Christian church, married in a Catholic church, baptized as an adult in a Baptist church, currently attend both Presbyterian and Catholic churches, and plan to have my ashes stored in a Catholic prayer garden after I die, I view myself as mostly Presbyterian and completely Christian.

I appreciate the Presbyterian focus on financially and physically helping those in need. I like the Presbyterian view of having specific Christian beliefs, along with a tolerance of other Christian beliefs. However, I am uncomfortable with the Presbyterian USA organizational hierarchy forcing political views into seminaries and pulpits. I am careful about which particular church to attend.

I enjoy the Catholic traditions of preparing for and celebrating holy days, emphasizing Communion, verified miracles, and their ties to the early Christian church. I also feel closer to God when I worship in ornate cathedrals with stained glass windows, candles, religious statues and religious paintings. However, I am uncomfortable with the church history of corruption and child abuse, the hierarchy of the Catholic Church living lives of privilege, and the unwelcoming nature of restricting Communion from other Christians.

The local Catholic and Presbyterian churches, where Liz and I attend, combined both choirs to perform Mozart's *Requiem Mass* together. In addition to an organ, there were violins, violas, bassoons, trumpets, and trombones played by musicians from both churches. The joint choir sang in Latin, but the words were provided in English on the program handout. The sanctuary was full, with church members from both churches. The Presbyterian minister and Catholic priest each had a minor role in the service.

One year later, the two churches combined their choirs again to sing great hymns of the past. They were accompanied by a small orchestra of musicians from both churches. A trained soprano soloist sang two of the songs. Both performances were wonderful, ecumenical, Christian events. They each serve as a bridge to Christian unity. Building more bridges between Catholic Christians and Protestant Christians across the world would be very beneficial for the Christian religion.

The Love of God

Parents typically love their children so much, they would do almost anything to ensure their happiness. In order to protect the lives of their children, parents would gladly sacrifice their time, money, career, and even their own lives. If a child failed in something, parents would be there to help. If a child married and later divorced or became an alcoholic, parents would be there for support. If a child murdered someone, parents would forgive and provide support.

God is our heavenly Father. He loves each of us much more than we love our own children. If we fail, he forgives and provides support. After the apostle Paul wreaked havoc on the early church with support for Christian imprisonment and the murder of Stephen, God forgave and provided support. God is there for us, with a continuous offer of forgiveness and support, no matter what we do. His love is boundless.

Entrance into Heaven

I read a book by Mary C. Neal, called *To Heaven and Back*, which told a true story of how the author drowned in a kayak accident, went to heaven, and was asked by Jesus if she believed in him, before learning it wasn't her time to remain in heaven yet. After reading that book and other stories like it, I do not believe we can say there is any specific individual on earth who will miss going to heaven: not fallen Christians, Jews, Muslims, Buddhists, atheists, agnostics, or murderers. I believe the love of Christ is so great that when we see him in heaven, in all of his power and glory, we will each have one last chance to believe in him. Only those with hardened hearts who deny him in that moment may perish.

Billy Graham held a similar view. In a 1997 interview with his friend, Robert Schuller, Billy Graham said, "I think that everybody that loves or knows Christ, whether they are conscious of it or not, they are members of the Body of Christ.… [God] is calling people out of the world for his name, whether they come from the Muslim world, or the Buddhist world or the non-believing world, they are members of the Body of Christ because they have been called by God. They may not know the name of Jesus but they know in their hearts that they need something they do not have, and they turn to the only light they have, and I think that they are saved and they are going to be with us in heaven."

Just as we learned in Luke's story of the thief on the second cross, a criminal simply asked to be remembered in Christ's kingdom. That criminal was unfamiliar with Christianity. Yet his faith was rewarded with entry into heaven that very day.

I also believe while Christians live their lives here on earth, there is no need to feel guilty about breaking any human-made religious rule. There is no need to sacrifice so much that we have unbearable burdens. As Christians, we understand Jesus paid the price for our shortcomings by dying on the cross. We just need to believe in Christ through faith and love others as Christ loves us.

It's that simple. It's the Good News.

Catholic Terms and Phrases

-A-

Ad limina – a meeting between a country's bishops and the pope. It is usually held once every five years.

Alb – a white robe worn by a priest at Mass.

Apologetics – clear, rational rebuttals to various attacks on the Catholic faith. Its writings include explanations of Catholic doctrines.

Apostolic succession – the handing of authority over to successor popes, beginning two thousand years ago with Peter.

Apparition – the appearance of a person who previously died. A vision that fully resembles the real person can occur with or without verbal interaction. Apparitions are real and objective interventions of divine power whose purpose is to recall and emphasize some aspect of the existing Christian message, not to create new Christian messages.

Archbishop – church leader over a geographic region consisting of multiple dioceses and multiple bishops.

Archdiocese – a geographic region under the authority of an archbishop. It typically includes multiple dioceses and multiple bishops.

-B-

Basilica – a large church designated by a pope as important. It typically has multiple aisles and large ceilings. It is not the main church in a diocese, where a bishop is located.

Beatification – the third of four steps in the process of being named a saint.

Bishop – church leader over a geographic region consisting of multiple priests and multiple parishes.

Bishop's staff – a wooden pole with a curved top, used by Catholic bishops. It is a sign of being a Good Shepherd, one who leads his faithful flock and protects them. A bishop's staff is also known as a crosier, paterissa, or pastoral staff.

Blessed Sacrament – another name for the Communion host or bread wafer.

-C-

Canon – a priest who is selected to run a cathedral.

Canon law – the system of rules and principles made and enforced by the church's hierarchical authorities to regulate its external organization and to direct the activities of Catholics toward the mission of the church.

Canonization – the fourth and final step in the process of becoming a saint.

Cardinal – an archbishop selected by a pope to also serve as an advisor to the pope.

Catechism – a book for teaching the principles of the Catholic religion. The term *catechism* is also used for the training classes of Catholic youth on the principles of Catholicism.

Cathedral – a large church located where a bishop is appointed to serve. It is the mother church of a diocese. There is typically no more than one cathedral in a diocese. Other large churches in a diocese with a cathedral may be named basilicas.

Chalice – the large cup used for Communion wine; multiple parishioners drink from a common cup.

Chrism – holy oil used in baptism and confirmation. Chrism consists of olive oil and a perfume, usually balsam. Chrism and two other holy oils are kept in a container called a chrismaria, usually near the baptismal font.

Ciborium – a chalice-like vessel used to hold Communion hosts. A ciborium is often made of metal and has a separate lid.

Cincture – a type of belt used by a Catholic priest with a white robe. Catholic monks often use a rope as a cincture with their robe.

Conclave – a meeting of cardinals to elect a new pope. Cardinals age eighty and older are unable to vote.

Convent – an enclosed religious house where nuns live and dedicate themselves to prayer.

Crucifix – a cross with the figure of the crucified Jesus Christ on it.

Curia – the administrative unit in the Vatican that assists the pope in governing the Catholic Church. It is more commonly known as the Roman Curia.

Cursillo – a group focused on increasing the spirituality and effectiveness of Catholic leaders. Candidates complete a three-day instructional retreat and attend ongoing group meetings.

-D-

Deacon – an ordained minister who normally has no desire to become a priest. Deacons wear vestments and can perform baptisms, officiate at weddings, and preach during Mass. Deacons must complete training in scripture, theology, and Canon law. It can take up to four years to become a deacon.

Didache – a book written in the first century by the original apostles of Jesus to document early Christian church teachings and church organization. This book was not included in the Bible. *Didache* is also a type of preaching that utilizes instructional teaching, typically with detailed interpretations of the Bible.

Diocese – a geographic region under the authority of a bishop. It typically includes multiple parishes and multiple priests.

-E-

Encyclical – a pastoral letter written by the pope to explain a teaching issue.

Eucharist – a term that is synonymous with Holy Communion or the Lord's Supper.

Eucharistic minister – a layperson who assists in dispersing the elements, bread and wine, of Holy Communion to the congregation.

-F-

Font – a small fountain of holy water usually located near the back of every Catholic church sanctuary. Most Catholics dip their fingers in the font on the way into the church and again on the way out of the church. After touching the holy water, Catholics then make the sign of the cross on themselves.

-G-

Genuflect – a half-bow by bending a knee. Catholics genuflect before entering a church pew and just before walking near the front of the sanctuary.

Great Amen – the part of every Catholic service where parishioners sing a short song repeating the word "Amen." It is based in the book of Revelation, where Jesus referred to himself as "the Amen."

-H-

Hail Holy Queen – a short Catholic prayer to Mary, the Mother of Jesus, using standard wording. There are several different standard prayers to Mary.

Hail Mary – a short Catholic prayer to Mary, the Mother of Jesus, using standard wording. It is based on Bible verses from Luke chapter 1. It is one of several different standard prayers to Mary. The prayer is: "Hail Mary, full of grace. The Lord is with thee. Blessed art thou among women, and blessed is the fruit of thy womb, Jesus. Holy Mary, Mother of God, pray for us sinners, now, and at the hour of our death. Amen."

Holy days of obligation – days during the year, in addition to Sunday, when Catholics should attend Mass. There are ten holy days of obligation celebrating the following: Nativity of Jesus; the Epiphany; the Ascension; the Body and Blood of Christ; Holy Mary the Mother of God; Mary's Immaculate Conception; Mary's Assumption; Saint Joseph; Saint Peter and Saint Paul the apostles; and All Saints. A conference of bishops can suppress some holy days of obligation or move them to Sunday. Because of that, some countries celebrate fewer than ten holy days of obligation.

Holy Orders – a special sacrament that creates the hierarchy of deacon, priest, and bishop. The men who are ordained by a bishop with Holy Orders serve the spiritual needs of others in the Catholic Church.

Holy water – water that was blessed by a Catholic priest. It is usually located in a small font in the rear of the sanctuary. On special holy days, the priest may walk through the congregation and spray parishioners with holy water to bless them. Holy water is a Catholic symbol of purification.

Homily – a short sermon usually focused on Christian principles as applied to everyday life. The homilia type of preaching is less educational and more practical in nature.

Host – a thin round wafer used as bread during Communion. Once a host is consecrated by a Catholic priest during the Communion process, it becomes the actual body of Christ. It is also known as the Blessed Sacrament.

-I-

Incorruptible – a dead body that does not decay. There are Catholic saints who died long ago, but their bodies show no sign of decomposition and no odor. Some are in Rome, Italy. Others are in places throughout the world. Some are displayed in glass-covered coffins. Others are interred under church altars, buried underground, or placed in church basement crypts.

Indulgences – the making of amends as a consequence of sin. Sins may be forgiven, but making amends or making restitution for those sins may still be needed. Indulgences can include paying for damage, doing good works, making a confession, praying, or reading the Bible. When sins are confessed to a Catholic priest, the priest may forgive those sins on behalf of God and then recommend specific indulgences to make amends for the sins.

-K-

Kerugma – a short sermon that announces something or makes a plain statement of fact. This type of preaching is used to announce that Jesus died on the cross to save us from sin.

Kyrie eleison – Greek words for "Lord, have mercy." These words are either said or sung by the congregation during a Catholic Mass. They can also be used responsively and intermittently with "Christ, have mercy."

-L-

Lectionary – a book or listing that contains the specific scripture readings and responsorial psalms read at Holy Mass for each day of the liturgical year.

Lent – a time to prepare for Easter through prayer, reflection, self-examination, repentance, and self-denial. The Lenten season begins on Ash Wednesday and ends on Easter Saturday. It lasts forty days, excluding Sundays.

-M-

Madonna – a representation of Mary, either alone or with her child, Jesus. It is most often a statue or a painting.

Magnificat – the Blessed Virgin Mary's hymn of praise to the Lord. It is taken from the book of Luke. Mary proclaims the Lord's greatness with humility and grace. It is also known as the Canticle of Mary.

Mass – a Catholic church service. The highlight of every Mass is Holy Communion, not the sermon.

Memorare – a short Catholic prayer to Mary, the Mother of Jesus, using standard wording. There are several different standard prayers to Mary.

Missal – a book containing the order of services and prayers of the Mass.

Mitre – a hat worn by a Catholic bishop. A bishop's hat is triangular and is used as a sign of victory in Christ Jesus.

Monastery – a residence and church where a group of monks live, separate from the world.

Monstrance – an ornate holder of a Communion host or bread wafer, after the host was consecrated by a priest to become the actual body of Christ. A typical monstrance is about two feet in height and made of brass, gold, or silver. Some are in the shape of a cross or sunburst. They are typically located in a side chapel where Catholics can pray in the presence of the body of Christ.

Mystery of faith – a reference made in every Catholic Mass to the Eucharist or Holy Communion. The mystery is how Jesus Christ becomes present, body and blood, in the consecrated host. It is considered God's greatest gift to humankind because Christ becomes intimately united to us by becoming the bread of life.

-N-

Novena – a lengthy Catholic prayer that occurs over nine consecutive days to meet a critical need. During a Novena, devotees make petitions through worship of Jesus and a request for intercession from a saint. They may express love and honor by kneeling, burning candles, or placing flowers in the church.

-O-

Ordinary time – all those parts of the Catholic Church's liturgical year that are not included in the major seasons of Advent, Christmas, Lent, and Easter. Ordinary time, which means ordered or numbered time, is celebrated in two segments of the year. The first segment begins on the Monday following the Lord's Baptism and ends on Ash Wednesday. The second segment runs from Pentecost Monday to the First Sunday of Advent. There are either thirty-three or thirty-four Sundays of ordinary time in each calendar year.

-P-

Paraklesis – an exhortation type of preaching. This type of sermon is used to inspire and encourage.

Parish – a small church under the authority of a priest.

Patron saint – a Catholic saint who is considered special to a town or Catholic church. Throughout much of Italy, each small town has a patron saint. The town keeps a statue of the patron saint in their church. They hold an annual celebration to honor the saint and to celebrate their religion.

Postulate – a governing board in the Vatican who investigates and approves each saint.

Presence – the actual body of Christ in a Communion host or bread wafer after a Catholic priest consecrates the host. The actual presence of Christ's body is contained in a consecrated host. The actual presence of Christ's blood is contained in the consecrated wine. Catholics eat the consecrated host and drink the consecrated wine in accordance with Christ's command. Catholics believe they receive the full Christ by either just eating a consecrated host or by only drinking a sip of the consecrated wine. Only one Communion element is needed to receive the full presence of Christ.

Pyx – a small round container that holds a Communion host or wafer after the host was consecrated by a priest to become the actual body of Christ. Volunteer Eucharistic ministers from the congregation use a pyx to carry a host to homebound parishioners so they can celebrate Communion.

-R-

Relic – items associated with Jesus, the apostles, or saints. They can be pieces of the True Cross of Jesus or the Holy Crown of Thorns. First-class relics come from a saint's body, such as a sliver of bone or a wisp of hair. Second-class relics come from something belonging to a saint, such as piece of their clothing. Many miracles occur in answer to prayer when a relic is present. The relic has no power in and of itself. The Catholic Church considers relics to be strong reminders of their faith.

Reliquary – a small ornate holder of a relic. Each official Catholic relic is verified by the Vatican with written documentation, and the reliquary is secured with a wax seal.

Requiem – music that is normally played to respect those who have died. The term is also used to refer to a Catholic Mass to remember those who have died.

Rosary – praying the rosary is a lengthy Catholic prayer using standard prayers based on the Bible. The rosary begins with the Apostle's Creed, followed by the Lord's Prayer. The standard Catholic prayers of Hail Mary and Glory Be are recited multiple times. The Lord's Prayer is repeated and followed by multiple Hail Mary and Glory Be prayers. This sequence is repeated five more times. Other standard Catholic prayers are included throughout the rosary prayer. When praying the rosary, the Lord's Prayer is repeated six different times. It may take fifteen to twenty minutes to pray the rosary properly.

Rosary beads – a necklace-type rosary is usually held in your hand when praying the rosary. Because of the number of repetitions of prayers, the rosary beads help keep count to insure a complete rosary prayer is made. It consists of fifty-nine beads, a Crucifix, and a medal. You begin by making the sign of the cross. Next, hold the cross on the necklace-type rosary and say the Apostle's Creed. Move your fingers to the first bead on the rosary and pray the Lord's Prayer. You move from bead to bead along the rosary when praying each prayer or set of prayers. Conclude use of the rosary beads by making the sign of the cross.

-S-

Sacrament – important moments in a Christian life. Catholics celebrate seven sacraments: Baptism, Confirmation or Chrismation, Eucharist or

First Communion, Penance and Reconciliation, Anointing of the Sick, Holy Orders or Ordination, and Matrimony.

Sacristy – a room for keeping vestments, church furnishings, sacred vessels, and parish records. It is usually located adjacent to the sanctuary. In some countries, it is known as the vestry.

Sign of the cross – touching your forehead to represent the Father, touching the center of your chest to represent the Son, then touching your left and right shoulder to represent the Holy Spirit. A priest may also make the sign of the cross outward to the congregation or to an individual.

Stations of the cross – fourteen markers on the wall of every Catholic church sanctuary that represent the fourteen locations where Jesus stopped on his walk to the Crucifixion.

Stigmata – a condition where the wounds of Christ appear on someone's hands, feet, and side. Padre Pio and other priests lived with this condition and open wounds for years.

-T-

Tabernacle – a small ornate box where unused consecrated hosts are stored until the next Communion service.

Theca – a small ornate holder of a relic under glass. Each official Catholic relic is verified by the Vatican with written documentation, and the reliquary is secured with a wax seal.

Tribunal – a Catholic court used to judge cases that refer to religious matters. They are usually organized at the diocesan or regional level. They also determine marriage annulments.

Tridentine Mass – the Latin Mass used until 1969.

Triduum – a religious celebration of the three days of Easter. It begins on the evening of Holy Thursday and ends on the evening of Easter Sunday. Catholic liturgical services that take place during the Easter Triduum include Mass of the Lord's Supper, Good Friday of the Lord's Passion, and Mass of the Resurrection of the Lord.

-V-

Veneration – a respectful and prayerful viewing of relics of the Catholic Church.

Vestments – clothing and liturgical garments worn by Catholic priests and bishops.

Vigil – the eve of a religious holiday or celebration observed by special prayer services and devotional exercises.

Common Catholic Prayers

The Lord's Prayer

Our Father who art in Heaven, hallowed be Thy name.
Thy kingdom come.
Thy will be done on earth, as it is in heaven.
Give us this day our daily bread, and forgive us our trespasses,
as we forgive those who trespass against us, and lead us
not into temptation, but deliver us from evil. Amen.

Hail Mary

Hail Mary, full of grace; the Lord is with thee.
Blessed art thou amongst women, and blessed
is the fruit of thy womb, Jesus.
Holy Mary, Mother of God, pray for us sinners,
now, and at the hour of our death. Amen.

Glory Be

Glory be to the Father, and to the Son, and to the Holy Spirit, as it was
in the beginning, is now, and ever shall be, world without end. Amen.

The Apostles' Creed

I believe in God, the Father Almighty, creator of heaven and earth,
and in Jesus Christ, His only Son, our Lord, who was conceived

by the Holy Spirit, born of the Virgin Mary, suffered under
Pontius Pilate, was crucified, died, and was buried. He descended
into hell; on the third day He rose again from the dead.
He ascended into Heaven, and is seated at the right
hand of the God, the Father Almighty. From thence
He shall come to judge the living and the dead.
I believe in the Holy Spirit, the holy catholic
church, the communion of saints, the forgiveness of sins, the
resurrection of the body, and life everlasting. Amen.

St. Augustine's Night Prayer

Watch, O Lord, with those who wake, or watch, or weep tonight,
and give Your angels and saints charge over those who sleep.
Tend Your sick ones, O Loving Lord.
Rest Your weary ones.
Bless Your Dying ones.
Soothe Your suffering ones.
Pity Your Afflicted ones.
Shield Your joyous ones.
And all for Your love's sake. Amen.

Grace before Meals

Bless us, O Lord, and these Your gifts, which we are about to
receive from Thy bounty, through Christ our Lord. Amen.

Grace after Meals

We give you thanks, Almighty God, for these and for all Your
blessings; You who live and reign, forever and ever. Amen.

Come, Holy Spirit

Come, Holy Spirit, fill the hearts of Your faithful,
and kindle in them the fire of your love.

Send forth Your Spirit, and they shall be created;
and You will renew the face of the earth.
O God, You taught the hearts of Your faithful by the light
of the Holy Spirit, grant that by the gift of that same Spirit,
we may be truly wise and always rejoice in His consolation.
We ask this through Christ our Lord. Amen.

An Act of Contrition

O my God, I am heartily sorry for having offended You.
And I detest all my sins because they have offended You, my
God, who are all good and deserving of all my love.
I firmly resolve, with the help of Your grace, to sin no
more, and to avoid the near occasions of sin. Amen.

Anima Christi

Soul of Christ, sanctify me.
Body of Christ, save me.
Blood of Christ, inebriate me.
Water from the side of Christ, wash me.
Passion of Christ, strengthen me.
O good Jesus, hear me.
Within Your wounds, shelter me.
Never permit me to be separated from You.
From the evil one, protect me.
In the hour of my death, call me, and bid me come to You.
That with Your saints I may praise You, forever and ever. Amen.
—St. Ignatius of Loyola

Divine Mercy Prayer

Eternal Father, I offer You the Body and Blood, Soul and
Divinity of Your dearly beloved Son, Our Lord Jesus Christ,
in atonement for our sins and those of the whole world.

For the sake of His sorrowful passion, have
mercy on us and on the whole world.

Prayer before Bed

Lord, grant me a safe and restful sleep, that I might
awaken refreshed and eager to serve You. Amen.

Prayer to Mary, Help of the Helpless

Holy Mary, help the helpless, strengthen the fearful, comfort
the sorrowful, pray for the people, plead for the clergy, intercede
for all women and men consecrated to God; may all who honor
you experience the powerful help of your assistance.
Amen.

Padre Pio's Prayer to Jesus

O my Jesus, give me Your strength when my weak nature
rebels against the distress and suffering of this life of exile, and
enable me to accept everything with serenity and peace.
With my whole strength I cling to Your merits, Your
sufferings, Your expiation, and Your tears, so that I may be
able to cooperate with You in the work of salvation.
Give me strength to fly from sin, the only cause of Your
agony, Your sweat of blood and Your death.
Destroy in me all that displeases You and fill my heart with
the fire of Your holy love and all Your sufferings.
Clasp me tenderly, firmly, close to You that I may
never leave You alone in Your cruel Passion.
I ask only for a place of rest in Your heart.
My desire is to share in Your agony and be beside You in the Garden.
May my soul be inebriated by Your love and nourished
with the bread of Your sorrow. Amen.

Padre Pio's Prayer for Trust and Confidence

O Lord, we ask for a boundless confidence and trust in Your Divine
Mercy, and the courage to accept the crosses and sufferings which
bring immense goodness to our souls and that of Your Church.
Help us to love You with a pure and contrite heart, and to
humble ourselves beneath Your Cross, as we climb the mountain
of holiness, carrying our cross that leads to heavenly glory.
May we receive You with great faith and love in Holy Communion,
and allow You to act in us, as You desire, for Your greater glory.
O Jesus, most adorable heart and eternal fountain
of Divine Love, may our prayer find favor before the
Divine Majesty of Your Heavenly Father. Amen.

Padre Pio's Prayer to Accept God's Will

Lord, God of my heart, You alone know and see all my troubles.
You alone are aware that all my distress springs from my fear
of losing You, of offending You, from my fear of not loving
You as much as I should love and desire to love You.
If You, to whom everything is present and who alone can see
the future, know that it is for Your greater glory and for my
salvation that I should remain in this state, then let it be so.
I don't want to escape from it.
Give me strength to fight and to obtain the
prize due to strong souls. Amen.

Saint Pio's Blessing

May Jesus comfort you in all your afflictions.
May He sustain you in dangers, watch over you always with His
grace, and show you the safe path that leads to eternal salvation.
And may He render you always dearer to His Divine
Heart and always more worthy of Paradise. Amen.

Blessing of St. Francis

May the Lord bless you and keep you.
May He show His face to you and be merciful to you.
May He turn His countenance to you and give you peace.
May the Lord bless you.

Peace Prayer of St. Francis of Assisi

Lord, make me an instrument of Your peace.
Where there is hatred, let me sow love.
Where there is injury, pardon; where there is doubt,
faith; where there is despair, hope; where there is
darkness, light; and where there is sadness, joy.
O Divine Master, grant that I may not so much seek to be consoled
as to console; to be understood as to understand; to be loved as to
love. For it is in giving that we receive; it is in pardoning that we are
pardoned; and it is in dying that we are born to eternal life. Amen.

Prayer of St. Ignatius of Loyola

Take, O Lord, and receive my entire liberty, my
memory, my understanding, and my whole will.
All that I am and all that I possess, You have given me.
I surrender it all to You to be disposed of according to Your will.
Give me only Your love and Your grace.
With these I will be rich enough and will desire nothing more.

Prayer for My Family

Loving God, I offer thanks for the gift of my family.
Help us to work together for peace and harmony in our relationships.
Grant us the grace to accept each other's faults and weaknesses.
Protect us from harsh words and hurt feelings.
Assist us to encourage one another's strengths and abilities.
Lead us to mutual understanding and support.

May we always forgive each other's failings and
rejoice in one another's successes.
Watch over my family, Dear Lord. Bless us
with good health and happiness.
Fill our hearts with love, patience, and kindness
for one another, now and always. Amen.

Prayer for Our Children

Loving God, I prayerfully entrust our children
and teenagers to Your special care.
Bless them with Your love and goodness. Grant them
continued growth in wisdom, knowledge and virtue.
Protect them day and night, at home, in school, at play.
Inspire them each day to do their best. Strengthen them
during times of discouragement and disappointment.
Make them ever mindful of the needs of others, kind and
caring toward the elderly and all those less fortunate.
May our children walk in the paths of holiness, as Your instruments
of joy, love, and peace in our family and in our world. Amen.

Prayer in Time of Personal Illness

O Loving Jesus, You responded to the needs of the sick with
a generous and compassionate heart. Be with me when I am
ill, and stay by my side when I am faced with infirmity.
Help me to experience Your great healing
power in my mind, body, and soul.
If I am burdened with suffering, lead me to unite myself
to Your Cross, so that my pain and sorrow can bring
spiritual benefit to me as well as to others.
May bearing the cross of illness here on earth help me to be
better prepared for the eternal joy of perfect happiness and
fullness of life with God forever in heaven. Amen.

Thanksgiving for All God's Gifts

O God, whose mercies are without number, and whose goodness is an inexhaustible treasure, I give You thanks for the gifts You have given me, evermore beseeching Your goodness, that while You hear the prayers of all those who ask, You also prepare them for the blessings yet to come. Amen.

Prayer for a Journey

Almighty and merciful God, You have commissioned
Your angels to guide and protect us.
Command them to be our careful companions, from our setting out until our return; to clothe us with their invisible protection; to keep us from all danger of collision, of fire, of explosion, of falls and bruises; and finally, having preserved us from all evil, and especially from sin, to guide us to our heavenly home. Through Jesus Christ our Lord. Amen.

Suggested Reading

1. Girzone, Joseph. 1987. *Joshua: A Parable for Today*. New York: Simon & Schuster.
2. Neal, Mary. 2012. *To Heaven and Back*. Colorado Springs: WaterBrook Press.
3. O'Reilly, Bill and Martin Dugard. 2013. *Killing Jesus*. New York: Henry Holt and Company.
4. Vardey, Lucinda. 1995. *Mother Teresa: A Simple Path*. New York: Ballantine Books.
5. Barclay, William. 1975. *The Daily Study Bible Series*. Philadelphia: Westminster Press.

Notes

Chapter 1

1. (Chimayo) *Heritage Magazine.* Heritage Hotels & Resorts, Inc. Winter/Spring 2018, pp. 32–36. Background information on El Santuario de Chimayo in Chimayo, New Mexico. Bernardo Abeyta, a farmer in 1810, uncovered the crucifix and moved the crucifix three times to a neighboring village.
2. (Black Madonna) CatholicNewsAgency.com/resources/blackmadonna. Catholic News Agency. Luke painted the Black Madonna. It appears dark due to centuries of smoke from candles for light. It is stored in the Jasna Gora Monastery in Czestchowa, Poland. In 1430, Hussite robbers tried to steal the painting.

Chapter 2

1. (Loretto) Heritage Magazine. Heritage Hotels & Resorts, Inc. Winter/Spring 2018, pp. 15–17. In 1853, the Sisters of Loretto opened the Academy of Our Lady of Loretto for girls. The Loretto Chapel was completed in 1878 in Santa Fe, New Mexico. Some claim Joseph built the double-helix thirty-three-step staircase.
2. (Lourdes) Funk & Wagnalls New Encyclopedia, Vol. 16. Funk & Wagnalls Corp. 1993, p. 239. The first church in Lourdes, France was built in 1876. A three-story basilica was added in 1889, which holds four thousand people. An underground basilica was added in 1958, holding twenty thousand people, with access to the spring's healing powers.

3. (praying the rosary) USCCB.org/how-to-pray-the-rosary. United States Catholic Conference of Bishops, "How to Pray the Rosary." Praying the rosary is a lengthy Catholic prayer using standard prayers based on the Bible. The rosary begins with the Apostle's Creed, followed by the Lord's Prayer. The standard Catholic prayers of Hail Mary and Glory Be are recited multiple times. The Lord's Prayer is repeated and followed by multiple Hail Mary and Glory Be prayers. This sequence is repeated five more times. Other standard Catholic prayers are included throughout the rosary prayer. It may take fifteen to twenty minutes to pray the rosary properly. A necklace-type rosary is usually held in your hand when praying the rosary. It consists of fifty-nine beads, a Crucifix, and a medal. You begin by making the sign of the cross. Next, hold the cross on the necklace-type rosary and say the Apostle's Creed. Move your fingers to the first bead on the rosary and pray the Lord's Prayer. You move from bead to bead along the rosary when praying each prayer or set of prayers. Conclude the rosary by making the sign of the cross. Because of the number of repetitions of prayers, the rosary beads help keep count to insure a complete rosary prayer is made.
4. (Hail Mary) *My Saint Pio Prayer Book*. The Padre Pio Foundation of America. 2018, p. 7.
5. (Glory Be) *My Saint Pio Prayer Book*. The Padre Pio Foundation of America. 2018, p. 7.
6. (Lourdes) CatholicNewsAgency.com/resources/ourladyoflourdes. Catholic News Agency. Multiple apparitions of Mary were seen in Lourdes, France. In 1858, Bernadette Soubirous saw eighteen apparitions of Mary. At age twenty-two, she became a nun in the Sisters of Charity.
7. (Fatima) CatholicNewsAgency.com/resources/ourladyoffatima. Catholic News Agency. Multiple apparitions of Mary were seen in Fatima, Portugal. In 1917, Lucia dos Santos, Francisco Marto, and Jacinta Marto saw apparitions of Mary. They were told three secrets, including the future shooting of Pope Paul II. Lucia became a Carmelite nun and lived to age ninety-seven.
8. (Guadalupe) Catholic.org/saints. Catholic Online. 2018. An apparition of Our Lady of Guadalupe occurred in 1531 to Juan Diego. Within six years, six million Aztecs converted to Catholicism. The Basilica of Our

Lady of Guadalupe on Tepeyac Hill houses the tilma and painting of Mary.

9. (Guadalupe) CatholicNewsAgency.com/resources/ourladyofguadalupe. Catholic News Agency. Juan Diego, a humble peasant, saw an apparition of Mary in 1531 near Mexico City. Mary placed her image on Juan Diego's tilma. The tilma and painting are undeteriorated 470 years later.

10. (Padre Pio) *A Child's Story of Padre Pio*. Paul Mandina. Capuchin Monastery. 1975. Francesco Forgione was born on May 25, 1887, in Pietrelcina, in southern Italy. His father worked in America to pay for his schooling.

11. (Padre Pio) padrepiodevotions.org. "A Short Biography." 2017. Padre Pio lived in San Giovanni Rotondo. He studied seven years to be a priest. He died on September 23, 1968. Eight million pilgrims visit San Giovanni Rotondo each year for miracle healings and to be close to God.

12. (Padre Pio) *My Saint Pio Prayer Book*. The Padre Pio Foundation of America. 2018, pp. 5–6. Padre Pio developed visible stigmata. La Casa Sollievo della Sofferenza (the Home for the Relief of Suffering) is a hospital that was dedicated in 1956 in San Giovanni Rotondo. Padre Pio was canonized a saint by Pope John Paul II on June 16, 2002.

13. (La Vang) divineministries.info. 2017. *Our Lady of La Vang: Vietnam, 1798*. John Carpenter. An apparition of Mary occurred in La Vang, Vietnam. In 1798, Catholics saw apparitions of Mary. A hundred thousand Catholics in Vietnam were killed for religious persecution. A church was built on the apparition site in 1901. A larger church was built in 1928.

14. (Jesus speaks of works of the Holy Spirit) Bible. New American Standard. A. J. Holman Company. 1973. John 14:11–21. Whoever believes in Jesus will do works greater than he accomplished, with the help of the Holy Spirit.

15. (miracles as evidence of the Holy Spirit) Bible. New American Standard. A. J. Holman Company. 1973. Mark 16:9–20. A resurrected Jesus said to the apostles, "Go into all the world and preach the gospel to all creation. He who has believed and has been baptized shall be saved; but he who has disbelieved shall be condemned. And these signs will

accompany those who have believed … they will lay hands on the sick, and they will recover."
16. (miracles as evidence of the Holy Spirit) Bible. New American Standard. A. J. Holman Company. 1973. Acts 15:6–12. Peter stood up and said Gentiles should also hear the Gospel and believe. God will give them the Holy Spirit. The whole assembly was silent and listened to Barnabas and Paul as they told the story of all the signs and wonders God had done amongst the heathen through them.
17. (Noah and the Ark) Bible. New American Standard. A. J. Holman Company. 1973. Genesis 5:32–10:1. An Old Testament miracle exhibited God saving Noah, his family, and the animals from a great flood.
18. (Daniel in the lion's den) Bible. New American Standard. A. J. Holman Company. 1973. Daniel 6. An Old Testament miracle exhibited God saving Daniel after he was thrown into a den of lions.
19. (David and Goliath) Bible. New American Standard. A. J. Holman Company. 1973. 1 Samuel 17. An Old Testament miracle exhibited God helping David kill a giant named Goliath with a simple sling.
20. (Jonah and the whale) Bible. New American Standard. A. J. Holman Company. 1973. Jonah 1. An Old Testament miracle exhibited God protecting Jonah while he was in the belly of a whale.
21. (parting of the Red Sea) Bible. New American Standard. A. J. Holman Company. 1973. Exodus 14. An Old Testament miracle exhibited God protecting the exiting Jews from Egypt by parting the Red Sea for them during their escape from the enemy.
22. (healing miracles) Bible. New American Standard. A. J. Holman Company. 1973. Matthew 8:6–34. Jesus healed a paralyzed servant and Peter's mother when she was sick. Jesus cast out demons and calmed the seas.
23. (healing miracles) Bible. New American Standard. A. J. Holman Company. 1973. Matthew 9:20–34. Jesus healed a blind man and raised a girl from the dead.
24. (healing miracles) Bible. New American Standard. A. J. Holman Company. 1973. Matthew 12:13. Jesus healed a man with a withered hand.
25. (healing miracles) Bible. New American Standard. A. J. Holman Company. 1973. Matthew 20:30–34. Jesus healed two blind men.

26. (healing miracles) Bible. New American Standard. A. J. Holman Company. 1973. Matthew 21:19–20. Jesus withered a fig tree.
27. (Jesus heals blind with mud and water) Bible. New American Standard. A. J. Holman Company. 1973. John 9:1–41. Jesus mixes spit and dirt to place mud on a blind man's eyes. He tells the man to go to the pool of Siloam to wash, and his vision returns.
28. (Moses and Elijah apparition) Bible. New International Version. Zondervan. 1984. Matthew 17:1–9. During the Transfiguration, there were apparitions of Moses and Elijah with Jesus and three apostles.

Chapter 3

1. (Protestant Reformation) Encyclopedia Britannica. "Reformation Christianity." 2017. Luther posted Ninety-Five Theses on October 31, 1517, charging church leaders with corruption for selling indulgences.
2. (Protestant Reformation) *Roots of the Reformation*. Karl Adam. CH Resources. 2012, pp. 11–41. There was a moral collapse of the popes. Taxation, payment for indulgences, nepotism, lust for power and money inflicted the church. Martin Luther posted Ninety-Five Theses at the Castle Church at Wittenburg. Luther espoused faith, not works. He is excommunicated. After fifteen hundred years in existence, Protestants split from the Catholic Church.
3. (Elijah to announce the Messiah) Bible. New American Standard. A. J. Holman Company. 1973. Malachi 3:1. "My messenger will prepare the way." Christians believe John the Baptist was the messenger.
4. (Elijah to announce the Messiah) Bible. New American Standard. A. J. Holman Company. 1973. Malachi 4:5–6. Elijah will announce the arrival of the Messiah. Christians believe John the Baptist fulfilled this prophesy by serving as Elijah's messenger.

Chapter 5

1. (Martin Luther) The Daily Study Bible Series. Dr. William Barclay. "The Gospel of Mark." p. 61. Martin Luther and John Wesley initially wanted the Catholic Church to make changes. They did not want to break away.

2. (Old Testament) *30 Days to Understanding the Bible*. Max E. Anders. Word Publishing. 1988, pp. 6–12. The Old Testament explains the history of the Hebrew people over two thousand years. It contains books on history, poetry, and prophecy. The New Testament covers a period of less than one hundred years.
3. (Protestant Reformation) Encyclopedia Britannica, Inc. Reformation Christianity. 2017. Luther posted Ninety-Five Theses on October 31, 1517. It included charges of corruption and selling indulgences.
4. (future Messiah) Bible. New American Standard. A. J. Holman Company. 1973. Isaiah 53. The Lord will be scourged and die as a lamb for sacrifice.
5. (future Messiah) Bible. New American Standard. A. J. Holman Company. 1973. Psalm 22. They will pierce His hands and feet, and cast lots for His clothes.
6. (death on the cross) Bible. New American Standard. A. J. Holman Company. 1973. John 19:28–42. A soldier lanced his side instead of breaking his legs.
7. (Elijah to announce the Messiah) Bible. New American Standard. A. J. Holman Company. 1973. Malachi 4:5–6. Elijah will announce the arrival of the Messiah. Christians believe John the Baptist fulfilled this prophesy by serving as Elijah's messenger.
8. (Elijah to announce the Messiah) Bible. New American Standard. A. J. Holman Company. 1973. Malachi 3:1. My messenger will prepare the way. Christians believe John the Baptist was the messenger.
9. (scribes and Pharisees) *The Daily Study Bible Series*. Dr. William Barclay. Westminster Press. 1975. "The Gospel of Matthew, Vol. 2." pp. 280–84. There are different types of Pharisees. There are fifty volumes of Jewish regulations managed by the Pharisees.
10. (scribal law) *The Daily Study Bible Series*. Dr. William Barclay. Westminster Press. 1975. "The Gospel of Matthew, Vol. 1." pp. 126–33. The law is used as an expression in four different ways: The Ten Commandments, the Pentateuch, the whole of scripture, and the Scribal Law. When the Scribal Law was finally put in writing in the third century, it was nearly eight hundred pages long.
11. (love to gain eternal life) Bible. New American Standard. A. J. Holman Company. 1973.Luke 10:25–37. A man asked Jesus: "Teacher, what

shall I do to inherit eternal life?" Jesus asked what was written in the law. The man responded: "Love the Lord your God with all your heart, and with all your soul, ... and your neighbor as yourself." Jesus agreed.

12. (Pharisee appearance) *The Daily Study Bible Series*. Dr. William Barclay. Westminster Press. 1975. "The Gospel of Matthew, Vol. 2." p. 132. Pharisees are concerned about laws, rules, and regulation, not the state of a person's heart.

13. (Peter as rock) Bible. New American Standard. A. J. Holman Company. 1973. John 1:40–42 and Matthew 16:17–19. Jesus said: "Upon this rock I will build my church." Jesus names Simon "Cephas," translated as Peter, which means "rock."

14. (Peter as rock) *The Daily Study Bible Series*. Dr. William Barclay. Westminster Press. 1975. "The Gospel of Matthew, Vol. 2." pp. 139–42. Catholics and Protestants hold different views on Peter being the basis of the Christian church.

15. (Peter as shepherd) Bible. New American Standard. A. J. Holman Company. 1973. John 21:15–19. Jesus met with his disciples for the third time after the resurrection and before his ascension. After eating a breakfast of bread and charcoaled fish, Jesus asked Peter three times if he loved him. After each response, Jesus told Peter sequentially "tend my lambs," "shepherd my sheep," and "tend my sheep." Jesus also informed Peter he would also die of crucifixion on a cross someday.

16. (Peter as shepherd) *The Daily Study Bible Series*. Dr. William Barclay. Westminster Press. 1975. "The Gospel of John, Vol. 2." pp. 284–87. Peter was told by Jesus to shepherd the Christian church. John recorded this incident to show Peter as the great shepherd of Christ's people after Jesus ascended to heaven.

17. (Jesus as shepherd) Bible. New American Standard. A. J. Holman Company. 1973. John 10:11–15. In response to questions from Jewish scribes and Pharisees, Jesus called himself the "Good Shepherd." Jesus was speaking about Christianity and how he would lay down his life for his sheep. The scribes and Pharisees were trying to trap him under the laws of Judaism. They did not understand what Jesus was saying.

18. (*Didache*) *The Daily Study Bible Series*. Dr. William Barclay. Westminster Press. 1975. "The Letters to the Galatians and Ephesians." pp. 145–48. The *Didache* is a book of the teaching of the twelve apostles. It

includes the order of sacrament, prayers to be used in church, and directions about office-bearers of the church. The *Didache* was written just after 100.

19. (official books of the New Testament) *Catholic Biblical Apologetics. Divine Revelation by Letter. Major Church Pronouncements on the Bible.* Paul Flanagan and Robert Schihl. 1985–2014. New Testament writings were decided in AD 382 at the Council of Rome.

20. (Protestant Reformation) *Roots of the Reformation*. Karl Adam. CH Resources. 2012, pp. 11–41. There was a moral collapse of the popes. Taxation, payment for indulgences, nepotism, lust for power and money ruined the church. Martin Luther posted Ninety-Five Theses at the Castle Church at Wittenburg. Luther espoused faith, not works. He is excommunicated. He calls the book of James an "epistle of straw."

21. (city-states) Encyclopedia Britannica. "Leo X." 2017. Pope Leo X, of the Medici family from the city-state of Florence, became pope and appointed relatives as cardinals.

22. (corrupt popes) *The Pursuit of Italy*. Sir David Gilmour. Farrar, Straus and Giroux. 2011, pp. 84–93. City-state popes ruled the church for seventy years beginning in 1455, including members of the families of Borgia, Piccolomini, della Rovere, and Medici. The Spanish Borgia pope, Alexander VI, had a mistress. Nepotism was used for two hundred years. The Lateran Council, 1513–1517, failed to reform the church. The pope also ruled the Papal States in central Italy.

23. (*sola scriptura*) *Catholicism and Fundamentalism*. Karl Keating. Ignatius Press. 1988, pp. 121–22, 134–35. The concept of sola scriptura, inspired by God, started at the Reformation. It eventually ignored tradition.

24. (*sola scriptura*) *Sola Scriptura. In the Vanity of Their Minds*. Fr. John Whiteford. Luther never sought to eliminate tradition altogether, only the parts that were corrupt.

25. (dual source of revelation) *Catechism of the Catholic Church*. Doubleday. 1994. Part 1. Section 1. Chapter 2. Article 2.III.84. Catholicism uses both scripture and tradition to determine church doctrine.

26. (the Crusades) Encyclopedia Britannica. "Crusades." 2017. Religious wars occurred between the Catholic Church and Muslims over control of the Holy Land. There were eight wars from 1096 to 1291.

27. (early Protestantism) Pew Research Center. *Religion & Public Life. Five Centuries after Reformation, Catholic-Protestant Divide in Western Europe Has Faded.* August 31, 2017.
28. (Council of Trent) *Roots of the Reformation.* Karl Adam. CH Resources. 2012, pp. 57–63. The papacy was spiritualized after the Council of Trent. Not one of Luther's accusations could be made today. The papacy is now strictly religious, Christian, and ecclesiastical.
29. (remove seven books from the Old Testament) *Catholicism and Fundamentalism.* Karl Keating. Ignatius Press. 1988, p. 132. Luther rejected seven books of the Old Testament because of conflicts with some of his theories, including purgatory. The books were moved to an appendix and considered the lesser books. They were Tobit, Judith, Wisdom, Ecclesiasticus, Baruch and the two books of Maccabees, as well as sections of Esther and Daniel.
30. (number of Christians) Pew Research Center's Forum on Religion & Public Life. *Global Christianity.* December 19, 2011.
31. (CMA members) cmalliance.org/about. 2013–2017. Part of a global alliance six million members strong.
32. (Church of God members) www.jesusisthesubject.org/our-history. 2017. The Church of God based in Anderson, Indiana, has 887,000 members worldwide.

Chapter 6

1. (mind control techniques) *The Heresy of Mind Control.* Stephen Martin. ACW Press. 2009, pp. 97–114. Mind control techniques are simple to employ.
2. (mind control techniques) *The Heresy of Mind Control.* Stephen Martin. ACW Press. 2009, pp. 143–53. Fundamentalists are right, everyone else is wrong. The Taliban also employ this thinking.
3. (transfiguration) Bible. New International Version. Zondervan. 1984. Matthew 17:1–9. God told Peter, James, and John to listen to Jesus.
4. (turning water into wine) Bible. New American Standard. A. J. Holman Company. 1973. John 2:1–11. At a wedding where his mother was also in attendance, Jesus performed a miracle by turning water into wine using six stone water pots, each holding thirty gallons.

5. (eating unclean meat according to Jesus) Bible. New International Version. Zondervan. 1984. Mark 7:14–20. Jesus said, "Nothing that enters a man from outside can make him unclean.... What comes out of a man is what makes him unclean ... from within, out of men's hearts."
6. (causing new Christians to stumble) *The Daily Study Bible Series*. Dr. William Barclay. Westminster Press. 1975. "The Letters to the Corinthians." pp. 74–76. Because many new Christians in the church at Corinth came from idol worship, they felt uncomfortable with eating meat offered to idols. Until their level of faith increases, Paul advises the experienced Christians to not eat that meat. 1 Corinthians 8:1–13.
7. (causing converted Jews to stumble) *The Daily Study Bible Series*. Dr. William Barclay. Westminster Press. 1975. "The Letter to the Romans." pp. 179–80. Many new Jewish converts to Christianity retained their Jewish dietary practices and would not associate with Gentile converts to Christianity in the same church. Paul recommends welcoming new Christians without pressuring them to change their past practices. Romans 14:1–6.
8. (no rules in Christianity: Paul) Bible. New American Standard. A. J. Holman Company. 1973. Galatians 2:14–21. Paul declares the end of the law. Faith in Christ has nothing to do with the law. We are not justified by works. If you get right with God through the law, then Christ died needlessly.
9. (Paul wanting to be liked) Bible. New American Standard. A. J. Holman Company. 1973. Galatians 1:6–10. Paul affirms there are no rules for Christians.
10. (justification through works: James) Bible. New International Version. Zondervan. 1984. James 2:14–26. James says, "You see that a person is justified by what he does and not by faith alone."
11. (book reference) *Killing Jesus*. Bill O'Reilly and Martin Dugard. Henry Holt and Company. 2013.
12. (Opus Dei) *Uncommon Faith: The Early Years of Opus Dei (1928–1943)*. John F. Coverdale. Scepter Publishers, Inc. 2002. Opus Dei encourages living a life of sanctity and holiness for parishioners, as well as priests. Opus Dei was founded by Saint Josemaria Escriva, from Spain. The organization is approved by the Catholic papacy.

Chapter 7

1. (Communion) Bible. New American Standard. A. J. Holman Company. 1973. Matthew 26:26–30 and Mark 14:22–26. Jesus said, "This is my body.... This is my blood, the blood of the new covenant which is being shed for many."
2. (number of Christians) Pew Research Center's Forum on Religion & Public Life. *Global Christianity*. December 19, 2011.
3. (Communion) Bible. New International Version. Zondervan. 1984. John 6:51–59. When teaching in Capernaum, Jesus said, "My flesh is real food and my blood is real drink. Whoever eats my flesh and drinks my blood remains in me and I in him."
4. (believe in Jesus for eternal life) Bible. New American Standard. A. J. Holman Company. 1973. John 3:16. Whosoever believes in Jesus will have eternal life.

Chapter 8

1. (Apostolic Canons and Constitutions) The Daily Study Bible Series. Dr. William Barclay. Westminster Press. 1975. "The Letters to Timothy, Titus, and Philemon." pp. 98–109. Early Christian church writings include the Apostolic Canons. Later, in the third century, the Apostolic Constitutions were written.
2. (Greek words for love) *The Daily Study Bible Series*. Dr. William Barclay. Westminster Press. 1975. "The Gospel of Matthew, Vol. 1." pp. 173–74. There are four Greek words for the more general English word "love".
3. (Lord's Prayer translation) Catholic News Agency. "Analysis: What Is the Context of Pope Francis' Words on the Lord's Prayer?" Andrea Gagliarducci. December 11, 2017. "Lead us not into temptation" should be more accurately interpreted in English to say "Do not abandon us to the temptation." Catholic Italian biblical scholars have been working on this reinterpretation since 1988.
4. (*sola scriptura*) *Sola Scriptura. In the Vanity of Their Minds*. Fr. John Whiteford. Luther never sought to eliminate tradition altogether, only the parts that were corrupt.

5. (dual source of revelation) *Catechism of the Catholic Church.* Doubleday. 1994. Part 1. Section 1. Chapter 2. Article 2.III.84. Catholicism uses both scripture and tradition to determine church doctrine.
6. (Jehovah or Yahweh) catholic.com/qa. "Catholic Answers." August 4, 2011. YHWH is the original Hebrew word for God. Using Greek records, Yahweh is probably the correct pronunciation. Jews substituted Adonai for YHWH. Incorrectly combining the two words resulted in a translation error creating the name Jehovah.
7. (cloak and two miles) *The Daily Study Bible Series.* Dr. William Barclay. Westminster Press. 1975. "The Gospel of Matthew, Vol. 1." pp. 167–68. A coat is given to someone you owe until you pay your debt and get your coat back. A tunic is the inner garment worn in those days. Under Roman occupation, Roman soldiers could require people to carry their things for up to one mile.
8. (occupied territory) *The Daily Study Bible Series.* Dr. William Barclay. Westminster Press. 1975. "The Gospel of Mark." p. 119. Romans occupied the Palestinian territory during the time of Jesus.
9. (Simon carries the cross) Bible. New American Standard. A. J. Holman Company. 1973. Matthew 27:32. A Cyrenian named Simon was pressed into service by a Roman soldier to carry the cross of Jesus to Golgotha, after Jesus became too weak.
10. (Second coming) Bible. New American Standard. A. J. Holman Company. 1973. Mark 13:28–37 and Matthew 24:32–41. Jesus said that no man knows about the day and the hour of the Second Coming, not even the angels in heaven, not even the Son, no one except the Father.
11. (Gentiles to be Jews first) Bible. New American Standard. A. J. Holman Company. 1973. Acts 15:1–21. Apostles, elders, and Paul meet to discuss whether Gentiles must first convert to Judaism before becoming Christians. James, the stepbrother of Jesus, is an apostle who still followed all the Jewish laws. He offered a compromise, which is accepted. Gentiles must follow four Jewish laws temporarily.
12. (Gentiles to be Jews first) Bible. New American Standard. A. J. Holman Company. 1973. Acts 21:17–26. James, the apostle, and other elders who still follow all the Jewish laws tell Paul that since he is accused of abandoning the Law of Moses, he must go through a Jewish purification

ritual. Paul did it, but it ultimately led to his demise, since he was caught and arrested in the Jewish temple while completing the rituals.

13. (Apostles disagree) Bible. New American Standard. A. J. Holman Company. 1973. Galatians 2:11–21. The compromise, in Acts 15:1–21, of Gentiles having to follow four Jewish laws, mostly on eating meat, was approved against Paul's wishes. James advocated for retaining some laws. Peter compromised.
14. (eating unclean meat according to Jesus) Bible. New International Version. Zondervan. 1984. Mark 7:14–20. Jesus says, "Nothing that enters a man from outside can make him unclean.... What comes out of a man is what makes him unclean ... from within, out of men's hearts."
15. (eating unclean meat) *The Daily Study Bible Series*. Dr. William Barclay. Westminster Press. 1975. "The Gospel of Mark." pp. 170–73. Jesus says eating unclean meat is not a sin, even though it violates Jewish law. Leviticus chapter 11 has a list of unclean foods.
16. (love commandment) Bible. New American Standard. A. J. Holman Company. 1973. John 15:11–17. Jesus said, "This is my commandment, that you love one another, just as I have loved you."
17. (miracles as evidence of the Holy Spirit) Bible. New American Standard. A. J. Holman Company. 1973. Mark 16:9–20. A resurrected Jesus said to the apostles, "Go into all the world and preach the gospel to all creation. He who has believed and has been baptized shall be saved; but he who has disbelieved shall be condemned. And these signs will accompany those who have believed ... they will lay hands on the sick, and they will recover."
18. (miracles as evidence of the Holy Spirit) Bible. New American Standard. A. J. Holman Company. 1973. Acts 15:6–12. Peter stood up and said Gentiles should also hear the Gospel and believe. God will give them the Holy Spirit. The whole assembly was silent and listened to Barnabas and Paul as they told the story of all the signs and wonders God did amongst the heathen through them.
19. (gifts of the Holy Spirit) Bible. New American Standard. A. J. Holman Company. 1973. 1 Corinthians 12:4–11. Paul explains that each man is given his own gift by the Holy Spirit. Gifts may include wisdom, knowledge, faith, healing, power, prophecy, spirit recognition, speaking in tongues, or interpreting tongues.

20. (Luther's view of the book of James) *The Daily Study Bible Series*. Dr. William Barclay. Westminster Press. 1975. "The Letters of James and Peter." pp. 3–33. The books of James, Jude, Hebrews, and Revelation are secondary books. James disagrees with Paul and the rest of the Bible. Luther prefers to remove the book of James from the Bible.
21. (Luther's Ninety-Five Theses) *Martin Luther's Ninety-Five Theses*. Timothy J. Wengert. Augsberg Fortress Publishers, 2015. A list of Luther's Ninety-Five Theses was posted publicly. Luther questioned the money required for indulgences and benefits from saints. He also questioned the pope's authority.
22. (Protestant Reformation) *Roots of the Reformation*. Karl Adam. CH Resources. 2012, pp. 11–41. There was a moral collapse of the popes. Taxation, payment for indulgences, nepotism, and lust for power and money corrupted the church. Martin Luther posted Ninety-Five Theses at the Castle Church at Wittenburg. Luther espoused faith, not works. He is excommunicated. He calls book of James an "epistle of straw."
23. (seven removed books from the Old Testament) EWTN.com/vexperts. Global Catholic Network. Rev. Mark J. Gantley. 2018. Martin Luther moved seven books to an appendix at the end of the Old Testament. These books are the most recent books of the Old Testament. The books were not accepted by Judaism because they were found to be written in Hebrew, not Greek. But Hebrew versions of two of these books were found in the Dead Sea Scrolls.
24. (the four Gospels) *The Daily Study Bible Series*. Dr. William Barclay. Westminster Press. 1975. "The Gospel of Mark." pp. 1–9. Mark was from Jerusalem. His Gospel was written first. Mark probably used firsthand accounts from Peter, including Peter's sermons. Part of Matthew and part of Luke were copied from Mark.
25. (the four Gospels) *The Daily Study Bible Series*. Dr. William Barclay. Westminster Press. 1975. "The Gospel of Luke." pp. 1–6. Luke was the only Gentile writer of a Gospel. Luke was from Macedonia, where they held women in higher esteem. Jewish men prayed every morning thanking God they were not Gentile, slave, or woman. Mark was written more realistically as a report on the life of Jesus.
26. (the four Gospels) *The Daily Study Bible Series*. Dr. William Barclay. Westminster Press. 1975. "The Gospel of John, Vol. 1." pp. 1–10. The

information in the Gospels were passed on orally first, then written later. Mark was likely first to be written, followed by Matthew and Luke. John was written around AD 100 in Ephesus. John covers more of the early ministry of Jesus. John has a more accurate timeline of events than the other Gospels.

27. (John's Gospel) *The Daily Study Bible Series*. Dr. William Barclay. Westminster Press. 1975. "The Gospel of John, Vol. 2." pp. 284–87. Peter was assigned by Jesus to shepherd the Christian church. John recorded this incident to show Peter as the great shepherd of Christ's people after Jesus ascended to heaven. John wrote and thought more deeply so future generations would better understand.

28. (Paul's letters) *The Daily Study Bible Series*. Dr. William Barclay. Westminster Press. 1975. "The Letter to the Romans." pp. x–xii, 1. Except for Romans, Paul's letters were in response to immediate situations faced by early Christian churches. Paul's letters were in response to information he received about the church. Because we only have Paul's responses, we are missing half of the conversation.

29. (Paul's letters) *The Daily Study Bible Series*. Dr. William Barclay. Westminster Press. 1975. "The Letters to the Corinthians." pp. 5–8. Paul was in Ephesus when he heard about problems in the church at Corinth. Paul writes a letter in reply, to address specific issues in that church. Many of the church members in Corinth were previously pagan and did not understand how they should now behave as new Christians.

30. (judging) Bible. New International Version. Zondervan. 1984. Matthew 7:1–5. In the Sermon on the Mount, Jesus said, "Do not judge others, in order that you may not be judged; for with the standard of judgment with which you judge, you will be judged; and with the measure you measure to others it will be measured to you. Why do you look for the speck of dust in your brother's eye, and never notice the plank that is in your own eye? ... Hypocrite."

31. (only Jesus knows what's in a man's heart) Bible. New American Standard. A. J. Holman Company. 1973. Luke 9:47. Jesus knows the reasoning of their hearts.

32. (judging) Bible. New American Standard. A. J. Holman Company. 1973. Romans 2:1–11. Paul says, if you judge others, you condemn yourself.

33. (judging: only Jesus knows what's in a man's heart) Bible. New American Standard. A. J. Holman Company. 1973. 1 Corinthians 4:1–5. Paul says to make a practice of passing no judgment. "Wait until the Lord comes ... and discloses the motives of men's hearts."
34. (judging) Bible. New American Standard. A. J. Holman Company. 1973. James 4:11–12. James says, who are you to judge your neighbor?
35. (judging) Bible. New American Standard. A. J. Holman Company. 1973. John 5:21–23. John says, neither does the Father judge anyone, but he has given the whole process of judging to the Son.
36. (slavery in Philemon) *The Daily Study Bible Series*. Dr. William Barclay. Westminster Press. 1975. "The Letters to Timothy, Titus, and Philemon." pp. 269–83. Philemon's runaway slave, Onesimus, became Christian and worked with Paul in Rome. Paul writes to Philemon and asks him to free his slave and accept him as a Christian brother. The church in Laodicaea and the nearby church in Colosse were in present-day Turkey. Galatians 3:28 says in Christ, there is neither Greek, nor Jew, slave nor free man, male nor female.
37. (Paul is a trained Pharisee) *The Daily Study Bible Series*. Dr. William Barclay. Westminster Press. 1975. "The Letters to the Philippians, Colossians, and Thessalonians." pp. 59–60. Paul was born into an aristocratic Jewish family, as an Israelite. He was trained in the law as a Pharisee and can speak Hebrew. Paul was previously a persecutor of the church.
38. (Luther's *sola scriptura*) *Christianity Today* (Christian history magazine). "Dr. Luther's Theology." Dr. Timothy George. 1992. Luther started *sola scriptura* but never rejected tradition.
39. (Luther's use of tradition) *Roots of the Reformation*. Karl Adam. CH Resources. 2012, p. 48. Luther still attended confession and honored Mary.
40. (CMA history) cmalliance.org/about. 2013–2017. CMA is part of a global alliance, six million members strong. A. B. Simpson, founder and former Presbyterian minister, wanted a global outreach.
41. (Holiness Church) Funk & Wagnalls New Encyclopedia. Vol. 13. Funk & Wagnalls Corporation. 1993, pp. 155–56. The Holiness movement began in the US after the Civil War. It had a focus on living a holy

life by following many laws. CMA, Church of God, Nazarene, and Pentecostal denominations came from the Holiness movement.

42. (Methodist Church) Funk & Wagnalls New Encyclopedia. Vol. 17. Funk & Wagnalls Corporation. 1993, pp. 242–44. Methodism began in 1729 by breaking away from Anglican Church. They focused on Christian perfection in a less formal environment.

43. (Anglican Church) Funk & Wagnalls New Encyclopedia. Vol. 6. Funk & Wagnalls Corporation. 1993, pp. 279–81. The Anglican Church broke away from Catholicism in 1534. Methodist and Episcopal churches later split from the Anglican Church.

44. (Disciples of Christ Church) Funk & Wagnalls New Encyclopedia. Vol. 6. Funk & Wagnalls Corporation. 1993, pp. 249–50. The Disciples of Christ started in the early 1800s in Pennsylvania and Kentucky. Their two leaders separately left Presbyterianism. It also included Churches of Christ, Christian Church and Churches of Christ, and the Christian Congregation. They later separated.

45. (Presbyterianism) Funk & Wagnalls New Encyclopedia. Vol. 21. Funk & Wagnalls Corporation. 1993, pp. 256–59. Presbyterianism broke from Catholicism in the Protestant Reformation. It was mainly located in Scotland and England. Local churches were led by a session of ordained elders.

46. (number of Christian denominations) World Christian Encyclopedia. Barrett, Kurian, and Johnson. Vol. 1. Oxford University Press. 2001, p. 16. There are 33,000 Christian denominations, including 22,000 independent, 9,000 Protestant, 1,600 marginal (cult-like), 781 Orthodox organizations, 242 Catholic rites, and 168 Anglican organizations.

47. (denomination growth) GordonConwell.edu/StatusofGlobalMission. Gordon-Conwell Resources. 2015. The Gordon Conwell Seminary completes an annual survey on Christianity. Christian denominations grow on average by 2.3 denominations per day.

48. (Paul claims faith alone) Bible. New American Standard. A. J. Holman Company. 1973. Galatians 2:14–21. Paul declared the end of the law. Faith in Christ has nothing to do with the law. No one can be right with God by doing the works of the law. If you get right with God through the law, then Christ died unnecessarily.

Chapter 9

1. (law versus faith: Paul) Bible. New International Version. Zondervan. 1984. Romans 3:19–26. No one will be declared righteous in his sight by observing the law; rather, through the law we become conscious of sin. This righteousness from God comes through faith in Jesus Christ to all who believe.
2. (no rules in Christianity: Paul) Bible. New American Standard. A. J. Holman Company. 1973. Galatians 2:14–21. Paul declares the end of the law. Faith in Christ has nothing to do with the law. We are not justified by works. If you get right with God through the law, then Christ died needlessly.
3. (justification through works: James) Bible. New International Version. Zondervan. 1984. James 2:14–26. James says, "you see that a person is justified by what he does and not by faith alone."
4. (perfect Christian life by behaviors) Funk & Wagnalls New Encyclopedia. Vol. 13. Funk & Wagnalls Corporation. 1993, pp. 155–56. The Holiness movement began after the Civil War. They had a focus on living a holy life by following many laws. The CMA, Church of God, Nazarene, and Pentecostal denominations came from the Holiness movement. Living a perfect Christian life according to a set of behaviors was their focus.
5. (judging) Bible. New International Version. Zondervan. 1984. Matthew 7:1–5. In the Sermon on the Mount, Jesus said, "Do not judge others, in order that you may not be judged; for with the standard of judgment with which you judge, you will be judged; and with the measure you measure to others it will be measured to you. Why do you look for the speck of dust in your brother's eye, and never notice the plank that is in your own eye? ... Hypocrite."
6. (only Jesus knows what's in a man's heart) Bible. New American Standard. A. J. Holman Company. 1973. Luke 9:47. Jesus knows the reasoning of their hearts.
7. (judging) Bible. New American Standard. A. J. Holman Company. 1973. Romans 2:1–11. Paul said, if you judge others, you condemn yourself.

8. (judging: only Jesus knows what's in a man's heart) Bible. New American Standard. A. J. Holman Company. 1973. 1 Corinthians 4:1–5. Paul said, make a practice of passing no judgment. "Wait until the Lord comes ... and discloses the motives of men's hearts."
9. (judging) Bible. New American Standard. A. J. Holman Company. 1973. James 4:11–12. James said, who are you to judge your neighbor?
10. (judging) Bible. New American Standard. A. J. Holman Company. 1973. John 5:21–23. John said, neither does the Father judge anyone, but he has given the whole process of judging to the Son.
11. (Gentiles to be Jews first) Bible. New American Standard. A. J. Holman Company. 1973. Acts 15:1–21. The apostles, elders, and Paul met to discuss whether Gentiles must first convert to Judaism before becoming Christians. James, the stepbrother of Jesus, is an apostle who still follows all the Jewish laws. He offers a compromise, which is accepted. Gentiles must follow four Jewish laws temporarily.
12. (James proposes four laws for Gentiles) *The Daily Study Bible Series*. Dr. William Barclay. Westminster Press. 1975. "The Acts of the Apostles." pp. 112–16. For Jews to interact with unclean Gentiles, Gentiles must eat meat according to Jewish law and abstain from fornication. The apostle James proposed this compromise to allow growth of the church to include Gentiles.
13. (eating unclean meat according to Jesus) Bible. New International Version. Zondervan. 1984. Mark 7:14–20. Jesus says, "Nothing that enters a man from outside can make him unclean.... What comes out of a man is what makes him unclean ... from within, out of men's hearts."
14. (Jesus condemned the law) *The Daily Study Bible Series*. Dr. William Barclay. Westminster Press. 1975. "The Gospel of Matthew, Vol. 1." pp. 126–30. Jewish Pharisees had volumes of oral and Scribal Law that burdened the religious people. Jesus and Paul condemned this law.
15. (Paul claims faith alone) Bible. New American Standard. A. J. Holman Company. 1973. Galatians 2:14–21. Paul declares the end of the law. Faith in Christ has nothing to do with the law. No one can be right with God by doing the works of the law. If you get right with God through the law, then Christ died unnecessarily.
16. (Christianity is open to all) Bible. New American Standard. A. J. Holman Company. 1973. Colossians 3:9–13. "There is no distinction

between Greek and Jew, circumcised and uncircumcised, barbarian, slave and free man, but Christ in all."

17. (St. Francis of Assisi) *Mother Teresa: A Simple Path*. Lucinda Vardey. Ballantine Books. 1995. p. xviii. St. Francis chose to live a life of poverty.
18. (tithing at 10 percent) Bible. New American Standard. A. J. Holman Company. 1973. Leviticus 27:32. "And for every tenth part of herd or flock, whatever passes under the rod, the tenth one shall be holy to the Lord."
19. (tithing) Webster's New World Dictionary and Thesaurus. Wiley Publishing, Inc. 2002. p. 662. The word *tithe* comes from the Old English word "teothe," meaning a tenth. It means giving a tenth of your income.
20. (tithing) Bible. New American Standard. A. J. Holman Company. 1973. Matthew 23:23. While calling the scribes and Pharisees hypocrites for tithing lesser crops like dill and mint, Jesus said tithing should be done with a deep concern for justice, mercy, and faithfulness.
21. (giving to the church) Bible. New American Standard. A. J. Holman Company. 1973. 2 Corinthians 9:7. Paul says God loves a cheerful giver, not someone who gives grudgingly.
22. (giving to the church) Bible. New American Standard. A. J. Holman Company. 1973. 2 Corinthians 8:12. Paul encourages giving what you can afford and not to go needy yourself by giving too much.
23. (giving to the church) Bible. New American Standard. A. J. Holman Company. 1973. 1 Timothy 5:17–18. Those who work hard at preaching and teaching are worthy of their wages.
24. (giving to the church) Bible. New American Standard. A. J. Holman Company. 1973. Acts 11:29. In the proportion that any of the disciples had means, each of them determined to send a contribution to the hungry.
25. (giving to the church) Bible. New American Standard. A. J. Holman Company. 1973. James 1:27. Pure religion is to visit and help needy widows and orphans.
26. (Jesus helps the poor) Bible. New American Standard. A. J. Holman Company. 1973. Luke 14:12–14. Jesus said you will be blessed when you invite the poor, the crippled, the lame, and the blind to a meal.

27. (Old Testament) *30 Days to Understanding the Bible*. Max E. Anders. Word Publishing. 1988, pp. 6–12. The Old Testament explains the history of the Hebrew people over two thousand years. It contains books on history, poetry, and prophecy. The New Testament covers a time period of less than one hundred years.
28. (Pharisees focus on laws and appearances) Bible. New American Standard. A. J. Holman Company. 1973. Luke 11:37–44. Jesus accuses the Pharisees of cleaning the outside of the cup and platter, but on the inside, they are full of wickedness.
29. (pray in secret) Bible. New American Standard. A. J. Holman Company. 1973. Matthew 6:5–8. Jesus said you should not pray to be "seen by people" but you should "go into your inner room and shut the door, and pray to your Father who is in secret."
30. (Pharisee appearances) Bible. New American Standard. A. J. Holman Company. 1973. Luke 20:45–47 and Matthew 23:5–12. Jesus said to beware of the scribes who like to walk about in long robes, who love the best seats in synagogues and pretend to offer long prayers.
31. (Pharisees make religion a burden) Bible. New American Standard. A. J. Holman Company. 1973. Matthew 23:1–4. Jesus said that scribes and Pharisees bind burdens that are heavy and hard to bear.
32. (loved much) Bible. New American Standard. A. J. Holman Company. 1973. Luke 7:36–50. Jesus said this bad woman's many sins are forgiven for she loved much.
33. (faith) Bible. New American Standard. A. J. Holman Company. 1973. Matthew 8:5–13. Jesus healed a centurion's servant because the centurion had faith.
34. (healing on Sabbath) Bible. New American Standard. A. J. Holman Company. 1973. Luke 13:10–17. Jesus healed a woman who could not straighten up on the Sabbath. Jesus said it does not break the law to untie an ox on the Sabbath to lead him out to water.
35. (healing on Sabbath) Bible. New American Standard. A. J. Holman Company. 1973. Luke 14:1–6. Jesus healed a man with dropsy on the Sabbath and said it is not against the law because if an ox falls into a well on the Sabbath, he will be pulled out.
36. (Pharisees are missionaries of evil) *The Daily Study Bible Series*. Dr. William Barclay. Westminster Press. 1975. "The Gospel of Matthew,

Vol. 2." p. 291. The greatest of all heresies is the sinful conviction that any church has a monopoly of God or of His truth, or that any church is the only gateway to God's kingdom.

37. (unity of all Christian churches) *The Daily Study Bible Series*. Dr. William Barclay. Westminster Press. 1975. "The Gospel of John Vol. 2." p. 218. We should have a unity of all Christian churches, based on love, with no barriers.
38. (eats with sinners) Bible. New American Standard. A. J. Holman Company. 1973. Matthew 9:10–13. Jesus eats with tax gatherers and sinners.
39. (Mother Teresa) *Mother Teresa: A Simple Path*. Lucinda Vardey. Ballantine Books. 1995, pp. xiii–xix. Mother Teresa's built homes for the poor in Calcutta and lived a life of poverty. Prayer was her source of strength.
40. (Jesus anonymously returns to earth today) *Joshua: A Parable for Today*. Joseph F. Girzone. Simon & Schuster. 1987. A priest wrote a fictional story about Jesus returning to earth today under an assumed name, and how he is treated.

Chapter 10

1. (Old Testament) 30 Days to Understanding the Bible. Max E. Anders. Word Publishing. 1988, pp. 6–12. The Old Testament explains the history of the Hebrew people over two thousand years. It contains books on history, poetry, and prophecy. The New Testament covers a period of less than one hundred years.
2. (love the Lord with all your heart) *The Daily Study Bible Series*. Dr. William Barclay. Westminster Press. 1975. "The Gospel of Matthew, Vol. 2." pp. 277–79. Jesus said to love the Lord with all your heart, all your mind, and all your soul. Jesus said this in response to a question from a Jewish scribe about summarizing the most important Jewish laws. It is also considered by some to be a summary of all religions. It is included in the Shema, the Jewish creed, which is used to begin every service in a Jewish synagogue.

3. (love the Lord with all your heart) Bible. New American Standard. A. J. Holman Company. 1973. Deuteronomy 6:4–7. Under Judaic law, God said to love the Lord with all your heart, all your soul, and all your mind.
4. (love others as yourself) Bible. New American Standard. A. J. Holman Company. 1973. Leviticus 19:9–18. Under Judaic law, God said to love your neighbor as yourself.
5. (love one another) Bible. New American Standard. A. J. Holman Company. 1973. John 15:11–17. With the onset of Christianity, a new command by Jesus for Christians was to love one another, just as Jesus loves you.

Chapter 11

1. (love to gain eternal life) Bible. New American Standard. A. J. Holman Company. 1973. Luke 10:25–37. A man asked Jesus, "teacher, what shall I do to inherit eternal life?" Jesus asked what was written in the law. The man answered, "love the Lord your God with all your heart, and with all your soul, ... and your neighbor as yourself." Jesus agreed.
2. (love commandment) Bible. New American Standard. A. J. Holman Company. 1973. John 15:11–17. Jesus said, "This is my commandment, that you love one another, just as I have loved you."
3. (judging) Bible. New International Version. Zondervan. 1984. Matthew 7:1–5. In the Sermon on the Mount, Jesus said, "Do not judge others, in order that you may not be judged; for with the standard of judgment with which you judge, you will be judged; and with the measure you measure to others it will be measured to you. Why do you look for the speck of dust in your brother's eye, and never notice the plank that is in your own eye? ... Hypocrite."
4. (only Jesus knows what's in a man's heart) Bible. New American Standard. A. J. Holman Company. 1973. Luke 9:47. Jesus knows the reasoning of their hearts.
5. (judging) Bible. New American Standard. A. J. Holman Company. 1973. Romans 2:1–11. Paul said, if you judge others, you condemn yourself.
6. (judging: only Jesus knows what's in a man's heart) Bible. New American Standard. A. J. Holman Company. 1973. 1 Corinthians 4:1–5. Paul

said, make a practice of passing no judgment. "Wait until the Lord comes ... and discloses the motives of men's hearts."

7. (judging) Bible. New American Standard. A. J. Holman Company. 1973. James 4:11–12. James said, who are you to judge your neighbor?
8. (judging) Bible. New American Standard. A. J. Holman Company. 1973. John 5:21–23. John said, neither does the Father judge anyone, but he has given the whole process of judging to the Son.
9. (causing new Christians to stumble) *The Daily Study Bible Series*. Dr. William Barclay. Westminster Press. 1975. "The Letters to the Corinthians." pp. 74–76. Because many new Christians in the church at Corinth came from idol worship, they felt uncomfortable with eating meat offered to idols. Until their level of faith increases, Paul advises the experienced Christians to not eat that meat. 1 Corinthians 8:1–13.
10. (causing converted Jews to stumble) *The Daily Study Bible Series*. Dr. William Barclay. Westminster Press. 1975. "The Letter to the Romans." pp. 179–80. Many new Jewish converts to Christianity retained their Jewish dietary practices and would not associate with Gentile converts to Christianity in the same church. Paul recommends welcoming new Christians without pressuring them to change their past practices. Romans 14:1–6.
11. (Gentiles to be Jews first) Bible. New American Standard version. A. J. Holman Company. 1973. Acts 15:1–21. Apostles, elders, and Paul meet to discuss whether Gentiles must first convert to Judaism before becoming Christians. James, the stepbrother of Jesus, is an apostle who still follows all the Jewish laws. He offers a compromise, which is accepted. Gentiles must follow four Jewish laws.
12. (Apostles disagree) Bible. New American Standard. A. J. Holman Company. 1973. Galatians 2:11–21. The compromise, in Acts 15:1–21, consisted of Gentiles having to follow four Jewish laws, against Paul's wishes. James advocates for retaining some laws. Peter compromises.
13. (*sola scriptura*) *Catholicism and Fundamentalism*. Karl Keating. Ignatius Press. 1988, pp. 121–22, 134–35. The term *sola scriptura*, inspired by God, was initiated at the Reformation. Tradition was later removed from use when interpreting the Bible.

14. (dual source of revelation) *Catechism of the Catholic Church*. Doubleday. 1994. Part 1. Section 1. Chapter 2. Article 2.III.84. Catholicism uses both scripture and tradition to determine church doctrine.
15. (second cross: criminal) *The Daily Study Bible Series*. Dr. William Barclay. Westminster Press. 1975. "The Gospel of Luke." pp. 286–87. Two criminals died on crosses beside Jesus. One criminal asked Jesus to remember him in his kingdom. Jesus replied he would be in Paradise that day.
16. (Jesus anonymously returns to earth today) *Joshua: A Parable for Today*. Joseph F. Girzone. Simon & Schuster. 1987. This is a fictional story about Jesus returning to earth today under an assumed name, and how he is treated.

Chapter 12

1. (the four Gospels) The Daily Study Bible Series. Dr. William Barclay. Westminster Press. 1975. "The Gospel of Luke." pp. 1–6. Luke was the only Gentile writer of a Gospel. He was from Macedonia, where they held women in higher esteem. Jewish men prayed every morning thanking God they were not Gentile, slave, or woman.
2. (honoring Mary) *Beginning Apologetics 6*. Father Frank Chacon and Jim Burnham. San Juan Catholic Seminars. 2000–2012, pp. 12–35. Mary is the mother of God. Archangel Gabriel honors Mary and calls her blessed. The book of Luke contains a prophesy of Mary being called blessed for all ages. Catholics honor the Blessed Virgin Mary, but do not worship her.
3. (honoring Mary) Bible. New American Standard. A. J. Holman Company. 1973. Luke 1:26–56. The archangel Gabriel says Mary is filled with the Holy Spirit, calls her blessed twice in four verses. All ages will call her blessed.
4. (praying to saints) *Catholic Biblical Apologetics. The Communion of Saints. Praying to the Saints*. Paul Flanagan and Robert Schihl. 1985–2014. Catholics pray to saints in heaven, but do not worship them.
5. (prayer to Mary) *Mother Teresa: A Simple Path*. Lucinda Vardey. Ballantine Books. 1995. pp. xxv–xxvi. Mother Teresa and the Missionaries of Charity often recited a prayer to Mary.

6. (Hail Mary) Bible. New American Standard. A. J. Holman Company. 1973. Luke 1:28. The archangel Gabriel greets Mary with a respectful greeting used for royalty. Gabriel says Mary is full of the Lord's grace.
7. (Hail Mary) Bible. New American Standard. A. J. Holman Company. 1973. Luke 1:39–45. Elizabeth told Mary, "Blessed among women are you, and blessed is the fruit of your womb." "Blessed is she who believed that there would be a fulfillment of what had been spoken to her by the Lord."
8. (Hail Mary) *My Saint Pio Prayer Book*. The Padre Pio Foundation of America. 2018, p. 7. The Hail Mary prayer is: "Hail Mary, full of grace; the Lord is with thee. Blessed art thou among women, and blessed is the fruit of thy womb, Jesus. Holy Mary, Mother of God, pray for us sinners, now, and at the hour of our death. Amen."
9. (Jesus speaks of works of the Holy Spirit) Bible. New American Standard. A. J. Holman Company. 1973. John 14:11–21. Whoever believes in Jesus will do works greater than he accomplished, with the help of the Holy Spirit.
10. (miracles as evidence of the Holy Spirit) Bible. New American Standard. A. J. Holman Company. 1973. Mark 16:9–20. A resurrected Jesus said to the apostles, "Go into all the world and preach the gospel to all creation. He who has believed and has been baptized shall be saved; but he who has disbelieved shall be condemned. And these signs will accompany those who have believed … they will lay hands on the sick, and they will recover."
11. (miracles as evidence of the Holy Spirit) Bible. New American Standard. A. J. Holman Company. 1973. Acts 15:6–12. Peter stood up and said Gentiles should also hear the Gospel and believe. And God will give them the Holy Spirit. The whole assembly was silent and listened to Barnabas and Paul as they told the story of all the signs and wonders God had done amongst the heathen through them.
12. (gifts of the Holy Spirit) Bible. New American Standard. A. J. Holman Company. 1973. 1 Corinthians 12:4–11. Paul explains that each man is given his own gift by the Holy Spirit. Gifts may include wisdom, knowledge, faith, healing, power, prophecy, spirit recognition, speaking in tongues, or interpreting tongues.

13. (World Youth Day) worldyouthday.com. 2017. World Youth Day began in 1985 under Pope John Paul II and is held every two or three years in a different city around the world. At the first World Youth Day, at St. Peter's Basilica in the Vatican, three hundred thousand people gathered. In Krakow in 2016, 1.6 million people attended the last Mass.
14. (Saint Pier Giorgio) frassatiusa.org. The biography of Blessed Pier Giorgio Frassati indicates he died as a young man from a disease he obtained while helping the poor and sick.

Chapter 13

1. (Longinus and his lance) Bible. New American Standard. A. J. Holman Company. 1973. Mark 15:39. A centurion saw Jesus breathe his last breath and said, "Truly this man was the Son of God."
2. (Paul's clothing as relics) *The Daily Study Bible Series*. Dr. William Barclay. Westminster Press. 1975. "The Acts of the Apostles." pp. 142–43. Early church leaders used Paul's sweatbands and aprons as relics to aid in healing miracles, when Paul was unavailable. Diseases left them, and evil spirits departed.
3. (Jesus's cloak as relic) Bible. New American Standard. A. J. Holman Company. 1973. Luke 8:43–48. A bleeding woman touched Jesus's cloak for healing. Jesus felt power leaving his body.

Chapter 14

1. (praying the rosary) USCCB.org/how-to-pray-the-rosary. United States Catholic Conference of Bishops. "How to Pray the Rosary." Praying the rosary is a lengthy Catholic prayer using standard prayers based on the Bible. The rosary begins with the Apostle's Creed, followed by the Lord's Prayer. The standard Catholic prayers of Hail Mary and Glory Be are recited multiple times. The Lord's Prayer is repeated and followed by multiple Hail Mary and Glory Be prayers. This sequence is repeated five more times. Other standard Catholic prayers are included throughout the rosary prayer. It may take fifteen to twenty minutes to pray the rosary properly. A necklace-type rosary is usually held in your hand when praying the rosary. It consists of fifty-nine beads, a Crucifix,

and a medal. You begin by making the sign of the cross. Next, hold the cross on the necklace-type rosary and say the Apostle's Creed. Move your fingers to the first bead on the rosary and pray the Lord's Prayer. You move from bead to bead along the rosary when praying each prayer or set of prayers. Conclude the rosary by making the sign of the cross. Because of the number of repetitions of prayers, the rosary beads help keep count to insure a complete rosary prayer is made.

2. (Hail Mary) Bible. New American Standard. A. J. Holman Company. 1973. Luke 1:28. The archangel Gabriel greets Mary with a respectful greeting used for royalty. Gabriel says Mary is full of the Lord's grace.

3. (Hail Mary) Bible. New American Standard. A. J. Holman Company. 1973. Luke 1:39–45. Elizabeth told Mary, "Blessed among women are you, and blessed is the fruit of your womb." "Blessed is she who believed that there would be a fulfillment of what had been spoken to her by the Lord."

4. (Hail Mary) *My Saint Pio Prayer Book*. The Padre Pio Foundation of America. 2018, p. 7. The Hail Mary prayer is: "Hail Mary, full of grace; the Lord is with thee; Blessed art thou among women, and blessed is the fruit of thy womb, Jesus. Holy Mary, Mother of God, pray for us sinners, now, and at the hour of our death. Amen."

5. (Glory Be) *My Saint Pio Prayer Book*. The Padre Pio Foundation of America. 2018. p. 7. The Glory Be Prayer follows: "Glory be to the Father, and to the Son, and to the Holy Spirit, as it was in the beginning, is now, and ever shall be, world without end. Amen."

6. (Apostles' Creed) CatholicOnline.org. 2018. The Apostles' Creed follows: "I believe in God, the Almighty, Creator of heaven and earth, and in Jesus Christ, His only Son, our Lord, who was conceived by the Holy Spirit, born of the Virgin Mary, suffered under Pontius Pilate, was crucified, died and was buried; He descended into hell; on the third day He rose again from the dead; He ascended into heaven, and is seated at the right hand of God the Father Almighty; from there He will come to judge the living and the dead. I believe in the Holy Spirit, the Holy Catholic Church, the communion of Saints, the forgiveness of sins, the resurrection of the body, and life everlasting. Amen."

7. (infallibility) *Catechism of the Catholic Church*. Doubleday. 1994. Part 1. Section 2. Chapter 3. Article 9. Paragraph 4: 871–96.

8. (bind on earth, bind in heaven) *The Daily Study Bible Series*. Dr. William Barclay. Westminster Press. 1975. "The Gospel of Matthew, Vol. 2." pp. 144–46. The apostles discuss whether Gentiles need to first comply with Jewish laws before becoming Christian.
9. (pope's infallibility) Bible. New American Standard. A. J. Holman Company. 1973. Luke 10:16. Jesus spoke to his followers saying, "The one who listens to you listens to me."
10. (pope's infallibility) Bible. New American Standard. A. J. Holman Company. 1973. Matthew 18:18. Jesus, speaking to his disciples, said, "Whatever you shall bind on earth shall have been bound in heaven, and whatever you loose on earth shall have been loosed in heaven."
11. (Gentiles to be Jews first) Bible. New American Standard. A. J. Holman Company. 1973. Acts 15:1–21. Apostles, elders, and Paul meet to discuss whether Gentiles must first convert to Judaism before becoming Christians. James, the stepbrother of Jesus, is an apostle who still follows all the Jewish laws. He offers a compromise, which is accepted. Gentiles must follow four Jewish laws temporarily.
12. (number of priests) National Catholic Reporter. Vatican statistics. March 7, 2016. There are 415,792 Catholic priests and 5,237 bishops worldwide.
13. (number of nuns) Pew Research Council. "U.S. Nuns Face Shrinking Numbers and Tensions with the Vatican." August 8, 2014. There are over seven hundred thousand Catholic nuns worldwide.
14. (number of saints) *Faith in Real Life*. Kathleen Manning. "How Many Saints Are There?" October 31, 2013. There are over ten thousand saints in the Catholic Church. Pope John Paul II canonized more saints than all the popes during the past five hundred years.
15. (four kinds of preaching) *The Daily Study Bible Series*. Dr. William Barclay. Westminster Press. 1975. "The Acts of the Apostles." pp. 22–24. There are four kinds of early Christian church preaching. Kerugma is an announcement or plain statement of fact. *Didache* is instructional teaching. Paraklesis is exhortation. Homilia is an application to life. A well-rounded sermon has all four.
16. (light of the world) Bible. New American Standard. A. J. Holman Company. 1973. John 8:12. Jesus said he is the light of the world. His followers would not be in darkness.

17. (versions of the Lord's Prayer) *The Catholic Virginian*, vol. 93, no. 2. November 20, 2017. Article by Father Kenneth Doyle of the Catholic News Service. The last phrase of the Lord's Prayer was not included in the earliest Greek manuscripts of the Gospels, so Jesus probably never said it. That phrase is included in the *Didache* and later manuscripts of the Gospels. The phrase remains theologically sound.
18. (the Lord's Prayer) Bible. New American Standard. A. J. Holman Company. 1973. Matthew 6:9–13. Jesus taught the disciples how to pray by saying the Lord's Prayer.

Chapter 15

1. (indulgences) Beginning Apologetics 8. pp. 28–32. Father Frank Chacon and Jim Burnham. San Juan Catholic Seminars. 2005. Catholic view the consequence of sin to be guilt and punishment. Restitution or punishment is also called indulgences.
2. (Protestant Reformation) Encyclopedia Britannica, Inc. "Reformation Christianity." 2017. Luther posted ninety-five theses publicly on October 31, 1517. He charged the church leaders with corruption and wrongfully selling indulgences.
3. (Medici family) Encyclopedia Britannica, Inc. "Medici Family." 2017. The Medici family had four popes and two queens.
4. (Protestant Reformation) Roots of the Reformation. Karl Adam. CH Resources. 2012, pp. 11–41. There was a moral collapse of the popes. Taxation, payment for indulgences, nepotism, and lust for power and money almost destroyed the church. Martin Luther posts his objections at the Castle Church at Wittenburg. Luther espouses faith, not works. He is excommunicated. He calls the book of James an "epistle of straw."
5. (corrupt popes) *The Pursuit of Italy*. Sir David Gilmour. Farrar, Straus and Giroux. 2011. pp. 84–93. There were unholy city-state popes leading the church for seventy years beginning in 1455. They included popes from the families of Borgia, Piccolomini, della Rovere, and Medici. The Spanish Borgia pope, Alexander VI, had a mistress. Nepotism was used for two hundred years. The Lateran Council, 1513–1517, failed to reform the church. The pope ruled the Papal States in central Italy and the church.

6. (church leaders forgiving sins) Bible. New American Standard. A. J. Holman Company. 1973. John 20:22–23. Jesus, speaking to his disciples after the resurrection, said "If you forgive the sins of any, they are forgiven; if you retain the sins of any, they are retained."
7. (church leaders forgiving sins) Bible. New American Standard version. A. J. Holman Company. 1973. Matthew 18:18. Jesus, speaking to his disciples, said, "Whatever you bind on earth shall be bound in heaven, and whatever you loose on earth shall be loosed in heaven."
8. (Council of Trent) *Roots of the Reformation*. Karl Adam. CH Resources. 2012, pp. 57–63. The papacy was spiritualized since the Council of Trent. Not one of Luther's accusations could be made today. The papacy is now strictly religious, Christian, and ecclesiastical.

Chapter 16

1. (Orthodox Church) Funk & Wagnalls New Encyclopedia. Vol. 20. Funk & Wagnalls Corporation. 1993, pp. 7–14. The Orthodox schism resulted from a gradual estrangement. Liturgy and doctrines remained very similar. Both groups remain very close today.
2. (Anglican Church) Funk & Wagnalls New Encyclopedia. Vol. 6. Funk & Wagnalls Corporation. 1993, pp. 279–81. The Anglican Church, or Church of England, schism occurred when England's Parliament passed a series of statutes denying the pope authority over the Church of England. Liturgy and doctrines remained very similar. Both groups remain respectful of each other today.
3. (Protestantism) Funk & Wagnalls New Encyclopedia. Vol. 21. Funk & Wagnalls Corporation. 1993, pp. 346–51. The history of Reformation included Luther, Zwingli, and Anabaptist radical sects. Calvin came along a generation later and revised Zwingli's views. There were many wars among Christians following the Reformation.
4. (Lutheranism) Funk & Wagnalls New Encyclopedia. Vol. 16. Funk & Wagnalls Corporation. 1993, pp. 264–67. Early Lutheranism believed in salvation by faith alone, the sacraments of infant baptism and Holy Communion. Like Catholics, they believed in the presence of Christ in the Communion elements. However, unlike Catholics, early Lutherans believed in the priesthood of believers and their role in evangelizing.

5. (Martin Luther) Funk & Wagnalls New Encyclopedia. Vol. 16. Funk & Wagnalls Corporation. 1993, pp. 261–64. Martin Luther, an Augustinian monk and professor of theology at the University of Wittenberg in Saxony, Germany, posted Ninety-Five Theses against the Catholic Church practice of indiscriminate charges for indulgences. Luther believed in salvation by faith alone, not by good works.
6. (Zwingli) Funk & Wagnalls New Encyclopedia. Vol. 28. Funk & Wagnalls Corporation. 1993, pp. 179–80. Huldrych Zwingli developed a separate Protestant group different from Lutheranism. He believed in less control by government over religion. He attacked Catholic beliefs in saints, relics, statues, and enforced celibacy. He did not believe in Christ's presence in the Communion elements. He died during a religious war.
7. (Anabaptist) Funk & Wagnalls New Encyclopedia. Vol. 2. Funk & Wagnalls Corporation. 1993, pp. 99–100. An Anabaptist means one who baptizes again, as an adult. Anabaptists consisted of many radical or unorthodox Protestant sects. They believed in a personal faith in God, no ritualism, and the right of independent personal judgment. They appealed to the poor and uneducated peasants. The Mennonites came from this tradition. Baptists did not come from the Anabaptist tradition.
8. (Calvinism) Funk & Wagnalls New Encyclopedia. Vol. 5. Funk & Wagnalls Corporation. 1993. p. 162. Calvin believed in justification by faith alone. He did not believe in the presence of Christ in the Eucharist. Calvin supported thrift, industry and hard work as forms of moral virtue, which helped lead to capitalism. Calvinism spread to France, Holland, Scotland, and became the basic creed of Presbyterians in Great Britain.
9. (John Calvin) Funk & Wagnalls New Encyclopedia. Vol. 5. Funk & Wagnalls Corporation. 1993. pp. 160–61. Calvin was a French theologian, reformer, writer, and pastor in the next generation after Luther and Zwingli.
10. (Protestant Reformation) Encyclopedia Britannica, Inc. Reformation Christianity. 2017. Luther posted Ninety-Five Theses publicly on October 31, 1517. He charged church leaders with corruption and selling indulgences.

11. (Medici family) Encyclopedia Britannica, Inc. Medici family. 2017. The Medici family had four popes and two queens.
12. (Protestant Reformation) *Roots of the Reformation*. Karl Adam. CH Resources. 2012, pp. 11–41. There was a moral collapse of the popes. Taxation, payment for indulgences, nepotism, and lust for power and money almost destroyed the church. Martin Luther posted Ninety-Five Theses at the Castle Church at Wittenburg. Luther espoused faith, not works. He was excommunicated. He called the book of James an "epistle of straw."
13. (corrupt popes) *The Pursuit of Italy*. Sir David Gilmour. Farrar, Straus and Giroux. 2011, pp. 84–93. Catholicism was ruled by city-state popes for seventy years, beginning in 1455. Popes came from the families of Borgia, Piccolomini, della Rovere, and Medici. The Spanish Borgia pope, Alexander VI, had a mistress. Nepotism was used for two hundred years. The Lateran Council, 1513–1517, failed to reform the church. The pope ruled the Papal States in central Italy in addition to the church.
14. (Council of Trent) *Roots of the Reformation*. Karl Adam. CH Resources. 2012, pp. 57–63. The papacy has been spiritualized since the Council of Trent. Not one of Luther's accusations could be made today. The papacy is now strictly religious, Christian, and ecclesiastical.

Chapter 17

1. (actual tithing statistics) aquinasandmore.com. 2018. "Catholic Tithing and Almsgiving." On average worldwide, Catholics give 1.1 percent of their income to the church. On average worldwide, Protestants give 2.2 percent of their income to the church.
2. (tithing) Bible. New American Standard. A. J. Holman Company. 1973. Malachi 3:10. Some American Protestant church leaders use a reference from Malachi, a book in the Old Testament or Hebrew Bible, to encourage giving offerings above 10 percent. "Bring the whole tithe into the storehouse … says the Lord Almighty, and see if I will not throw open the floodgates of heaven and pour out so much blessing that there will not be room enough to store it."

Chapter 18

1. (Islam) Pew Research Center. Michael Lipka. Muslims and Islam: Key Findings in the U.S. and around the World. August 9, 2017. Islam is the fastest growing major religion in the world. Its growth is due to Muslims having more children. Currently, there are 1.8 billion Muslims worldwide.
2. (love commandment) Bible. New American Standard. A. J. Holman Company. 1973. John 15:11–17. Jesus said, "This is my commandment, that you love one another, just as I have loved you."
3. (Gentiles to be Jews first) Bible. New American Standard. A. J. Holman Company. 1973. Acts 21:17–26. James, the apostle, and other elders who still follow all the Jewish laws tell Paul that since he is accused of abandoning the Law of Moses, he must go through a Jewish purification ritual. Paul did it, but it ultimately led to his demise, since he was caught and arrested in the Jewish temple while completing the rituals.
4. (no rules in Christianity: Paul) Bible. New American Standard. A. J. Holman Company. 1973. Galatians 2:14–21. Paul declares the end of the law. Faith in Christ has nothing to do with the law. We are not justified by works. If you get right with God through the law, then Christ died needlessly.
5. (believe in Jesus for eternal life) Bible. New American Standard. A. J. Holman Company. 1973. John 3:16. Whosoever believes in Jesus will have eternal life.
6. (Jesus prays for unity) *The Daily Study Bible Series*. Dr. William Barclay. "The Gospel of John, Vol. 2." pp. 213–16. Jesus prays to the Father that his disciples be one, just as Jesus is one with the Father.
7. (Methodist reunification) Funk & Wagnalls New Encyclopedia. Vol. 17. Funk & Wagnalls Corporation. 1993, pp. 242–44. Methodism began in 1729 by breaking away from the Anglican Church. Methodists work to reunite various Methodist denominations through joint annual conferences.
8. (World Methodist Council) worldmethodistcouncil.org. 2011. The World Methodist Council promotes unity among eighty Methodist-related denominations and their eighty million people. They hold a world conference every five years. The Council is headquartered in

Lake Junaluska, North Carolina, and has an ecumenical office in Rome. They have been successful in reuniting three denominations into one denomination called United Methodist.

Chapter 19

1. (worldwide ministry) Bible. New American Standard. A. J. Holman Company. 1973. Matthew 28:16–20. After the resurrection, Jesus told his disciples to "go and make all nations my disciples."
2. (number of Christians) Pew Research Center's Forum on Religion & Public Life. *Global Christianity*. December 19, 2011.
3. (number of saints) *Faith in Real Life*. Kathleen Manning. "How Many Saints Are There?" October 31, 2013. There are over ten thousand saints in the Catholic Church. Pope John Paul II canonized more saints than all the popes during the past five hundred years.
4. (Pope John Paul II) CBN.com/churchandministry/pope-john-paul-II. Christian Broadcasting Network. 2017. Pope John Paul II canonized more saints than all the popes during the past five hundred years combined. He traveled internationally 104 times, far more than any other pope. It had been 455 years since the last non-Italian cardinal was elected pope.
5. (Pope Benedict XVI) CatholicNewsAgency.com/resources/benedict. Catholic News Agency. Pope Benedict, from Germany, was elected pope on April 19, 2005.
6. (Pope Francis) popefrancisvisit.com/pope-francis-biography. "Catholic to the Max." 2015. Pope Francis was elected as the 266th pope on March 13, 2013. He was the first non-European pope since year 741.
7. (Operation Blessing) ob.org. Pat Robertson. Operation Blessing invested $3.6 billion in goods and services to help disadvantaged and disaster victims in over a hundred countries.
8. (Samaritan's Purse) samaritanspurse.org. "Samaritan's Purse." 2017. Franklin Graham helps the poor, sick, and suffering in over a hundred countries.
9. (World Methodist Council) worldmethodistcouncil.org. 2011. The World Methodist Council promotes unity among eighty Methodist-related denominations and their eighty million people. The World

Conference meets every five years. It is headquartered in Lake Junaluska, North Carolina, and has an ecumenical office in Rome. The Council was successful in reuniting three denominations into one denomination called United Methodist.

10. (Methodist reunification) Funk & Wagnalls New Encyclopedia. Vol. 17. Funk & Wagnalls Corporation. 1993, pp. 242–44. Methodism began in 1729 by breaking away from the Anglican Church. They continue to work to reunite various Methodist denominations through joint annual conferences.
11. (Global Christian Forum) globalchristianforum.org. 2017. The Global Christian Forum fosters mutual respect among Christian churches who have not been in conversations with each other previously. Their initial organizing meeting was held in 2002. Their first official conference was held in 2007.

Chapter 21

1. (Paul's letters) The Daily Study Bible Series. Dr. William Barclay. Westminster Press. 1975. "The Letter to the Romans." pp. x–xii, p. 1. Except for Romans, Paul's letters were written in response to immediate situations faced by early Christian churches. Paul's letters were in response to information he received about the church. Because we only have Paul's responses, we are missing half of the conversation.
2. (Paul's letters) *The Daily Study Bible Series*. Dr. William Barclay. Westminster Press. 1975. "The Letters to the Corinthians." pp. 5–8. Paul was in Ephesus when he heard about problems in the church at Corinth. Paul writes a letter in reply, to address specific issues in that church. Many of the church members in Corinth were previously pagan and did not understand how they should now behave as new Christians.
3. (Communion) Bible. New American Standard. A. J. Holman Company. 1973. Matthew 26:26–30 and Mark 14:22–26. Jesus said, "This is my body.... This is my blood, the blood of the new covenant which is being shed for many."
4. (number of Christian denominations) World Christian Encyclopedia. Barrett, Kurian, and Johnson. Vol. 1. Oxford University Press. 2001. p. 16. There are 33,000 Christian denominations, including 22,000

independent, 9,000 Protestant, 1,600 marginal (cultlike), 781 Orthodox organizations, 242 Catholic rites, and 168 Anglican organizations.

Chapter 22

1. (Old Testament) 30 Days to Understanding the Bible. Max E. Anders. Word Publishing. 1988, pp. 6–12. The Old Testament explains the history of the Hebrew people over two thousand years. It contains books on history, poetry, and prophecy. The New Testament covers a period that is less than one hundred years.
2. (Luther's view of the book of James) *The Daily Study Bible Series*. Dr. William Barclay. Westminster Press. 1975. "The Letters of James and Peter." pp. 3–33. The books of James, Jude, Hebrews, and Revelation are secondary books. James disagrees with Paul and the rest of the Bible. Luther prefers to remove the book of James from the Bible.
3. (no rules in Christianity: Paul) Bible. New American Standard. A. J. Holman Company. 1973. Galatians 2:14–21. Paul declares the end of the law. Faith in Christ has nothing to do with the law. We are not justified by works. If you get right with God through the law, then Christ died needlessly.
4. (Paul wanting to be liked) Bible. New American Standard. A. J. Holman Company. 1973. Galatians 1:6–10. Paul affirms there are no rules for Christians.
5. (justification through works: James) Bible. New International Version. Zondervan. 1984. James 2:14–26. James said, "You see that a person is justified by what he does and not by faith alone."
6. Living a perfect Christian life according to a set of behaviors was their focus.
7. (Apostles disagree) Bible. New American Standard. A. J. Holman Company. 1973. Galatians 2:11–21. The compromise, in Acts 15:1–21, of Gentiles having to follow four Jewish laws, was against Paul's wishes. James advocates for retaining some laws. Peter compromises.
8. (Paul's letters) *The Daily Study Bible Series*. Dr. William Barclay. Westminster Press. 1975. "The Letter to the Romans." pp. x–xii, p. 1. Except for Romans, Paul's letters were in response to immediate situations faced by early Christian churches. Paul's letters were in

response to information he received about the church. Because we only have Paul's responses, we are missing half of the conversation.
9. (Paul's letters) *The Daily Study Bible Series*. Dr. William Barclay. Westminster Press. 1975. "The Letters to the Corinthians." pp. 5–8. Paul was in Ephesus when he heard about problems in the church at Corinth. Paul writes a letter in reply, to address specific issues in that church. Many of the church members in Corinth were previously pagan and did not understand how they should now behave as new Christians.
10. (tithing at 10 percent) Bible. New American Standard. A. J. Holman Company. 1973. Leviticus 27:32. "And for every tenth part of herd or flock, whatever passes under the rod, the tenth one shall be holy to the Lord."
11. (tithing) Webster's New World Dictionary and Thesaurus. Wiley Publishing, Inc. 2002, p. 662. The word *tithe* comes from the Old English word "teothe," meaning a tenth. It means giving a tenth of your income.
12. (tithing) Bible. New American Standard. A. J. Holman Company. 1973. Matthew 23:23. While calling the scribes and Pharisees hypocrites for tithing lesser crops like dill and mint, Jesus said tithing should be done with a deep concern for justice, mercy, and faithfulness.
13. (giving to the church) Bible. New American Standard. A. J. Holman Company. 1973. 2 Corinthians 9:7. Paul says God loves a cheerful giver, not someone who gives grudgingly.
14. (giving to the church) Bible. New American Standard. A. J. Holman Company. 1973. 2 Corinthians 8:12. Paul encourages giving what you can afford and not to go needy yourself by giving too much.
15. (giving to the church) Bible. New American Standard. A. J. Holman Company. 1973. 1 Timothy 5:17–18. Those who work hard at preaching and teaching are worthy of their wages.
16. (giving to the church) Bible. New American Standard. A. J. Holman Company. 1973. Acts 11:29. In the proportion that any of the disciples had means, each of them determined to send a contribution to the hungry.
17. (giving to the church) Bible. New American Standard. A. J. Holman Company. 1973. James 1:27. Pure religion is to visit and help needy widows and orphans.

18. (perfect Christian life by behaviors) Funk & Wagnalls New Encyclopedia. Vol. 13. Funk & Wagnalls Corporation. 1993, pp. 155–56. The Holiness movement began after the Civil War. They focused on living a holy life by following many laws. CMA, Church of God, Nazarene, and Pentecostal denominations came from the Holiness movement.

Chapter 23

1. (parable of the mustard seed) The Daily Study Bible Series. Dr. William Barclay. Westminster Press. 1975. "The Gospel of Matthew, Vol. 2." pp. 75–78. Jesus told the parable of the mustard seed, known for being the smallest seed. An idea that can change an entire civilization begins with one person.
2. (Apostles' Creed) CatholicOnline.org. 2018. The Apostles' Creed follows: "I believe in God, the Almighty, Creator of heaven and earth, and in Jesus Christ, His only Son, our Lord, who was conceived by the Holy Spirit, born of the Virgin Mary, suffered under Pontius Pilate, was crucified, died and was buried; He descended into hell; on the third day He rose again from the dead; He ascended into heaven, and is seated at the right hand of God the Father Almighty; from there He will come to judge the living and the dead. I believe in the Holy Spirit, the Holy Catholic Church, the communion of Saints, the forgiveness of sins, the resurrection of the body, and life everlasting. Amen."
3. (Nicene Creed) CatholicOnline.org. 2018. The Nicene Creed follows: "We believe in one God, the Father, the Almighty, Maker of all that is, seen and unseen. We believe in one Lord, Jesus Christ, the only Son of God, eternally begotten of the Father, God from God, Light from Light, true God from true God, begotten, not made, consubstantial with the Father. Through him all things were made. For us men and our salvation he came down from heaven, and by the Holy Spirit was incarnate of the Virgin Mary, and became man. For our sake he was crucified under Pontius Pilate; he suffered death and was buried. On the third day he rose again in accordance with the scriptures; he ascended into heaven and is seated at the right hand of the Father. He will come again in glory to judge the living and the dead, and his kingdom will

have no end. We believe in the Holy Spirit, the Lord, the giver of life, who proceeds from the Father and the Son. With the Father and the Son, he is worshipped and glorified. He has spoken through the Prophets. We believe in one holy Catholic and apostolic Church. We acknowledge one baptism for the forgiveness of sins. We look for the resurrection of the dead, and the life of the world to come. Amen."

4. (Jesus speaks of works of the Holy Spirit) Bible. New American Standard. A. J. Holman Company. 1973. John 14:11–21. Whoever believes in Jesus will do works greater than he accomplished, with the help of the Holy Spirit.
5. (miracles as evidence of the Holy Spirit) Bible. New American Standard. A. J. Holman Company. 1973. Mark 16:9–20. A resurrected Jesus said to the apostles, "Go into all the world and preach the gospel to all creation. He who has believed and has been baptized shall be saved; but he who has disbelieved shall be condemned. And these signs will accompany those who have believed ... they will lay hands on the sick, and they will recover."
6. (miracles as evidence of the Holy Spirit) Bible. New American Standard. A. J. Holman Company. 1973. Acts 15:6–12. Peter stood up and said Gentiles should also hear the Gospel and believe. And God will give them the Holy Spirit. The whole assembly was silent and listened to Barnabas and Paul as they told the story of all the signs and wonders God had done amongst the heathen through them.
7. (gifts of the Holy Spirit) Bible. New American Standard. A. J. Holman Company. 1973. 1 Corinthians 12:4–11. Paul explains that each man is given his own gift by the Holy Spirit. Gifts may include wisdom, knowledge, faith, healing, power, prophecy, spirit recognition, speaking in tongues, or interpreting tongues.

Epilogue

1. (Saul wreaks havoc on the church) *The Daily Study Bible Series*. Dr. William Barclay. Westminster Press. 1975. "The Acts of the Apostles." pp. 59–72. Saul, later Paul, imprisons Christians, supports the killing of Stephen.

2. (book reference) *To Heaven and Back*. Mary C. Neal, MD. WaterBrook Press. 2012.
3. (Billy Graham quote on going to heaven) *Evangelicalism Divided*. Iain Murray. Banner of Truth. 2000, pp. 73–74. In a 1997 interview with Robert Schuller, Billy Graham says he believes Buddhists, Muslims, and nonbelievers will go to heaven if they know in their hearts they need something they do not have and turn to the only light they do have.
4. (second cross: criminal) *The Daily Study Bible Series*. Dr. William Barclay. Westminster Press. 1975. "The Gospel of Luke." pp. 286–87. Two criminals were crucified on crosses beside Jesus. The one who was penitent asked Jesus to remember him in His kingdom. Jesus replied he would be in Paradise that day.

Common Catholic Prayers

1. (common Catholic prayers) *Compendium of the Catechism of the Catholic Church*. 2005. Libreria Editrice Vaticana. The Compendium of the Catechism of the Catholic Church was promulgated by Pope John Paul II in 1992. It was written by a Commission of Cardinals under the direction of then Cardinal Joseph Ratzinger, now Pope Benedict XVI. It was released to the entire Catholic Church and to all people of God. Explanations of church doctrine and common prayers of the Catholic Church are included in the Compendium.
2. (common Catholic prayers) *My Saint Pio Prayer Book*. The Padre Pio Foundation of America. 2018, pp. 7–55. Common Catholic prayers were reprinted in Padre Pio's Prayer Book.

Index

A

Anabaptist 158
Anglican 23, 45, 49, 59, 66
Ave Maria 115

B

Bible 40, 44, 47, 48, 65, 69, 70, 73, 75, 89, 103, 109, 110, 198
Billy Graham 191, 223

C

Calvinism 159
Cana 57, 149
Catholic terms 142
Celebrate Their Religion 119
Child abuse 149
Chimayo 1, 3, 20
Christian & Missionary Alliance 30, 49, 78, 97, 183
Communion 65
Confession of Sins 131
Core Beliefs 37
Counter-Reformation 148
Crucifix 1, 116
Crusades 44

D

Dead Sea Scrolls 72

Didache 43, 48, 137, 140
Disciples of Christ Church 80
Dismas 109

E

Elijah 41
Evangelical 30

F

False narratives 52, 197
Far Right 104
Fatima 14
Four Gospels 75
Franklin Graham 190
Frauenkirche 171
Fundamentalist 30, 47, 57, 66, 104

G

Gifts of the Holy Spirit 74
Global Christian Forum 192
Greatest commandment 99
Guadalupe 16

H

Hail Mary 115
Holiness Movement 78
Holy Crown of Thorns 126
Holy Lance 125
Holy Water 138

I

Immigration 48
Incorruptible 14
Indulgences 145
Infallibility 133
Islam 176

J

James 106, 211
Jehovah 71
Judaism 25, 26, 40, 42, 90, 258
Judging Others 86

K

Katharine Drexel 111

L

Lenten season 101
Liturgy 199
Lord's Prayer 140
Loretto Chapel 10
Lourdes 12
Love the Lord with All Your Heart 99

M

Mahaffey 30, 31, 97
Marian Doctrine 113
Martin Luther 40, 47, 69, 75, 145, 153
Medici 146
Methodism 80
Miracles 2, 13, 17, 19, 112, 117
Monstrance 139
Mother Teresa 93, 188

N

No rules 60
Novena 11

O

Opus Dei 62
Orthodox 4, 23, 45, 49, 66, 104

P

Padre Pio 18, 119
Papal States 147
Pat Robertson 190
Patron saint 120
Paul's letters 76
Peter 42
Philemon 77
Pieta 39
Poland 178
Pope Benedict 189
Pope Francis 189
Pope John Paul II 179, 188
Praying to Saints 114
Presbyterianism 80
Protestant Reformation 23, 45, 47, 69, 131, 145, 153, 154, 160
Pyx 139

R

Relics 126
Rosary 3, 12, 14, 19, 115, 132

S

Saint Francis of Assisi 9, 89
Sanctification 89
Saved 92, 206
Schisms 44
Scribal Law 42
Second Cross 109
Seder 25
Sola scriptura 47, 69, 81, 161
Stations of the Cross 2, 10, 116, 136
Stigmata 18

T

Techniques Used by Cults 53
Tithing 89
Tradition 69
Transfiguration 56
True Cross 125

V

Vatican City 149
Venerate 128

W

World Methodist Council 192
World Youth Day 120

Y

Yahweh 71

Z

Zwingli 154, 156

CPSIA information can be obtained
at www.ICGtesting.com
Printed in the USA
BVHW030058180120
569780BV00001B/3